london cycling guide

MORE THAN 40 GREAT ROUTES FOR EXPLORING THE CAPITAL

TOM BOGDANOWICZ

In association with the London Cycling Campaign

≡lifestyle
∴ books™

Read. Learn. Do What You Love.

Published 2016 — IMM Lifestyle Books
www.IMMLifestyleBooks.com

IMM Lifestyle Books are distributed in the UK by Grantham Book Service,
Trent Road, Grantham, Lincolnshire, NG31 7XQ.

In North America, IMM Lifestyle Books are distributed by Fox Chapel Publishing,
1970 Broad Street, East Petersburg, PA 17520,
www.FoxChapelPublishing.com.

ISBN 978-1-5048-0019-8

Printed in the United States of America

2 4 6 8 10 9 7 5 3 1

CONTENTS

GETTING STARTED

One of the many attractive aspects of cycling is that you can do as little or as much as you like. You can choose where and when to ride and you can pick and choose who you ride with. You don't have to depend on gym opening times, bus timetables or petrol stations.

As a cyclist you can also take your pick from an enormous range of easy or challenging activities. Many people are unaware that there are active groups that play unicycle hockey, bicycle polo and off-road jumping. For the more relaxed, there are historical bike rides, architecture bike rides, visits to stately homes, repair workshops and night rides to watch the summer solstice. You'll find that there are free guided rides organized regularly by the London Cycling Campaign (LCC) and Cycling UK (formerly Cyclists' Touring Club [CTC]) groups along many of the routes described in this book. To join in, all you need is a bike.

Another wonderful resource in London is the set of 14 free cycle route guides that were produced by the LCC in partnership with Transport for London (TfL). They show you all the streets in London that are recommended by cyclists as having less traffic or being more convenient. You'll find that there are hundreds of little-known cycle cut-throughs that enable you to reach your destination more quickly and with less traffic.

If you already own a bike and it hasn't been out of the shed in a while, it's worth taking it in for a service to make sure it's roadworthy – the £30 to £60 a service costs is money well spent. Remember that a poor quality bike can be hard work, so if you are planning to keep up your resolve to cycle more, consider buying the best you can afford. The alternative is to hire a bike. This is easier in central London than elsewhere, but many bike shops offer cycle rental so it's worth asking (see pages 230–242).

If you haven't ridden a bike in a while, or even if you have, it's worth investing in some cycle training – in some boroughs you may find that classes are subsidized. The section on cycling technique (see page 19) provides an introduction to confident riding in cities but there is no substitute for a one-on-one lesson. Even experienced riders can discover that instructors spot errors in their road riding.

This book will help you with buying decisions, but don't forget that your local cycle group will be pleased to help, whether you are a novice looking for a bike, a triathlete looking for people to train with, or a mountain biker looking for good trails. And if they don't know, they will know someone who does.

Why cycle?

The freedom of riding a bicycle is a unique experience. When small children learn to ride they feel a sense of independence, the pleasure of the wind on their faces, and that extraordinary sensation of moving the pedals, gathering speed and overtaking mere mortals on foot. It's a pleasure that many adults rediscover when they take up cycling for health or for convenience. Some psychologists identify a sensation called 'free motion play' that can be used to explain both the child's delight on a swing and an adult's pleasure at riding a bike downhill or skiing.

Most cyclists ride bikes for the sheer enjoyment of it, but of course there are many more concrete benefits of getting on a cycle and pedalling for half an hour every day. For most of us it saves time and money as well as improves our fitness and contributes to our longevity. If someone were to invent a device that used no fuel, propelled you at 20 mph, improved your health, helped you lose weight, made you live longer, saved you money and got you to work faster they would surely be a celebrity, a Nobel Prize winner and a multi-millionaire. Such an invention would cost thousands of pounds and fly out of showrooms. Yet, extraordinarily, the humble bicycle is the cheapest form of transport you can buy and highly accessible to all. Indeed, the bicycle remains the world's most popular form of transport. Unfortunately, in Britain it declined in popularity as the country was redesigned for the motor car.

One of cycling's great assets, affordability, is also its weakness. Without the multi-million-pound advertising budgets from which car sales

benefit, there is little to make people aware that the cheaper though less profitable bicycle is a realistic and convenient mode of transport. The fact that cycling has survived and, in London, grown sharply, is a tribute to a brilliant and highly efficient invention that is primarily promoted by word of mouth. If it wasn't for the fact that urban design has been focused on motor vehicles for several decades, cycling, thanks to its obvious benefits, might well be the choice of many more people in Britain. Some experts say that as climate change becomes a more pressing problem and urban congestion increases, governments will have to consider not only road pricing but curbs on motor car promotion, as they did with the tobacco industry, in order to enable people to make transport choices based on convenience and

Above: *Fast, enjoyable and healthy – cycling is good for you and good for London. It is also an inexpensive and reliable mode of transport.*

common sense rather than the temptations of TV ads. Until then, many people will be missing out on cycling's undoubted benefits.

Enjoyment

The wind, the speed and human propulsion involved in cycling make it a delight for most people who try it. Some may dislike busy traffic, others may dislike rough tracks, but almost any-one will agree that pedalling through Hyde Park as the sun is setting has to be one of London's best attractions.

Convenience and flexibility

A bicycle gives you the freedom to choose when and where you want to travel. It's simply a case of picking up the bike and riding. Your journey can be door to door and, in Britain, you can take your bike on most trains outside of peak hours.

Reliability

On a bicycle you can time your journey to the minute. Congestion makes little difference, and you can walk around road works if needs be. You can travel short or long distances without relying on petrol pumps, bus timetables or rail tickets.

Affordability

Running a car, according to the RAC, costs approximately £2,500 a year, or £6,000 if you include insurance, depreciation and the cost of a loan. Maintaining a bicycle costs around £50 a year if you do your own repairs or £200 a year if you include a service, insurance and depreciation. New cars cost upwards of £5,000 whereas new bikes cost from £150. So even if you allow an annual £1,000 for occasional car rental and rail travel you come out winning as a bike owner. And you don't have to worry about finding a car parking space or leaving your car outside your home.

Sociability

On a bicycle you interact with the world and with people on the streets. You encounter friends and can stop and start at will. You can join cycling organizations and participate in hundreds of free guided bike rides. Many rides, like those in this book, will reveal places you didn't know existed.

Environmental benefits

Road transport in Britain accounts for 20 percent of carbon dioxide emissions. Cycling does not consume fuel or emit noxious fumes. Most cycles can last a lifetime if cared for and their manufacture consumes little in terms of raw materials. Even motoring organizations advocate cycling for shorter journeys.

Congestion

Congestion costs London upwards of £1 billion a year, but increased cycling helps to reduce motor traffic volumes as urban populations continue to grow. Six cycles can move in the space of one car on the road and you can park ten bicycles in one car-parking space. In London, the growing number of traffic-management schemes in residential areas means that a large proportion of cyclists don't use main roads at all but opt for cut-throughs and traffic-free routes. From the perspective of local and national government, cycling is a win-win option.

Health benefits

A study of 1,300 workers in Birmingham found that the one factor that made a difference to fitness levels was cycling to work. Men who rode bikes regularly had a fitness level of someone five to ten years younger. A study in Holland looked at longevity and found that cyclists over the age of 30 had a life expectancy two years greater than people who did not cycle. Regular cycling also appears to halve your chances of cancer and diabetes, and combined with a healthy diet it can help with weight loss. The British Medical Association concluded that the health benefits of regular cycling far outweigh any risks.

Parking

Many cycling households in London find that they do not need to own a car or they only need one car instead of two. That means lower costs and less trouble searching for parking spaces. Employers also gain if more of their staff cycle: one large London company estimates that it saves about £2,000 a year in parking space costs for every staff member who cycles to work.

Youthful appearance

This is not scientifically proven, but when guessing a cyclist's age you'll often find that you underestimate by five to ten years. Cyclists all know this and it encourages them to keep cycling. Madonna, Jeremy Paxman, Jon Snow and Eric Clapton are all cyclists.

Improved urban realm

A cycle-friendly city is a civilized city. There is little doubt that cycling cities such as Cambridge, Oxford and York all have a special attraction for

tourists. Abroad, too, people feel particularly welcome in cycle-friendly Amsterdam and Copenhagen. By working to improve cycling conditions, cities can become better places to live and work.

Cycling is good for you and good for London.

Above: *Cycle commuters at Canary Wharf. The health benefits alone are reason enough to consider commuting by bike.*

CHOOSING A BIKE

Bikes range from £25 second-hand roadsters to £5,000 road racing machines, but you need the right bike at the right price to suit your needs, otherwise you simply won't use it. A cheap bike may be perfect for the local trip where theft could be a worry, while a good-quality racing bike may be ideal for a long commute. A good choice will bring decades of enjoyable cycling and all the benefits that come with a more active lifestyle. Before buying, it's worth seeing if your employer offers loans for bikes or is signed up to the Cycle to Work scheme, which may get you a discount on the price of the bike. Whether you are buying new or second-hand, be sure to try before you buy.

What not to buy

It generally pays to avoid buying two kinds of bike: a new sub-£100, full-suspension imitation mountain bike (MTB) or a second-hand racing bike with steel wheel rims. Both types are slow, heavy and often unreliable. Such bikes, however, are less popular with thieves, so they can be useful for short trips during which you have to leave the bike outside, and if you have one in the shed, hang on to it – many are now being converted to trendy 'single-speeds'.

The right bike for you

The chart (below) is an easy-to-use guide to choosing the right bike for your circumstances and riding requirements (more stars equals more suitable). It covers the typical uses of a bicycle with the most appropriate type of bicycle for that type of cycling. Remember that you can always hire or borrow bikes to find out what suits you best, and you can upgrade as your needs and ambitions change.

You may find that with some minor changes you'll be able to own one bike that covers several needs. For example, you can fit a set of smooth tyres to a mountain bike to adapt it for city use, while a set of knobbly tyres will equip a touring bike for moderate off-road use.

Where to buy

A good local bike shop is the best place to buy your bike after trying out a selection. Your bike will be fully assembled and a shop can offer advice on models, correct sizes and accessories. Most shops include a 6- or 12-month service in the price. You'll also establish a useful contact for information, reliable repairs and news about cycling activities.

When buying a new bike, good shops will change the saddle, pedals or tyres for a small extra charge. This can be important in getting the right fit and better comfort or performance.

Members of your local cycle group or club (see Social Cycling, page 32) may be willing to offer expert help with buying, if you need it, and will point you to their favourite bike shops.

CHOOSING THE RIGHT BIKE FOR YOU							
USE	HYBRID	MOUNTAIN (MTB)	TOURING	RACING	FOLDING	CITY	LOW-COST MTB
Commuting	★★	★	★★	★	★	★★★	
Fast commuting	★★		★★	★★		★	
Bike/rail commuting					★★★		★
Leisure: on road/bike track	★★★	★★	★★★			★★	
Touring	★★	★	★★★	★★			
Mountain biking	★	★★★					
Road racing			★	★★★			
Child-carrying	★★★	★★	★			★★	
All-round use	★★★	★	★★			★★	
Price £	250–500	250–3000	400–2000	300–3000	300–600	200–2000	100
Weight kg/lb	11.3/25	12.2/27	11/24	9/20	11.3/25	11.3/25	13.6/30

Size

With bicycles, size matters, and most bicycle models come in several sizes. For example, mountain bikes and hybrids are usually sized in inches from 15 in to 21 1/2 in, or simply XS, S, M and L, but road bikes are sized in metric centimetres, from 48 cm to 62 cm in 2-cm increments. Many models now come in versions for men and women. Women's bikes can have either a step-through frame for easier dismounting, or can be like the equivalent men's models but with altered geometry to allow for relatively shorter torsos and longer legs. There are no hard-and-fast rules on what an individual should ride, so it's useful to try a variety of models including those designed for the opposite sex.

Usually, the correct frame size will be about 26 cm (10 in) less than your inside leg measurement for on-road use and 30 cm (12 in) less for off-road. You should be able to stand across the bike without your crotch touching the top tube, otherwise stopping at the lights could be painful. Allow at least 2.5 cm (1 in) clearance for bikes for on-road use, and 5–7.5 cm (2–3 in) for mountain bikes.

With the saddle height set correctly – your leg should be almost straight with the heel at the bottom of the pedal stroke (see Correct Set-up, page 14) – make sure you are not stretched too far forward or too low down on the handlebars. Handlebar stems on some bikes can be adjusted

Above: *A custom-made fixed-wheel bike with colourful matching components.*

up or down, and most competition bikes (on-road or off-road) tend to have more stretched-out positions. If the bike is too small, you will feel cramped and the saddle height may not go up far enough (there is a limit marked on most saddle seat pins). If you can't get into a position you like, consider another size, model or brand, because bike geometry varies between models and between brands.

Frame materials

Most modern bikes are made of aluminium. It's light and doesn't rust, but the bikes can be less comfortable than steel ones because the frames feel stiffer. Quality steels such as cro-moly or manganese molybdenum build into comfortable frames, and Columbus, Tange and Reynolds are popular tube brands. Lower grade hi-tensile steels are used on cheaper bikes. Most steel frames will rust if not cared for, unlike stainless steel and titanium frames, which are non-rusting, lightweight and durable but expensive. Carbon fibre offers the ultimate in low weight and high performance, but it's expensive and relatively fragile.

9

Key components

Modern components have made cycling much easier – gears shift with a click and brakes are more efficient. Shimano dominates the parts market but it has rivals in SRAM and Campagnolo. If you can afford it, aim for a bike with aluminium alloy components throughout, especially the wheel rims, to reduce weight and avoid rust. However, be aware that black components can be deceptive. At the top end of the market they are made of aluminium and anodized black for style; but at the bottom end the components can be made of cheap steel and coated with plastic or painted black to make them look expensive.

Handlebars and stems

Flat or slightly raised bars offer more convenient braking and a better view of the road ahead. Dropped bars, on the other hand, offer three riding positions (top of bars, on the brake hoods and on the drops) and better stream-lining for racing or touring. Many urban riders modify dropped bars by turning them upside down and cutting the tops off for a cow-horn effect. It helps with braking. There are other modifications you can make. For instance, adding forward extensions to flat bars will give you an additional position, and fitting auxiliary levers to the bar tops of dropped handlebars will give more convenient braking in town.

Gears

The two distinct types of gears are hub gears and derailleur gears. Gears that are enclosed in the hub of the rear wheel usually offer two to eight speeds and are common on city bikes. They are less exposed to external damage and require little maintenance, but usually have to be serviced in a shop if something does go wrong. You can change hub gears while at a standstill, which is convenient when you are stopped at the lights.

Virtually all racing and mountain bikes have derailleur gears. These are lighter than hub mechanisms, shift with a click and offer a range of up to 33 gears. They need fairly regular cleaning but this is an easy process and repairs are fairly simple. You have to shift derailleur gears while

pedalling so it's important to shift down before stopping.

On straight handlebars you have a choice of twist grips or push-button shifters depending on the brand. It's a personal choice.

Brakes

The modern calliper brakes used on racing bikes offer sensitive finger-tip control. V-brakes are used on hybrids and mountain bikes for their greater power, and disc brakes are used increasingly on higher priced bikes to provide strong braking in muddy or wet conditions. All brakes and brakepads need regular adjustment to maintain optimum performance, but brakes on cheap bikes are often of poor quality and require additional attention.

Saddle

Bike saddles are a personal choice and you should try several before buying. Some people swear by traditional leather saddles but others prefer gel. Grooves or holes in saddles can help avoid pressure on your sensitive bits, and most experienced cyclists use relatively firm, narrow saddles because they don't rub on your thighs on long rides. Some companies now offer saddles in different sizes and shapes to suit those with narrower or wider sit bones.

You will find that the cheaper plastic saddles, which come with some bikes, are only comfortable on shorter rides. Saddles designed for women are usually wider and shorter than those designed for men.

Wheels and tyres

Light wheels and tyres can make the biggest difference to your speed and acceleration. Changing the tyres of a bike is relatively easy and inexpensive and can be done when you are buying your new bike. Unless you plan to ride off-road frequently, aim for mixed-tread tyres rather than fat, knobbly MTB ones. If you want to cut down your commuting times, pick smooth or semi-smooth tyres and light, narrow rims. Although serious off-road use demands wide knobbly tyres, most park and canal paths can be ridden on mixed-tread tyres.

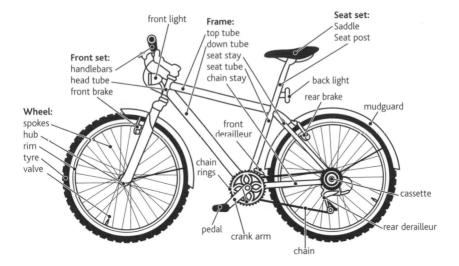

Above: *A basic mountain bike with parts labelled. They are applicable to most bikes.*

On full-size bikes there are several common, though incompatible, wheel sizes in use:
- **700 C** (aka 28" (road bikes) or 29er (mountain bikes)) wheel size used on road-racing bikes, touring bikes and most hybrids and city bikes as well as many newer (29er) mountain bikes. ISO rim size 622mm (Note: the ISO designation is the actual diameter of the rim rather than the 700C/28/29/650B/26 descriptions which relate to the estimated outer tyre diameter. The ISO number is more consistent but rarely used in bike shops).
- **650B** (aka 27.5") on mountain bikes and small size road racing bikes. ISO rim size 584mm.
- **26 inch** wheel size used on mountain bikes and some hybrids and city bikes. ISO rim size 559mm.

If your household already has bikes with one wheel size, it may be worth sticking to bikes with the same-sized wheels so that parts like inner tubes and tyres are compatible.

Pedals

Metal pedals are more durable than plastic ones. Experienced riders prefer clip-in pedals which make riding more efficient and release with a flick of the foot. For clip-ins you need special shoes, but many are designed for walking use as well as for riding.

Suspension

Suspension is useful off-road but on-road it carries a weight penalty and, unless it's of low quality, a higher cost. You can have suspension on the front forks or both front and rear. Some urban bikes have suspension front forks and a suspension seat post, offering a compromise between weight and cost.

Accessories

When pricing bikes and making comparisons, be sure to consider the cost of any accessories that are or are not included. Ask the shop to price up your preferred models with a full complement of accessories before you make your decision.

Bike brands

Most bikes, aside from custom-built jobs and some folders, are built in the Far East. Many of the popular brands sold in the UK, however, are either US- or UK-owned. Specialized, Marin, Trek, Ridgeback, Genesis and Giant are all well established, and London brands include the folding Brompton, Condor, Pinnacle and custom builders like Saffron, Donhou, Hartley, Oak and Rusby.

TYPES OF BIKE

Hybrid bikes are a mix of road bike and mountain bike, offering a comfortable upright position with flat handlebars, and are suitable for leisure riding as well as commuting. They generally have wheels in the 700 C size (larger than the typical 26 inch mountain bike wheel). They are not usually fitted with mudguards or a carrier but typically have attachment points for them. These are easy and relatively inexpensive upgrades.

City bikes are designed for pure urban use with an upright riding position, hub gears (3–8 speed) so you can change down once you've stopped rather than trying to time downshifts as you approach junctions. They usually include the key city essentials of mudguards, rack and lights. **Roadsters** are basically traditional city bikes with swept-bar handlebars and often a basket. They have retro styling but can be heavier than city bikes. Cruiser-style bikes are fun to ride, but their extra-wide handlebars make them awkward in traffic.

Mountain bikes with full-suspension can't be beaten for off-road exhilaration. In town, however, their extra weight and the drag of knobbly tyres can slow you down. You can improve the on-road performance significantly by fitting smooth or semi-smooth tyres. Expect to pay more than £400 for a new mountain bike with front suspension, and upwards of £600 for front and rear suspension. There are many sub-categories of mountain bike ranging from jump bikes to cross-country bikes. Most mid-priced bikes have disc brakes and several inches of suspension 'travel' in the front forks. Full-suspension bikes (even the cheap ones) aren't good all-rounders because of the difficulty of attaching fittings such as racks, mudguards and child seats.

Touring bikes' versatility and durability are their greatest attributes. They usually have dropped handlebars and are often made of high-quality steel for comfort and easier repair on tour. Comfort is critical on a touring bike, so make sure the saddle contact points are to your liking.

Long-distance riders usually like a firm, fairly narrow saddle. To reduce the risk of discomfort, it's a good idea to try your saddle over at least 80 km (50 miles) before using it on a bike tour, and the same for your handlebars and pedals. Touring bikes usually come with a full range of accessories and can be adapted easily for child- or load-carrying. In stripped down form, touring bikes can also be used for club racing or for fast commuting.

Racing or road bikes are worth considering if you have a long commute and you have a shower at work – you can turn your journey into a workout. Super-light machines are addictive and are more affordable since the advent of aluminium frames, but the lower you go in weight, the higher the incremental cost. Titanium and carbon fibre can take a bike's weight below 8 kg (18 lb) but the price can top £3,000 – you can buy a fine aluminium-framed bike that weighs 10 kg (23 lb) for around £500. For fast commuting you may need to fit tyres that are more durable than the usual race wear.

Folding bikes: one reason behind the boom in folders is that they can usually be taken indoors, making theft less likely. The others are that they can be taken on trains at peak times, packed into car boots and left in cupboards, either at home or at work. London's Brompton leads the pack in terms of foldability, but other folder specialists such as Dahon, Birdy, Mezzo and Airnimal offer both lightweight and sporty models. Most of the major brands now offer their own folders.

Single-speeds and fixed-wheel bikes are a recent fashion. They offer single-gear simplicity, low maintenance and a sporty look but lack the multiple gears you need for hills and faster starts at the lights. Single-speeds allow you to freewheel but on fixed-wheel bikes, or fixies, the pedals always rotate. You must have at least one independent brake on a fixed-wheel bike for safe on-road use.

BMX bikes are small-wheeled, single-geared bikes aimed at kids and for recreational use. They are usually lighter, faster and more durable than the equivalent kid's mountain bike so are a good choice as a first bike. However, prowess in BMX tricks does not mean your child has good road cycling skills. Ensure they attend cycle training (Bikeability) classes at school before cycling on the road.

Recumbents, tandems and all-ability cycles: many people are unaware of the range of cycles you can buy or hire. At one end of the scale are the human-powered vehicles (HPVs) that break speed records and even fly. At the other end are tricycles that can have two people pedalling side by side and cycles that have one person pedalling while the other simply sits. There are bikes suitable for people who can't balance, can't see, can't pedal with their feet (hand-cranked bikes), or are unable to use an ordinary bike for any other reason. Unusual cycles are a treat to ride, especially for children, and can be tried out at several London parks including Battersea and Dulwich as well as

Above: *Recumbent bikes are fast and suitable for many kinds of riders.*

at cycle events and bike shows. Bikefix in central London and London Recumbents in Dulwich specialize in recumbents and other unusual cycles.

Tandems are the secret of enjoyable family cycling. You can mix adult and child or two adults of differing strengths on a tandem trip and still make good time. Crank shorteners and kiddy-cranks make them suitable even for five-year-olds.

Electric bikes have progressed rapidly in terms of their range thanks to more long-lasting and lighter batteries. They are a growing part of the cycle market and road-racing and off-road versions are now available alongside the more typical electric city bikes. The distance range of 'ebikes' can reach 100 kms (60 miles) and some weigh less than 14Kg (30 lbs), but a 30 km (20 mile) range and a 30 Kg (66 lbs) weight is more typical. Their speed is limited, by legislation, to 15 mph on roads. Although you can contribute to

Above: *Veteran bicycles and riders at a Bike Week event in Battersea Park.*

the pedalling, e-bikes are obviously not the choice if you want a work out. They do however offer an option for longer journeys without great exertion. Be aware that their extra weight makes them a challenge if you have to store them up a staircase. Prices start at around £600 and rise to several thousand for better models. The AtoB website is a good source of information about e-bikes.

Second-hand bikes

Second-hand bikes can be great bargains but it's best to buy them from an established bike shop or from an individual who can show you proof of ownership and a photo ID. Bike magazines often advertise cycle jumbles where you can find good-value bikes, and there are several recycling projects in London offering reconditioned bikes. Steevr clear of bikes without frame numbers or those that have recently been repainted. It is always best go with a bike expert to help you, and members of local cycle groups or clubs may be able to help. Beware of buying second-hand bikes at street markets and on the Internet – you may get sold a lemon or a stolen bike. You can check if a bike has been registered as stolen at www. checkmend.com or bikeregister.com though these sites only list officially registered bikes (only a small proportion of all bikes in the UK). You

can also ask the seller if he or she has registered the bike at *www.bikeregister.com* or another registration scheme. They will need to transfer the registration to you.

Assess the cost of any repairs before buying. New tyres or wheels, for example, can double the cost of a £50 bargain. Don't buy a bike that's been crashed – cracked paint, wobbly wheels or bent forks are a giveaway, and mountain bikes in particular can receive some pretty harsh treatment. If you do buy a second-hand bike, check it thoroughly.

Correct set-up

Riding a well-set-up bike is a joy, while riding one that's badly set up can be agony. Your position on a bike can be adjusted in several ways – varying the saddle and the position of the handlebars and stem. Setting up is usually a case of personal preference but it's useful to start from the established rules of thumb and adjust from there. On a racing bike you will be bent over with your elbows slightly bent when holding the handlebars; on a bike with straight handlebars you should be a little more upright but with your arms still slightly flexed at the elbow (see illustration on opposite page). Owning a bike that is the correct size is also important (see Size page 9).

Saddle height: Your leg should be almost, but not quite, straight when your foot reaches the bottom of the pedal stroke (you should always pedal with the ball of your foot). You can calculate the advised setting for high efficiency by measuring from your crotch to the floor in socks and then multiplying by 1.09 – this gives the distance from the high point of the saddle measured in a straight line to the centre of the pedal spindle at its furthest point from the saddle. This assumes shoes with relatively thin soles, so if you wear thicker soles adjust accordingly. New riders may feel more comfortable at a lower saddle height initially because it is easier to put a foot down on the ground. You adjust the seat pin height by loosening the Allen key bolt or quick-release lever on the frame.

Saddle fore-and-aft: In theory, the point just behind your kneecap should be vertically above the pedal spindle at its forward-most point, but many people prefer to be a little further back. You may need assistance to set this position, and a plumb line held next to your kneecap can help.

Saddle level and tilt: Saddles are usually designed to be horizontal but some people prefer the nose a little lower. If you are still uncomfortable with more than a slight adjustment from level, consider changing saddles. Both the fore-and-aft position and the level are awkward to adjust on many saddles and may need to be changed simultaneously. Loosen the two nuts or Allen key bolts at the top of the seat pin, adjust and tighten.

Correct set-up

Handlebars and stem: Some bikes have fully adjustable handlebars and stem, but on others, to make changes you have to replace the stem for one that rises either more or less steeply, or is longer or shorter (an easy switch on bikes with modern stems). If a new stem does not give you enough height you can buy an extender. On older bikes you can adjust the stem up or down by about 5 cm (2 in) by easing off the Allen key bolt at the top (not too far), rapping it with a rubber mallet to release the wedge inside the frame, and pulling the stem up or down. Do not exceed the marked 'up' limit (for safety reasons) and don't forget to re-tighten the stem with the Allen key.

A rough guide for saddle nose to handlebar distance (nearest point on the handlebars) is elbow to fingertips. Handlebar height is typically level with the saddle for touring and city riding, and below saddle height for road racing and fast commuting. With mountain bikes it depends on the type of riding, and some riders use dropped handlebars upside down with the tops cut off for city riding.

Brakes: Set the brake levers so that you can reach the levers comfortably while riding. On straight flat bars you can adjust the levers inwards by means of a small screw/Allen key bolt set near the pivoting end of the lever.

Pedals: Instead of ordinary pedals you can fit pedals with toe-clips and straps which make pedalling more efficient but make taking your feet off the pedals slower. Clips should fit your shoe size and you should keep straps loose in urban traffic. Clip-in pedals, such as Shimano SPD or Look, are a further improvement in efficiency but remember to set them to a loose setting for urban riding. Adjust them by means of the small Allen key screw at the back of the pedal.

Gears: Most hybrid, racing and mountain bikes have a wide selection of gears, but you can change the gear range at relatively low cost (a different gear cassette costs about £25). If you find that your gear range is too high or too low, consider changing it.

ACCESSORIES AND CLOTHES

Some bikes, often Dutch or German models, come with a full set of accessories but most don't. If you're buying a bike without the accessories you want, you may get a better deal on them if you buy them with it, rather than buying them later or from a different store. Here's what you will need.

Pump and puncture kit

Correctly inflated tyres improve speed and deter punctures. Ideally, you should have two pumps: a track or foot pump with a pressure gauge to use at home and which can inflate tyres to 120 psi (8 bar) or more, as well as a small portable pump. You should inflate tyres to the pressure recommended on the tyre sidewall – generally expressed as a maximum and minimum range. Good pumps (track and portable) have a lever that tightens the pump head around the valve. Most modern pumps can be used with the two popular valve types – Presta (long and thin) and Schrader (car type) – by flipping a lever or by using a choice of two connectors. There is a third type of valve, the Woods, which has a collar nut and was used on older roadsters.

A spare inner tube of the right size for your tyres, a puncture kit, tyre levers and a 15 cm (6 in) adjustable spanner are what you'll need to fix a puncture.

Mudguards

These are useful in bad weather. The best are made of unbreakable plastic and come in sizes to fit 26 inch mountain bike wheels or the 700 C (sometimes called 28 inch) wheels fitted to hybrids and road bikes. Mudguards come in types to fit bosses (small holes near the wheel hubs) and those to fit bikes without bosses, such as racers or MTBs (mountain bikes).

Lock

A good lock is essential in London. Count on spending 10 to 20 percent of the value of your bike on a lock (see Storage, Security and Insurance, page 29).

Lights

In the UK you must have reflectors and front and rear lights, plus reflectors on your pedals. Flashing LED (light-emitting diode) lights are now permitted. These cost £5–£30 but are designed only to make you visible, not to light the road. Choose lights that are visible from the sides as well as head-on. Remember to remove your lights when leaving your bike. Rechargeable halogen lights light the road or track, but they cost £100 or more (take care in urban areas not to blind other cyclists or drivers by adjusting the intensity setting). Dynamos (£30–£60) need no batteries and are fixed permanently to the bike so they are less easy to steal. Modern dynamos have a rear 'standlight' that switches on when you stop pedalling and some, such as Reelights, exert no friction on your wheel.

Panniers, saddlebags, racks and trailers

The most comfortable way of carrying loads on a bike is in panniers attached to a rack. Panniers come in sets of two and the better ones, such as Ortlieb or Carradice, are water- proof (£60 upwards). You can buy them for front and rear racks. There are also bags designed to convert into briefcases and which have inserts for laptops. Rack-top bags are for smaller loads and sit on top of a rack. The racks themselves are made of aluminium or tubular steel and the better models, such as Tubus or Blackburn, take heavier loads for a given weight of rack.

Traditionalists scorn panniers and racks and opt for saddlebags, and retro fashion dictates that you have one made out of durable cotton-duck. Modern saddlebags have their own attachment devices and are usually secured to the seat pin. Alternatively, for smaller loads, you can use a courier bag. These keep all your kit in one place for quick stops, and the better ones have straps to secure them around your waist. For greater loads the best solution is a trailer that you drag behind your bike. One-wheeler trailers offer good balance but are relatively small; two- wheelers are bigger but can tip over if you ride too fast around

corners. Larger shops offer a good selection, as do specialists such as Bikefix (see Major London Cycling Shops, page 236).

Water bottles, hydration packs and rucksacks

Water bottles are essential on longer journeys, and when touring it's useful to have two. You can carry them in holders or cages attached to your bike, or opt instead for a hydration pack. This is a water container in a small backpack which allows you to sip water on the go. Rucksacks are often used to carry gear but you may find that a heavy weight on your back can lead to backache (and make you rather top-heavy).

Helmets

Cycling helmets are not compulsory in the UK but increasing numbers of cyclists are wearing them. If you chose to wear a helmet, remember that they do not prevent collisions and are made to withstand impact speeds of up to 12mph, not the higher speeds that usually occur in collisions with vehicles. Be wary of taking more risks, such

Above *Well-equipped cyclists on a leisure ride with water bottles, saddlebags, cycling clothing and safety gear.*

as riding at high speed, when wearing a helmet than when not wearing one. One of the best ways of avoiding collisions is to take some cycle training (see Urban Cycling Techniques, page 19).

When buying a helmet, make sure you choose one that's the right size, is comfortable and provides sufficient ventilation for your riding pace. It should fit snugly around your head and not be tilted to the back, front or side. Straps should be snug but not cut in to your chin or neck. The EU 1078 standard should be marked on the side of the helmet; Snell B90 and B95 are higher standards. If children are wearing helmets make sure they remove them when going on swings – the straps can catch on playground fixtures. It is also important to ensure that your child's helmet fits properly and doesn't slide around on his or her head.

Clothing

You can ride a bicycle in almost any clothing, but for longer rides proper cycle clothing offers convenience and comfort. In bad weather, cycling waterproofs enable you to arrive dry and presentable, while bright or reflective garments make you more noticeable. Layering is a good approach to a cycling outfit because you can add or remove items as the weather changes and as you ride more intensively, and carrying an extra T-shirt or a light jacket is always a good precaution. If wearing normal clothing, choose trousers and briefs with light seams or without seams at the back. Breathable garments make you less sweaty, and stiff-soled shoes transmit power more efficiently.

Jackets and reflective gear: reflective vests, belts and leg bands improve your visibility, especially at night. The leg bands double as trouser clips. Waterproof jackets are the best clothes to keep out the weather, although in an emergency a bin bag with a few holes in it can serve as an alternative. Cycle-specific jackets are light, and usually made of a material that is both waterproof and breathable. They are often brightly coloured for good visibility and slightly longer at the back. Armpit zips help reduce condensation inside, and pockets on the back rather than in front help make cycling more comfortable. The better (and more expensive) jackets incorporate highly breathable materials such as Gore-Tex, eVent, Ventile cotton and Epic.

Tops and bottoms: cycling tops are usually made of Lycra or merino wool and have several pockets at the back. Although most tops in shops are festooned with team sponsors' logos, you can also buy plain ones.

Lycra shorts offer excellent comfort for longer journeys, and those with built-in padding help keep you dry and provide some cushioning. Cycling shorts are designed to be worn next to the skin, and some riders rub antiseptic cream into the pad to improve hygiene. If you prefer a more casual look, you can buy regular shorts with padded inners. Leggings offer warmth for the knees and legs in winter months.

Shoes: modern cycling shoes are designed to be fitted with cleats that attach to pedals rather like ski bindings, and there are different brands of cleat that attach to specific brands of pedal. Cleats pop off the pedal with a sideways flick of the foot and are the preferred choice of most experienced riders who adjust them to the loose setting when riding in urban traffic. Racing shoes have cleats that are difficult to walk in while touring and mountain bike shoes have convenient recessed cleats. There are two popular brands of cleats: Shimano SPD and Look – they are not compatible so you have to have the corresponding type of pedal.

Gloves: padded cycling gloves not only keep your hands more comfortable but also protect your palms in the event of a fall. Mitts for the summer have no finger tips whereas winter gloves are full-fingered and often include some waterproofing.

Electronics

Cycle computers can provide details of speed, distance and heart rate. More sophisticated ones use sensors in the cranks to measure power output and can also link up to smartphones. Smartphone-based GPS systems or independently powered ones (useful if you want to conserve your phone battery) offer detailed mapping as well as noting your location so they can be used for route planning and competing with other riders using apps like Strava.

Bell

All new bikes must be fitted with a bell. Used considerately, they are a useful way to warn pedestrians of your approach, particularly along towpaths. On the other hand, ringing your bell incessantly is to be avoided! Saying 'ding, ding' is a good organic substitute for a bell.

Cameras

A growing number of cyclists mount small cameras on their helmets or bikes for both entertainment and to keep a record of any road incident. Because of their small size, the camera batteries do not last a long time.

URBAN CYCLING TECHNIQUES

Balancing on a bicycle is a skill most people already have, but confident cycling in urban traffic is a skill that needs to be learned.

Experienced urban cyclists rarely have conflicts with drivers and are not commonly involved in collisions. This is not simply chance, but the result of an effective strategy of road behaviour. In Britain, unlike the Netherlands, high quality separate facilities for cyclists are still rare; in Holland children are taught how to interact with other road users when they encounter motor vehicles.

Thanks to cycling expert John Franklin and the pioneering educational work of Cycle Training UK, the skills of confident, safe cycling are now part of a government-approved curriculum called Bikeability, which is taught in many schools. Similar training sessions are available to adults in most London boroughs, often at low cost.

While it is best to have a training session (see Key Contacts, page 234, to find a trainer), reading the short guide below will set you on the right road. If you have the opportunity it is worth reading John Franklin's Cyclecraft.

At the heart of confident cycling are good communication, positioning and awareness:

Clear communication with other road users is achieved by making eye contact with drivers, which ensures that they have seen you. Experienced riders anticipate the movements of other road users and signal their intentions clearly whenever necessary.

A satisfactory road position is one where you take as much of the road as you need to be safe. You need to ensure that drivers can see you and there is no ambiguity about what both of you are about to do next, such as pass, turn or wait.

Awareness means being constantly aware of other road users, looking back every few seconds and scanning ahead for hazards such as potholes, opening car doors, drivers indicating and pedestrians stepping off the kerb to cross. You should always look before signalling or moving.

Below *Start in a low gear and with your foot in the 2 o'clock position (like the rider in the yellow helmet third from right).*

Practice

If you haven't recently ridden in traffic, practise by riding in the park or on quiet streets. You need to be confident about doing the following:
• Using the brakes and carrying out an emergency stop – both brakes are applied at the same time with arms braced. Shift your weight towards the back of the bike.
• Using the gears – you should change down before coming to a stop.
• Riding while holding the handlebars with one hand, so that you can signal with the other hand safely.
• Looking behind while holding the handlebars with two hands. Try turning your head so your chin rests on your shoulder.
• Looking behind while holding the handlebars with one hand. Try putting your other hand on the back of the saddle or on your hip for stability.
• Looking back and signalling with one hand.

Before riding to work or another destination in weekday traffic, work out a preferred route on one of the 14 London cycle maps which show you routes with less traffic. Try to practise your route to work on a Sunday or enquire from your local cycling group about arranging for a 'bike buddy' who rides a similar route and can show you the ropes.

Highway Code

As a cyclist you have the same rights to use the road as a motorist and you also have the same responsibilities towards the more vulnerable road users – pedestrians. Most Highway Code rules therefore apply to cyclists as well as motorists. Cycling on pavements alongside roads is only per-mitted if there are signs indicating that this is the case. When using a shared pavement, give way to pedestrians and take extra care coming off the pavement into the road because drivers may not have noticed you. Traffic signals and zebra cross-ings in the UK must be obeyed by all road users including cyclists. Being considerate to other road users, whether you are driving or cycling, helps to reduce road danger to you and to others.

Starting and stopping

Don't just ride out into the road: place your bike out in the road where you can see and be seen by drivers first and then get on. Make sure you are in a low gear and set one pedal in the 2 o'clock position, where the pedal crank is in line with the down tube. First look behind you, letting anyone already moving on the road go first, then move off when the road is clear.

While riding, keep at least two fingers over the brake levers to be able to stop quickly if the need arises. Use both brakes at the same time and come to a halt before putting your foot down. This enables you to stay in full control before stopping.

Gears

Gears enable you to maintain a steady pedalling rate. If your bike has gears, practise using them, especially changing down before stopping (you can change at a standstill only if you have hub gears). It's most efficient to maintain a steady rate of pedalling – 60 to 80 revolutions per minute is best – by changing the gears.

Road positioning

New cyclists often think that the safest place to be on a bike is very close to the kerb. As Bikeability instructors will tell you, this is poor practice because you are less visible to drivers and you encounter drains and debris near the side of the road. Bikeability guidance is to ride either in the centre of the left lane (primary position, P, see illustration opposite) or 1 metre (3 ft) away from the kerb (secondary position, S) to allow drivers to pass when it is safe to do so. The space between you and the kerb gives you a margin for error. If you are in the primary position (the usual default position on minor roads, see diagram, page 21), and do not think it is safe for a vehicle to pass – for example when approaching a road narrowing, or cycling past parked cars – it is worth making it clear to the driver behind you that you know they are there with a quick look. Once you clear the obstacle, move over and let them pass. Courtesy by all road users is what sharing the road is about.

On busy roads adopt the secondary position to allow a stream of traffic to pass, but you may need to move into the primary position ahead of parked cars or while passing side roads.

Before making any changes of direction on the road remember to look behind you, and signal if anyone needs to know what you're doing. Looking behind is something you should be doing on a regular basis. You should allow at least a car door's width when passing parked cars in case one of them opens a door in front of you. It's always worth watching for people inside cars who may be about to get out. Ahead of junctions you should be in the primary position to get a better view of the side street and to prevent drivers over-taking and suddenly turning left in front of you.

Signalling

Before making a turn, check behind (over the turn-side shoulder) before signalling and only signal if there is someone behind you or ahead of you who needs to know your intentions.

Make your signal clear and decisive.

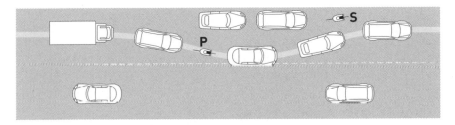

LONDON CYCLING CAMPAIGN'S GOOD CYCLING CODE

- **Be assertive:** You've the same right to use the road as vehicles. Keep well out from the kerb or parked cars. Make eye contact with drivers who might cross your path, and use hand signals when turning.
- **Give pedestrians** priority on shared paths; give them the kind of space you'd like to be given by car drivers.
- **Make sure you can be seen at night:** Use lights and consider wearing high-visibility clothing or adding reflective material to your bike.
- **Take extra care in the rain:** Give yourself extra room to manoeuvre or stop.
- **Jumping red lights** and riding on pavements is illegal and can also be dangerous or frightening for others. Don't do it!
- **Take special care at junctions** and never cut inside a left-turning lorry – it's potentially hazardous and not worth the risk for the few seconds saved.
- **Don't use a mobile phone** while cycling – it distracts your attention from the road. It's better to stop and take that call.

- **Consider investing in panniers,** a rack, basket or good rucksack: dangling heavy shopping from your handlebars or carrying bags under one arm will make you very unstable on your bike and it will be much harder to steer safely.
- **Look after your bike!** A well-maintained bike is your best ally on the road. Check your tyres and brakes regularly. If you want to learn how to service your bike, why not contact LCC to find your nearest bike maintenance course or organize a Dr Bike for your workplace, school or community group to get your bike checked and learn how to perform basic maintenance.
- **Do tell other road users** when their actions may have caused you to have an accident. But remember that being calm and polite is more likely to get your point across than aggression; you can also win more support for all cyclists by simply waving a thank you or otherwise making some acknowledgement when someone has been courteous to you.

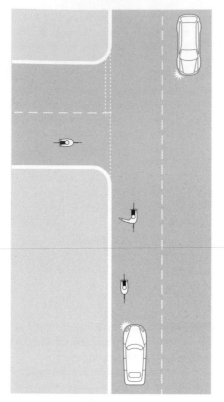
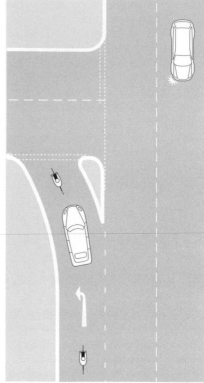

Cycle lanes

Segregated cycle lanes or tracks can be convenient but beware of assuming that they eliminate risk from traffic or pedestrians.

Drivers often cross them from side streets or driveways and you may not have priority over these vehicles. Even if you do, vehicles may not always observe that priority. So use cycle lanes if it is convenient and safe to do so and take care at all side streets. When using non- segregated cycle lanes take particular care when approaching traffic signals because drivers may turn left across your path. Also watch out for pedestrians crossing cycle lanes.

Turning left and right

Ahead of a left turn you should be in the primary position to prevent a driver passing and turning left across your path. Look back and signal to ensure drivers know you are about to turn (see both illustrations above).

Turning right may involve two manoeuvres: one to get into the right-hand lane and a second to turn right. Both should be preceded by checking for traffic and signalling if anyone needs to know your intentions. If you are unable to make the manoeuvre before a vehicle comes up behind, you will have to wait on the left until there is a gap in the traffic.

Overtaking

You should normally overtake slow or stationary vehicles on the outside. Look, signal and move out well before reaching the vehicle that you are about to overtake. If there are several parked cars to overtake, it is usually best to stay in the primary position until you have passed them all rather than moving in and out (see illustration, page 23).

Roundabouts

In *Cyclecraft*, John Franklin advises cyclists to negotiate roundabouts in the same way as they

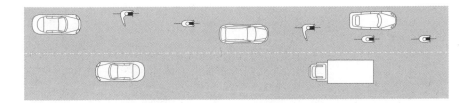

would do when driving a car – adopt the primary position at the entrance of the roundabout in the appropriate lane for the exit you are aiming for. So stay in the near lane for the first exit or the outer lane for subsequent exits. The problem with the alternative strategy of staying on the edge of a roundabout until you reach your exit is that you come into conflict with vehicles trying to leave the roundabout, and those trying to join the round-about at the mouth of each entrance/exit (see illustration, bottom left). Several major London roundabouts/gyratories (including Elephant and Castle, Hyde Park Corner, Wandsworth Bridge, Vauxhall Cross, Bricklayer's Arms, Swiss Cottage and Waterloo) have cycle bypasses or pavement / cycle track routes, although they may be poorly signed. If you are unfamiliar with a difficult junction consider walking on the pavement and using the signals.

Lorries and high-sided vehicles

Avoid getting caught on the inside of a left-turn-ing lorry or other high-sided vehicle: the so-called 'left-hook' is a common cause of injuries to cyclists. You should not edge forwards along the inside of a long vehicle – if necessary, wait behind it or overtake on the outside. Remember that if you can't see the driver in their mirror then they can't see you. Avoid the front left corner of a lorry cab, both in front of the cab and to its side, which is a particular danger area because it falls in one of the drivers 'blind spots.' The London Cycling Campaign is lobbying to make lorry cabs with minimal 'blind spots,' already in common use on refuse lorries and airport lorries, the standard for all trucks on London roads.

Articulated lorries swing out before turning left so if you are on their inside you have to beware of being overtaken by the cab but then finding that the centre and tail of the lorry comes closer to you (see illustration, bottom right).

If you are on the opposite side of the road you may find that the lorry encroaches onto your side of the street as it corners. So if you aim to turn right at a junction it is usually better to stop in the centre of a lane rather than over to the extreme right, where you may be in conflict with larger vehicles.

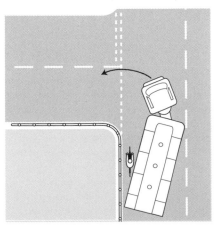

CANALS & RIVERS TRUST – LONDON TOWPATH CODE

Cyclists are allowed to ride along most towpaths in London, but Canals & Rivers Trust asks you to follow its towpath code and ride with consideration for others.

- Use a bell, giving two tings when approaching pedestrians. Be aware that some pedestrians may have visual or hearing impairments and might not hear your bell.
- Slow down when approaching pedestrians and only pass when it is safe to do so. Extra care should be taken when passing children, less able people and animals.
- Try to pass on the water side of the path. Pedestrians will tend to move to the back edge of the towpath to allow you to pass.
- Be patient and courteous to pedestrians. A 'thank you' is always appreciated.
- Ride at a sensible speed. The towpath is not suitable for fast cycling.

Left: *London's towpaths are a delight but always give way to walkers.*
Below: *Commuters making use of one of London's many cycle paths.*

Commuting by bike

The step from enjoying a leisure cycle ride to commuting by bike is an easy one, and cycle commuting will not only save you time and money but will also keep you fit. Thirty minutes of cycling a day (15 minutes each way) will satisfy the recommended daily exercise level for adults.

It's best to plan a pleasant route to work, with the help of the London cycling maps, and practise it on a weekend before trying it in heavier traffic. Make sure you have a secure place to leave your bike at work.

Employers stand to gain from having more staff cycle to work. Studies show that cyclists take fewer days off and are fitter and healthier than people who don't exercise. Employers can replace one car-parking space with ten for bicycles. One major employer estimates that every additional cycling employee saves it £1,500 annually in the cost of a car parking space. A cycle-friendly employer can provide the following:

- **Participation in the government Cycle to Work scheme**, which can save you up to 40 percent of the cost of a new bike. Your employer has to join the scheme which can easily be arranged by one of the facilitators such as Cyclescheme or Halfords. The employer has to buy the bike (reclaiming VAT) and you pay for it by deductions from your salary. As you don't pay tax or National Insurance on the income you forego, you save up to 40 percent. After a set period you buy the bike from your employer for a small proportion of its original cost.
- **Cycle stands, showers and lockers.** Employers with travel plans are eligible for the TfL workplace cycling scheme which provides free bike stands and a grant towards workplace showers and lockers.
- **Corporate affiliation** to a cycling organization which, in the case of London Cycling Campaign, provides discounted membership for staff and other services.
- **A tool kit** and drying room.
- **Periodic cycle repair** sessions for staff.
- **A pool bike** for use on company business.
- **Set up a Bicycle User Group** (BUG) to ensure good communication with staff.

For more on cycling to work go to *www.lcc.org.uk.*

TRANSPORTING YOUR BIKE

Cycling is easily combined with other forms of transport, including rail, car and plane. Almost all the rides in this book start at a railway station to which you can bring your bike by rail outside of peak times. You can also carry bikes on many sections of the London Underground, Overground and DLR outside of the rush hour. For more information about taking bikes on the railway network, contact National Rail on 08457 48 49 50 or see their leaflet Cycling by Train, available via their website *www.nationalrail.co.uk*. Carrying bikes on cars is easy if you have a rack, and most airlines and ferry services accept bikes though you usually have to pay a charge.

The information below applies to full-size bicycles. Folding bikes are allowed on all trains and on the Underground at all times, though in some cases you are asked to put them in a bag. Even though you are allowed to take folders on the Underground at peak times, the carriages are often too packed with passengers to make it a realistic proposition.

Short-distance trains

Most short-distance rail operators in London permit cycle carriage without any cost outside peak hours which are usually defined as:

- Trains that arrive in London between 7 and 10 am (or 7.45–9.45 am on some lines) Monday to Friday
- Trains that depart from London between 4 and 5 pm (4.30–6.30 pm on some lines) Monday to Friday.

The exact rules vary depending on the operator running a particular rail franchise, and the operators change periodically. For up-to-date rules check *www.nationalrail. co.uk/css/CycleLeaflet.pdf*. Some short-distance trains have a dedicated cycle space or a shared-use space (also available to wheelchair users). The carriage with a bike space is usually marked with a bicycle sign. If there is no dedicated space you can put your bicycle in a vestibule. It pays to ask about which side the platforms are likely to be on so

that you can be on the opposite side. On the rail line from Finsbury Park to Old Street, no bikes are allowed any time.

Long-distance trains

Cycle carriage is permitted on most long-distance trains but with restrictions at peak times. You usually have to book a reservation because intercity trains, now that they no longer have goods carriages, have limited amounts of space. Trains usually accommodate between two to six bicycles and, in a few cases, tandems. Full details are provided at: *www.nationalrail.co.uk/css/ CycleLeaflet.pdf*.

Airport trains

The Gatwick Express and Heathrow Express trains have dedicated space for bicycles at all times. The Heathrow Express can take about four bikes. The Stansted Express, however, does not permit bikes at any time unless they are packed for air travel. On trains to Luton airport, cycle carriage is only permitted off-peak but you may be able to board at peak times with a bike that is packed for air travel.

Docklands Light Railway

Cycle carriage is permitted off peak. Peak times are 07.30–09.30 am and 4–7 pm Mon.–Fri. Folding bikes can be taken any time.

London Overground

You can take bikes on most Overground trains outside peak times. Peak times are 07.30–09.30 am and 4–7 pm Mon.–Fri. Folding bikes can be taken any time.

London Underground

The map on page 28 (also on the web at *http://content.tfl.gov.uk/bicycle-tube-map. pdf*) shows where non-folding bicycles can be carried on the Underground outside peak times. There is no charge for cycle carriage. For more information on Underground services call 0343 222 1234.

Above: You can take bikes on most Overground trains outside peak times. Folding bikes can be taken any time.

- Peak hours are 7.30 am–9:30 am and 4 pm–7 pm, Monday to Friday
- You must not take a non-folding bicycle onto a moving escalator
- You cannot take a non-folding bicycle onto any rail replacement bus.

Non-folding bicycles are permitted on the Underground, outside peak times, on sections of lines that are above ground, notably the Circle, East London, Hammersmith & City and Metropolitan Lines. Additionally bikes are permitted on the following Underground lines as follows:

Bakerloo Line: Outside peak times in either direction between:
- **Queen's Park to Harrow** in morning peak
- **Harrow to Queen's Park** in evening peak.

Central Line: Outside peak times in either direction between:
- **White City–West Ruislip/Ealing Broadway**
- **Leyton–Epping**
- **Newbury Park/Woodford–Hainault.**

Jubilee Line: Outside peak times in both directions between:
- **Finchley Road–Stanmore**
- **Canning Town–Stratford.**

Northern Line: Outside peak times in both directions between:
- **Edgware–Colindale**
- **Hendon Central–Golders Green**

- **East Finchley–High Barnet/Mill Hill East.**

Piccadilly Line: Outside peak times in either direction between:
- **Barons Court–Hounslow West/Uxbridge**
- **Cockfosters–Oakwood.**

River, Buses and Trams

Riverboat services accept folding and non-folding bicycles at any time. Non-folding bicycles are not permitted on either buses or trams. Drivers can allow folding bikes on.

Emirates Air Line

Bikes are permitted at any time free of charge. You only pay for the passenger. Opening times are 8 am–8 pm daily except during high winds.

Coach

Most coach companies will accept dismantled and packed bicycles and some, such as those to Oxford, will take complete cycles in the luggage compartment. Check with the operators.

Car

With the appropriate rack almost any car can carry from one to three cycles. Don't forget the bikes on the roof when negotiating low bridges and other restricted spaces.

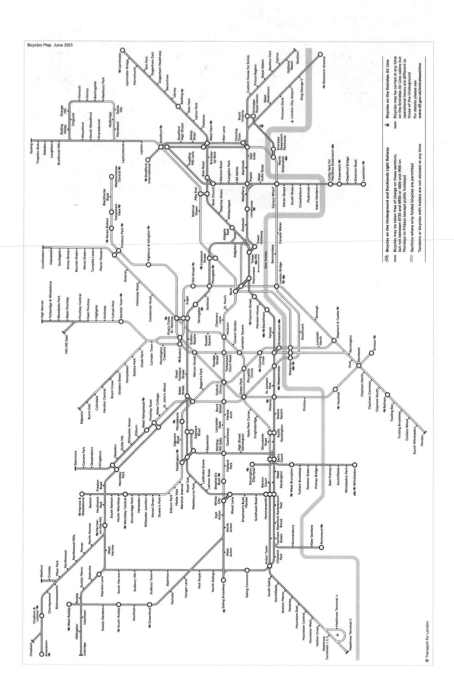

STORAGE, SECURITY AND INSURANCE

Owning a cycle is a delight, having one stolen is inconvenient and costly. In a decent world we would be able to leave our bikes on the street without locks and find them when we got back. The sad reality in London is that 17,000 bikes are reported stolen to the police each year and the actual number taken by thieves is much higher because many losses go unreported.

Good bicycle security depends on:
- The quality of the lock or locks
- The location
- The locking technique.

In case of theft you should consider security marking your bike and taking out insurance. It is also worth having third party insurance in case you are responsible for a collision.

Below: *Remember to lock the frame and both wheels of your bike to an immovable object. Consider using two locks, if necessary.*

Locks

Professionals can break virtually any lock but strong expensive locks take them longer to break and may deter them from trying. Opportunist thieves aim for easy targets. A basic rule of thumb is that you should spend 10% to 20% of the value of your bike on a lock or locks. A £2000 bike is a magnet for thieves; a £50 second hand roadster attracts little interest.

A company called Sold Secure grades locks from Gold down to Bronze and these grades are marked on better quality locks. The penalties for a stronger lock are price and weight. Some cyclists choose to leave heavier locks at regular destinations. If you do this, remember not to inconvenience other cyclists or pedestrians.

Strong locks include both D locks and heavy chains with solid padlocks. For higher security it is preferable to use two locks of different types: one locking the bike frame to a solid object (the D lock) and another to lock the two wheels to the frame.

D locks usually attach to your bike frame – some cyclists wrap chains around their waists.

Thin cable locks offer little security. Slightly heavier ones can be used to secure the wheels to the frame. Some 'extension' cables are designed to be looped around a D lock.

Locks come with two or three keys – put one in a safe place.

Parts get stolen as well as bikes, particularly if they are only held in place by quick-release levers. You can often improve security by replacing such levers with bolts, or with locking nuts with customized Allen keys. Pitlock, Pinhead and Atomic 22 all make lockable nuts and bolts.

Storing your bike indoors

If possible, store your bike indoors, whether at home, at work or at other destinations. It is good practice to lock it to a solid object even indoors, particularly if you regularly leave it in a hallway shared with others. Outdoor sheds are considered very vulnerable to theft and you should lock the bike to a fitting attached firmly to the wall of the shed. Bike shops sell heavy rings that can be attached to house walls and there are versions for sheds that bolt though the shed wall itself for added security.

If you are short of space at home you can hang your bike on a wall or from a ceiling, using hooks or brackets designed for this purpose (some people use the brackets designed for hanging heavy plant pots). Larger bike shops sell a range of brackets costing from £10 to £30.

There are also pulley systems that enable you to pull your bike right up to ceiling level.

At work you may have access to indoor bike stands. If not, then lock your bike's frame to the front wheel. If your employer has no facilities for bikes they may be able to apply for the Transport for London (TfL) workplace cycling programme. This programme offers free stands to companies that have a travel plan (TfL will help with these too) and where the company agrees to install the stands on its own premises.

Storing your bike outdoors

Public cycle-parking locations vary greatly in the levels of security they provide. Some are securely locked, others are supervised, and there are open

but well-observed bike stands and the less publicly visible bike stands. The longer you plan to leave your bike unattended the more secure a location you'll need.

The preferred locations are enclosed (card-entry) cycle-parking compounds. These charge a small fee, typically 50p – £2 per day, and include those at Finsbury Park Station, the Midtown Cycle Vault, and the Sekura-Byk facility at the car park in Bernard Street near Russell Square.

Cycle parking is also provided inside a number of car parks – including many in Westminster (see the council's website) and the City of London. It is usually free but access is not restricted by card and it is less secure than caged compounds.

An increasing number of rail stations now offer secure (card entry) cycle parking including Finsbury Park, St Pancras, Surbiton, Walthamstow, Battersea Park and Peckham Rye. Others like Waterloo and Ealing Broadway have cycle parking in well-lit public areas.

If leaving your bike in the street, always lock it to an immovable object and wherever possible, choose a bike stand in a well-lit public place. If one isn't available, government websites advise using street furniture or railings where your bicycle will not be an obstruction. Make certain that thieves can't make off with your bike by lifting it over a post or railing.

You should avoid:

- Dark alleys
- Stands that only grip your front wheel
- Posts that your bike could be lifted over
- The Westminster security zone where all bikes are removed immediately. The zone is not clearly defined but broadly covers the area between Buckingham Palace, Parliament and Trafalgar Square. There are bike stands along the Embankment, at the north end of Trafalgar Square, in Millbank and Victoria Street – all just outside the zone
- Railings with signs saying that your bike will be removed
- Anywhere that your bike is likely to cause an obstruction – the police can remove bicycles that are an obstruction without notice. If you think this has happened to your bike call the local police station.

Security marking

When you acquire a bike take a photo of it and note down its make, model and frame number. Frame numbers are usually under the bottom bracket (the part of the frame to which the chain wheel is attached) but can sometimes be near the seat pin or on the frame by the rear wheel slot. If in doubt, ask your shop. You should also note the make of all the major components such as gears, chainset, brakes, and wheels. When you have the frame number, add your bike to the Met Police preferred database www.bikeregister. com. London police forces use this database to help identify lost or stolen bikes. Registration is free, but you have to pay for frame marking kits and stickers. These are often provided at no cost by the police at special events: keep an eye on the events page at www.lcc.org.uk. Long-life battery powered devices concealed on your bike with a GPS signal linked to your phone are now available but they remain costly.

Theft insurance

No lock is perfect so it pays to have insurance. The number of thefts has raised premiums, and insurers require your bike to be locked to a solid object if left outside or in a shared hallway. Some specify the grade of lock. LCC offers purpose-designed cycle insurance which includes some personal accident cover as well. You may also be able to add your cycle to household insurance.

Third-party insurance

It is worth having third-party insurance to cover you for the unlikely eventuality that you damage a car or injure a pedestrian. Third-party insurance is provided as a free membership benefit of LCC and Cycling UK. There are more details on their websites.

What to do if your bike is stolen

Report your stolen bike to the police immediately by phone, in person or online at *https://online. met.police.uk/ocr.html#theft*. Ask the police if the bike may have been removed for security reasons (for example if it was near Parliament) or because it was an obstruction. Ask for the CAD (Computer Aided Despatch) or CRIS (Crime Reference Information System) number for the theft – your insurer will require this.

Register it as stolen at *www.bikeregister.com*.

In the unlikely event that you are mugged for your bike or personal belongings, the police advice is to give them up rather than face injury. Report the event immediately by dialing 999. The police have a prioritizing system so call 999 even if the incident is non-life threatening.

For more on cycle insurance and theft prevention go to *www.lcc.org.uk*.

SOUND LOCKING TECHNIQUE

- **Choose a well-lit public location** where your bike is not an obstruction.
- **Use two high-quality locks** of different types. Lock frame and one wheel to the bike stand, and use another lock to attach the other wheel to the frame.
- **If you have quick-release wheels** and only one lock, remove the front wheel and lock both wheels and frame together to the stand.
- **Fill the space within a D-lock** (for example, with a wheel) to prevent the lock being prised open with a car jack.

- **Take all lights** and removable accessories (and saddle if removable) with you.
- **Make sure your bike will not fall** and perhaps trip pedestrians.
- **Do not leave the chain** on the ground, where it can be easier to break.
- **Leave the lock facing downwards** to make lock-picking more difficult.
- **Do not accidentally lock** your bike to another bike.
- **Make your bike look unattractive** – torn tape and ugly paintwork can discourage some thieves.

SOCIAL CYCLING

One of the delights of cycling in London is the rich social life associated with this mode of transport. There are hundreds of opportunities to go on free guided bike rides, meet other cyclists, learn about bike repair or participate in local activities. Most of the rides in this book were created by local LCC groups and some are conducted as regular guided rides every month.

Major annual events

The two big annual events are Bike Week, which offers more than a hundred cycling-related activities all across London in June, and the annual Ride London event. During this event, usually held on a weekend in August or September, roads are closed in central London and 50,000 people ride a circuit that includes all the major landmarks in the capital. On the other day of the weekend, thousands of cyclists who have registered participate in a 100 km road race in Southern England. While professional riders compete to win, thousands of other riders try to achieve a personal best. The race makes for an enjoyable day out as spectator even if you are not participating.

There are also numerous charity events that start in London, of which the biggest is the London to Brighton ride in June.

Local rides, repair workshops and social events

Throughout the year there are thousands of activities that cater to the interests of new riders, leisure cyclists, racing cyclists, architecture fans, mountain bikers, people with disabilities, bicycle polo players and unicycle hockey fans. There are groups that not only organize rides and social activities but also work to improve provisions for cyclists in London, whether it's more cycle parking or safer routes to schools.

Southwark Cyclists, for example, organize an annual solstice ride and weekly 'afterworker' rides. Tower Hamlets Wheelers and the Islington Cyclists Action Group have regular bike repair workshops as well as weekly rides. Westminster Cyclists specialize in relaxed rides to stately homes, and the LCC Lambeth group organizes architectural rides. Kingston Cyclists are famous for their 'bread pudding' rides. The Barnet group has talks and entertainment before its regular meetings and runs weekly rides. Most groups also work to improve the conditions for cycling in London.

Non-LCC members are welcome at virtually all of the guided rides (but children must be accompanied by adults) and the announcement for each ride usually gives you a guide to the length, duration and degree of difficulty. Most rides include a stop or two and an opportunity to chat – one LCC group reports that one in five of the couples among its membership met through social cycling. Rides are posted on the LCC website (*www. lcc.org.uk*) under rides and events.

Below: *'Dr Bike' repair clinic at an LCC event in Hackney.*

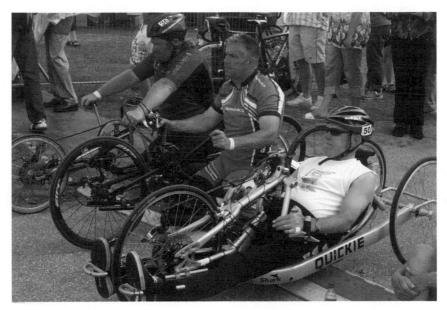

Above: *Riders of hand-cranked cycles taking part in a cycling event. These bikes can be hired at several locations.*

Racing – road, off-road, BMX and track

On the racing and triathlon front there are dozens of active clubs in London, ranging from track racing at Herne Hill and the Velopark in East London to triathlons in Kingston and Audax (against-the-clock) rides in north London. Some groups organize joint trips out of town to Wales, Scotland and abroad.

The new Velopark in Newham, built for the 2102 Olympics in London, offers a range of activities including track racing (a one hour introductory training session, including cycle hire, costs £35), a BMX track, a road racing circuit and an off-road circuit. Booking online at: *www.visitleevalley.org. uk/en/content/cms/london2012/velo-park/.*

Participation and contacts

Nothing could be easier than taking part in cycling activities – most rides and events are free, and the information is on the Internet. You'll find that you meet a range of different people from all walks of life and many different backgrounds. The London Cycling Campaign website offers an easy-to-use list of events going on in London and the South East. It also puts you in touch with the local cycling groups in each London borough, many of which have their own websites with separate lists of activities. For racing cyclists, British Cycling offers a similar listing of events on its website and for those outside London there is Cycling UK, the national cyclists' organization. Fixed-wheel and single-speed enthusiasts have their own website at *www.lfgss.com.*

Special needs and all-ability cycling

Virtually anyone, whatever their abilities, can cycle. There are now several locations in London where adaptive cycles (such as two-by-two and hand-cranked cycles, recumbents and tandems with a reclining seat) can be hired or bought. Locations include London Recumbent at Dulwich and Battersea parks, Bikeworks near Victoria Park, Companion Cycling in Bushy Park and Pedal Power in Finsbury Park.

There are full details to be found in the free, downloadable *All Ability Cycling Guide* booklet on the LCC website.

More details

For details of all organizations that can assist with cycling in London see Resources page 234.

CHILDREN AND CYCLING

Children love cycling, whether by themselves or on the back of a bicycle, tandem or trailer. Cycling gives children a first taste of independence and can be an activity shared with parents or other adults. The special section on rides for children (see page 224) identifies parks in Inner London where children and adults are allowed to cycle. If you are cycling with a child on the back of your bike you may prefer the rides in parks and along canals.

Equipment

You can buy trailers, child seats and tandems at larger cycle shops and at specialist family- oriented bike shops such as Bikefix.

Whatever you choose, make sure you practise riding using the child seat or special bike before venturing out in traffic. Trailers, child seats and tandems require different balancing and cornering techniques to ordinary cycles.

Below: *Trailer cycles allow children to ride in safety with adults.*

Trailers – 6 months to 6 years

An increasing number of Londoners use trailers for journeys that don't involve travelling through heavy traffic. They can usually carry up to two children weighing up to a total of 40 kg (88 lb). Prices start at about £200. There are also specialized tricycles that incorporate child seats, such as the Christiania, but these are more expensive.

Child seats – 9 months to 4 years

The most common way of transporting a small child on a bike is to use a child seat. Child seats are best attached to stable bikes such as hybrids or mountain bikes. You can buy a seat for the rear of the bike (some fit over a carrier) or one that fits on the front, over the top tube of the frame. Prices start at about £50. Make sure the seat has guards for the child's feet so that they do not slip into the front or rear wheels, and a convenient and secure harness. The type of seat that is suitable will depend on the weight of the child (9–15 kg/20–33 lb) so take advice from the shop when buying, and please note that a baby has to be able to hold its head up unsupported,

with a helmet on, before using a child seat. Take particular care when supporting a cycle with a child on it when you are not riding the bike because the weight of the child can cause it to overbalance and fall over.

Trailer cycles and tandems – 5 years upwards

The beauty of a trailer cycle or a tandem is that it allows an adult and a child to cycle together without exhausting the child. Younger children contribute less to the power input, older children contribute more.

Trailer cycles are like the back end of a bicycle with one wheel, saddle, pedals and chain. They attach to the seat post or carrier of an adult's cycle. They are less stable than tandems, but easier to transport and store and the child gets to pedal at its own pace while most of the work is done by the adult. Prices start from £120. You can also buy towbar-type devices that attach a child's bike to an adult's.

Tandems are ideal for travelling with children and, using devices such as kiddy cranks or crank adaptors which reduce the distance from the saddle to the pedals, they can last from ages 6 to 16. The problem with tandems is that they are difficult to store and they are not allowed on most trains (although some Virgin and First Great Western trains accept them). If you can afford it, you can buy and fit couplings that enable you to split your tandem in two, or even three, for storage and transport.

Children's cycles

It is now common to start children out on small bikes without pedals that teach them to balance as they scoot along. They can then move on to bikes with pedals and 30–35 cm (12–14 in) wheels. It is important to get the sizing right, and the child should be able to stand astride the bike with his or her feet on the ground. Bikes that are too small can cause knee pain.

While children are usually happy riding any bike, you will find that BMX-type bikes are lighter and more durable than imitation mountain bikes and easier to maintain.

Above: *A bike trailer can accommodate several small children quite comfortably.*

Kids' gear

Children's helmets should be correctly sized and fitted, and replaced when they get too small, or too worn. Make sure your child understands that helmets do not make them invulnerable and they should not take greater risks when wearing one.

Children are vulnerable to the effects of the sun and their clothes should provide sufficient covering. They are also vulnerable to cold and children in child seats in particular, who are not being active, need to be warmly wrapped on cold days.

Reflective or bright clothing helps visibility.

Cycle training

Modern cycle training, known as Bikeability, includes actual riding on roads and is offered at a large number of London schools. Such training is strongly recommended in order to ensure your child rides confidently and safely on streets with traffic. If your child's school does not offer cycle training you may be able to arrange it through your local council, or you can approach the head to see if such training can be arranged. Schools that have travel plans can take advantage of Transport for London (TfL) grants for cycle parking and can get advice on arranging cycle training.

For more on children and cycling go to *www.lcc.org.uk*.

ROADWORTHINESS CHECK AND PUNCTURE REPAIR

Before riding your bike for the first time you should conduct basic checks following the 'M' method, and after that a simple ABC (Air, Brakes, Chain) check before setting off should be sufficient. Unless you are a confident mechanic, however, you should take your bike in for an annual or bi-annual service. Several local LCC groups organize repair workshops at a low cost, and also arrange 'Dr Bike' sessions where bikes can be examined and some minor adjustments carried out.

You should clean your bike at least once a month and lubricate it weekly (use a proper chain lubricant for the chain) if you use it regularly. A simple way of cleaning a bike is to use a bucket of warm water with some car shampoo in it and a 'banister' brush. For the chain and gears use a dishwashing brush and a plastic dish-scouring sponge, or specialized equipment, then lubricate them when dry.

THE M-CHECK METHOD

This simple way of checking your bike gets its name from the M-shaped sequence of checks that you follow, from the bottom of the front wheel up to the handlebars, down to the chain- set, up to the saddle and then down to the bottom of the rear wheel. (See the illustration below, with the super-imposed M over the bike and its parts.)

Front wheel

- The tyre should be fully inflated (the required pressure in psi or bar is marked on the side wall of the tyre) and the tread free of cuts
- The hub quick-release or the wheel nuts should be well secured
- The wheel should not move from side to side
- The rim should spin true and the brake surfaces should not be badly worn
- All spokes should be tight and in place
- The inner tube valve should be straight, not at an angle.

Front brake

- Spin the wheel and then pull the brake tight with the lever – the brake should lock the front wheel firmly
- The brake pads should not rub on the rim and should hit the rim squarely
- Brake cables should be tightly attached and not frayed at either brake or lever ends
- Replace broken cable casings
- Replace worn brake pads
- The brake should not move backwards and forwards or judder – if it does, you may need to tighten the brake assembly.

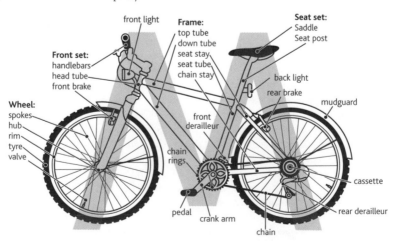

Forks

Forks usually curve away from the bike. Replace bent forks.

Headset

The headset should be tight, no movement when rolled back and forth with the front brake on, but allow free side to side movement of the handlebars.

Stem

The stem should be secured tightly, and stems that move up and down should not be above their upward limit marker. Your stem should be in line with the front wheel.

Handlebars

- Handlebars should be tightly secured to stem
- All bolts attaching brake levers and gear levers to the handlebars should be secure
- Replace handlebar end plugs if missing.

Frame

Check for dents and cracks.

Bottom bracket and chainset

- The chainset should rotate smoothly when you turn it backwards
- The chainset should not wobble from side to side – a wobbly chainset usually means the bottom bracket is loose
- Chainrings should be true and it should be difficult to pull the chain away from them – if the chain pulls away easily, the chainrings may be worn.

Chain

The chain should be free of mud and well lubricated. Use a degreaser to remove road dirt and apply proper chain lubricant (not WD40 or light oil). Replace the chain if it is worn – significant wear may require replacement of the gear sprockets at the same time.

Cranks

Both cranks should be firmly attached to the bottom bracket. Check by holding both firmly and moving them from side to side.

Pedals

Pedals should spin smoothly and be firmly attached to the cranks.

Front gears

- The cable should be firmly attached and not frayed. The cage should move smoothly from side to side
- If your front gears are not shifting properly you may need to adjust the upper and lower limits of the gear cage
- Gears that don't shift at all could mean a rusty or defective cable.

Seat post

The seat post should be set to the correct height (see Correct Set-up, page 14) and not exceed the upper limit mark.

Saddle

The saddle should be in line with the wheels, secure and level or set a fraction downward at the front if you prefer.

Rear brake

Checks as for front brake.

Rear wheel

Checks as for front wheel.

Rear gears

- Indexed gears should change with a click – if they do not, you may need to adjust the upper and lower limits
- Bent gear hangers may affect performance, and stiff or rusty cables may also affect shifting
- If hub gears do not shift properly you may need to adjust the cable tension.

Accessories

- Make sure lights are fitted properly
- Check the bolts on your mudguards and luggage carriers – these often come loose and then fall out.

Tyre inflation

- For inner tubes with Schrader (car type) valves, you push or screw on the pump connector firmly (the pin in the pump has to contact the pin in the

37

valve), unfold the thumb lock on the pump (if it has one) and inflate. To deflate, press the pin inside the valve.

- To inflate a Presta (long and thin) valve, unscrew the small nut on the tip of the valve, press it gently to release a little air, push or screw on the connector, then set the thumb lock and inflate. To deflate, unscrew the small nut and press.
- To inflate a Woods valve (used on roadsters - fat at the bottom , thin at the top), do not unscrew the retaining knurled nut but screw or push on the connector (same as for Presta) and inflate.

PUNCTURE REPAIR

Knowing how to repair a puncture is a key skill. You can repair punctures at the roadside if you have the kit with you, but it is much easier to carry a spare inner tube and replace the punctured one rather than try to patch a punctured tube on the spot.

- First try to find the cause of the puncture. If you find the offending item, remove it and mark the place on the tyre so that you can ensure that any other bits of glass or thorn are not still there on the inside.
- Release the brake cable and remove the wheel.
- Let out any remaining air in the tyre by pressing the pin (inside a Schrader valve) or unscrewing the nut (on a Presta valve) and pressing it lightly

(see illustration a opposite, top left), or undoing the knurled nut (on a Woods valve)

- If you have a Presta valve, remove the knurled nut that locks it to the rim.
- Flex the tyre around the rim, pushing the bead to the centre where there is a small dip – this makes removal easier.
- Use two tyre levers to lift one tyre bead over the edge of the rim by inserting them about 50 mm from each other and pressing downwards. Once the tyre has lifted away on a small section you can slip in a third lever to extend the lifted section, then slip the lever sideways to ease the rest of the tyre off (see illustration b opposite, top right).
- If you have not identified the cause of the puncture, keep the tyre in the same place on the wheel and note the position of the inner tube with respect to the tyre as you remove it, taking care not to damage the valve.
- Inflate the tube and put the tyre near to your lips to feel the air coming out. If this doesn't work, you have to put the tyre in a bucket of water and look for the bubbles.
- Once you've established where the hole is, mark it with a biro. Then line up the tube with the tyre, and check again for the offending item and make sure it has been removed.
- To repair the puncture on the road, deflate the tube, roughen the surface where the hole is with

TOOL KITS

Travel kit
- Portable pump suitable for your type of inner tube valve
- Spare inner tube to match your tyre size (check width and wheel diameter – usually 700 C or 26 inches)
- Puncture repair kit with patches, glue and sandpaper
- Three strong plastic tyre levers
- Multi-tool or set of Allen keys in sizes to fit all the bolts on your bike (including 8 mm for the chainset and the right size for brake pad adjustment)
- An adjustable spanner

- Small Phillips and flat-head screwdrivers
- Plastic gloves (from chemist)
- Zip ties
- Duct tape

Additions for basic home kit
- Track pump with gauge
- Spanners in 8, 9, 10, 15 and 17 mm sizes
- Chain removal tool
- Bicycle wire cutters
- Pliers
- Sharp knife

sandpaper and cover it with a thin layer of puncture solution, spreading it slightly wider than the patch you are going to use.

- Leave the adhesive to dry for 5 minutes, or the time specified on the box. Then peel away the metallic covering on the patch and press the patch (still covered on one side by the light plastic film) over the hole (see illustration c below, bottom left). You can, but don't have to, remove the plastic film by cracking it and peeling from the centre outwards. Don't start peeling from the edge because the patch will come up.
- To refit the tube and tyre, place one bead of the tyre onto the rim (you usually leave it in this position).
- Inflate the spare or repaired tube slightly and put the valve in the hole, making sure it is straight. Then ease the tube inside the tyre.
- Use your fingers to roll the second tyre bead back onto rim, starting at the valve and working away from your chest. The tyre will get tighter as you near the final section and you may need to use a tyre lever to lift it over (see illustration d below, bottom right). Take care not to pinch the tube with the tyre or the lever. Some tyres, especially

those on Brompton folders, are more difficult to refit than others. Replace the knurled nut on Presta-valved inner tubes.

- Replace the wheel, inflate the tyre (on a Woods valve replacing the knurled nut) and remember to tighten the nuts or quick-release and to replace the brake cable if you have released it.

IF YOU HAVE A COLLISION

In the unlikely event of being involved in a collision, you should note the names, addresses and phone numbers of at least two witnesses. Call the police or ask someone else to do so. Make a sketch of the collision and take photos if you have access to a phone camera. Record or write down the incident as you remember it. When the police come, note down the CAD (Computer Aided Dispatch) or CRIS (Crime Reference Information System) number that the police will allocate to the incident.

Once home, call a lawyer who specializes in cycling cases. LCC provides contacts for lawyers, and members are entitled to free legal advice. If you are responsible for a collision, contact your insurer – LCC provides its members with third-party insurance.

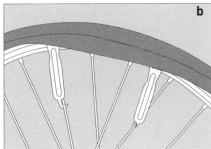

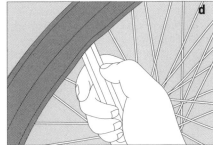

IMPROVING LONDON'S CYCLING FACILITIES

You arrive at a shop and there is no bike stand, you ride down a street and it's full of potholes, or you cycle down a bike route to find it just stops. These are common experiences for those who cycle regularly in London. But it doesn't have to be that way. Thanks to constant lobbying by the London Cycling Campaign and its local groups, cycling provision has been improved at thousands of locations across London. These may be small changes, such as a couple of bike stands on a street (more than 80,000 have been installed since 2000) or a bicycle cut-through, or they may be bigger changes like the cycle super-highway alongside the Thames Embankment, routes through a park or cycle crossings at major roundabouts. By becoming an LCC member you support the continuation of such work (see Contacts, page 234).

Your efforts can make a difference. It's not that difficult to get conditions improved, particularly if you are working with others. Politicians and engineers are often unaware of the needs of cyclists, so alerting them to potential problems can help them save time and money later on, or it can help them satisfy local targets for increased cycling and reduced car use in their boroughs.

If you have issues that you want to raise then contact or join your local cycle campaigning group – this will usually be an LCC- affiliated group or a combination of LCC and Cycling UK members. Groups usually meet monthly (for discussion of socials, rides and lobbying) and some have special working groups that talk to the council about, for instance, improving cycle routes, installing cycle parking, making one-way streets have two-way access for cyclists and providing cycle training in schools. You can also handle some matters yourself.

Potholes

Transport for London (TfL) has a pothole reporting system for the capital: *www.tfl.gov.uk/tfl/roadusers/reportastreetfault/newfault.aspx* or just go to the LCC website which has a link to the pothole reporting form.

Cycle parking

If you want bike stands outside a shop or work-place your local cycling officer may be able to help. At the website *www.urbancycleparking.org.uk* you can suggest locations for parking stands which are passed on to councils, or share information about existing stands.

School cycle training

If your child's school doesn't provide cycle training you can arrange for it to do so by working with your headmaster and the council's school travel planner. Details on the LCC website.

Workplace facilities

Your employer can meet corporate social responsibility aims and save money (on car parking) by assisting cyclists. Transport for London offers free bike stands to qualifying employers, and by joining the government's Cycle to Work scheme your employer can enable you to buy a bike at a discount (see Commuting, page 25).

Right: *Cycle parking provision, like this set of stands at London University, encourages more people to cycle to school, college and work.*

INTRODUCTION TO THE ROUTES

The bike routes in this book were designed by members of the London Cycling Campaign (LCC), who have been riding many of them for decades as part of regular guided ride programmes. They include classics such as the Thames Banks ride and the Tamsin Trail in Richmond Park, as well as lesser-known routes including the Crane River, and Markets and Squares: North and East London. There is also a special section of rides for children (see page 224). You can find out about free guided rides at *www.lcc.org.uk* – see the Social Cycling section (page 32).

In addition to the rides described in this book there are three popular and easily followed longer routes along London waterways. The Grand Union and Regent's canals can be ridden from the Thames to Birmingham (with an interruption in Islington); the South Bank of the Thames can be ridden eastwards all the way to the coast, and

the Thames banks can be ridden west-wards from Putney. All three routes are marked in green on the relevant *Local Cycling Guides*.

The maps of the routes in this book, along with the descriptions, provide guidance on directions and where to stop for refreshments, but you are advised to order a complete set of the free *Local Cycling Guides* developed by LCC with Transport for London (TfL). These fully detailed maps, with their comprehensive guidance on preferred streets for cycling, will enable you to develop the rides further and discover your own routes. Each ride in this guide provides the number of the *Local Cycling Guide* that covers the route area. Maps can be ordered via the LCC and TfL websites, or by calling TfL on 0343 222 1234. Several of the rides are in central London, where you can take advantage of the London Cycle Hire scheme (see Santander Cycles, page 230).

The rides range in time from about 1.5 to 4 hours (not taking into account stops for tea). The marked times do not allow for longer stops and, since many pleasant places to take a break are

Below: *A number of the rides take advantage of routes through lovely local parks across London.*

suggested, you may wish to factor some extra time into your journey planning. Many rides are designed to link up easily with others. You can, for example, ride along the Lee Valley and then along the Thames Banks, or link up with the rides in Barnet and Enfield. The Epping Forest, North London Heights and Ham and High Hills rides all require some strenuous climbing.

When embarking on a ride, make sure your bike is roadworthy (see page 36) and that you have sufficient water, food, puncture repair kit, spare inner tube, basic tools, lock, lights, waterproof jacket, map (TfL/LCC Local Cycle Guide) as well as your phone and money.

Personal safety can be an issue along some routes that are not heavily used and there have been, albeit relatively rare, instances of muggings of cyclists. The police advise you to give up your bike or belongings rather than risk injury, and to call 999 immediately and report the incident.

Such incidents are more likely in less-populated areas such as along canals and in parks. Routes in north, south and east London are generally less secure than those in the centre of town and in the west. You may wish to ride in company in these areas (see Social Cycling, page 32), or ride on Sundays when there are more people around on the leisure routes.

The routes in the book are designed as daytime rides and many of the parks mentioned are closed after dusk. If you fancy an evening ride, consider the well-lit rides in central London and the Soho and Bloomsbury sections of the Camden and Soho ride (see page 166), but take lights and reflective outerwear and be careful after dark. While every effort has been made to note where you have to walk your bike, permissions can vary. Please respect signs along routes and always give way to pedestrians on shared paths.

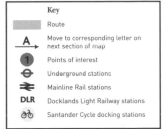

Key

	Route
A→	Move to corresponding letter on next section of map
1	Points of interest
⊖	Underground stations
⇌	Mainline Rail stations
DLR	Docklands Light Railway stations
🚲	Santander Cycle docking stations

Barnet Parks and Brooks

Barnet's delightful hidden cycling routes seem unknown to its residents even though they are well promoted by the enthusiastic Barnet Cyclists group. The ride includes Dollis Brook and Pymme's Brook as well as the old villages of Chipping Barnet, Monken Hadley and Hadley Green. Barnet's once-famous horse fair gave rise to 'Barnet' as Cockney rhyming slang for hair (Barnet fair = hair). An attraction of the ride is the trees, which can look spectacular in the autumn. A minor detour from the ride takes you to the very unusual Southgate tube station. The ride can be divided easily into two sections, both of them starting and finishing at Oakleigh Park station. Both sections include short stretches of fairly busy roads, which can be walked if you prefer, and there is rough ground near Monken Hadley.

1. Oakleigh Park overground station is reached from King's Cross or Finsbury Park. Exit the station on the side of platforms 1 and 2 and follow the bike signs towards Alverston Avenue.
2. As you descend the hill you will have fine views of north London's suburbs.
3. At the park, follow the cycle route signs for Arnos Grove to a small bridge over **Pymme's Brook**. Crossing the bridge, head straight up the small hill where you will see steps. Opposite the steps, follow the narrow passage marked 'cycle route' which leads to Ridgeway Avenue, and head up the steep hill. Take care crossing the fast road (Cat Hill) into Belmont Avenue and turn down Norrys Avenue, the first left. Norrys Avenue, at which one turns left, has no street sign.
4. A left and right lead to Bevan Road, which is a no-through-road except for cyclists.
5. You can stop for refreshment at the **Cock** pub in Chalk Lane or, for a nice cup of tea, follow Chalk Lane to the very fast A111, which you cross on foot, and walk to the right for 50 metres (165 ft) to **Trent Park** – the café (open daily 10.30 am–5 pm) is a favourite Barnet Cyclists pit stop.
6. Returning to Chalk Lane, bear right down Games Road to Hadley Wood, part of which (just past the railway bridge), served as Greece in the Cliff Richard film *Summer Holiday*. The downhill off-road path through the wood can be muddy after rain.
7. When you reach the road (through the white

LOCAL INFO

Local Cycle Guide: 2
Start point: Oakleigh Park station
Length: 21 km (13 m)
Time: 4 hours
Type of ride: Medium. Mostly off-road and on quiet streets. Some hills, and two short stretches of busy road

Sights and places to visit
- Pymme's Brook
- Southgate Underground station (optional)
- Livingstone Cottage, Hadley Green
- Barnet Museum, 31 Wood St, Barnet EN5 4BE. Tel 020 8440 8066
- St Mary's Church, Monken Hadley, EN5 5PZ
- Dollis Brook

Eating and drinking
- Cock, Chalk Lane, Barnet, Hertfordshire, EN4 9HU Tel 020 8449 7160
- Trent Park café, Cockfosters Road, Enfield, Barnet, EN4 0PS Tel 020 8449 1359
- The Monk, 193 High Street, Barnet, Hertfordshire, EN5 5SU Tel 020 8449 4280
- Café Pacino, 1 Church Passage, Wood St, Barnet, EN5 4QS. Tel 020 8440 3489
- Oakhill Park café, Church Hill Road, East Barnet, EN4 8SY. Tel 020 8361 1013

Rail stations: Oakleigh Park, New Barnet, New Southgate
Underground stations: Totteridge, Whetstone, Woodside Park, High Barnet

gate), turn left and immediate right into **the Crescent** to pass a house with a turret that belonged to the comedian Spike Milligan. Return to the busy road and bear left to join the quieter Hadley Green Road.

8. The village of **Monken Hadley** was built on land formerly owned by the Abbey of Saffron Walden. Its grand Georgian villas (one sold for £9m) stand near the more modest home of the explorer David Livingstone. **St Mary the Virgin's Church** had one of the beacons that warned Britons of the approaching Spanish Armada in 1588.

9. Hadley Green is where Edward IV defeated the Earl of Warwick at the Battle of Barnet in

Above: Admiring St Mary the Virgin's Church in the old village of Monken Hadley. A church has stood on this location for over 800 years.

1471. Thousands died in the four-hour battle.

10. Turn left into Barnet High Street, which offers a selection of food and drink stops including **the Monk** (just as you turn into the High Street), known by locals as the Monk-en-Drunk.

11. Cross the road by the pedestrian crossing's lights just before **St John's Church** and walk up the path (Church Passage) next to it or stop off at the Guns and Smoke café. The church was rebuilt in 1873 by William Butterfield.

45

B (from page 49)

47

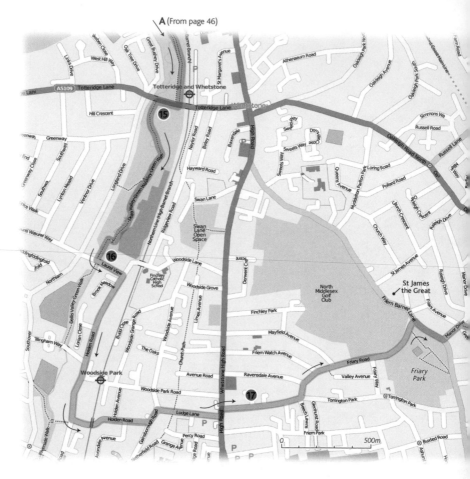

A (From page 46)

Across the road, to the left, is the medieval **Tudor Hall** (behind the car park) and to the right, at no. 31 Wood St, is **Barnet Museum** (Tue–Thu 2.30–4.30 pm, Sat 10.30 am–12.30 pm and 2–4pm).

12. Turn left after the museum (into Manor Road), but note the quaint 19th-century alms-house on the other side of the road.

13. At the end of the steep hill, a quick right and left into Leeside takes you to Riverside Walk where you turn left (east) – do not cross the small bridge – and follow **Dollis Brook**. You have to cross a busy road and return to the brook by taking the path next to the Barnet Table Tennis Centre. The brook you are following passes through what was once Brook

Farm. Wheat was grown here to fuel London's transport horses in the 18th century.

14. Where you see a pavilion on the left you can either head back to Oakleigh Park station – take the path just to the left of the pavilion – or carry on along the brook.

15. If you carry on along the brook, cross the next road by turning right and left to stay by it.

16. At the next road, leave the path and follow cycle route signs to reach the High Road at North Finchley — see map.

17. Walk across busy Whetstone High Road. At the fork in Torrington Park bear left along **Friary Road** to Friary Park where there is a café (open daily, 10 am–5 pm). Opposite is the neo-Gothic church of **St James the Great**. Cross

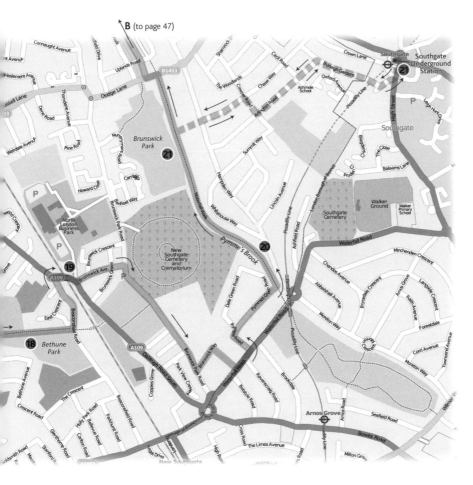

Friern Barnet Lane with care, turn right and then first left down Manor Drive.

18. At the bottom of the hill you enter **Bethune Park** via a gate. TfL maps show cycling is permitted. Go straight through the park.

19. Turn left as you exit the park into Beaconsfield Road, then turn right over the bridge. Beware of fast traffic down Brunswick Park Road. As you ride uphill duck left into the small industrial estate (Brunswick Way) and turn immediately left after you come out of it.

20. Turn immediately left and then right into Pymme's Green Road. At its end you enter a path to **Pymme's Brook**, which you cross and follow northwards (left) looking out for wildlife, including herons and woodpeckers.

21. Architecture enthusiasts may wish to follow a path to the right, when you reach open ground, to visit the spaceship-like **Southgate Tube station**, one of Charles Holden's designs for London Transport in the 1930s. Follow the marked route, and then return to the brook.

22. After crossing one busy road (Osidge Lane) you have a final coffee opportunity at the **Oakhill** Park café that is on the left near the corner of the park, where Parkside Gardens meets Church Hill Road (open daily, from 10.30 am).

23. Continue along the brook until you reach a blue iron bridge on the left. Cross it and follow the marked cycle path back to Oakleigh Park station.

Enfield Gentry

Enfield is one of London's largest boroughs and includes several fine parks and grand houses. In the 17th century the area played a key role in providing fresh water for London's growing population when a waterway, the New River, was built from Ware in Hertfordshire to Islington in North London. This ride includes sections of the New River as well some of the homes of the local gentry, who included the developer of the New River, Sir Hugh Myddelton. The route is a favourite with the Westminster Cyclists group as well as local riders who enjoy the parklands featured on the ride – these were once part of a royal deer park or chase (meaning hunting ground). The ride includes short sections of busy road as well as some off-road tracks that can get muddy after rain – knobbly tyres are advisable. Appropriately, the ride starts at Enfield Chase station.

1. Leaving **Enfield Chase** station, cross the busy road (A110) and head east. Just after the railway bridge on the left you pass Chase Green Gardens, where you can see the **New River**. Turn left into Gentleman's Row, which takes you past some fine 18th- and 19th-century mansions to a narrow section of path where you have to walk. Cross the New River and turn right. Cross two further bridges, passing the nicely located **Crown & Horseshoes** pub, to reach Parsonage Gardens. After rejoining the road, keep turning right to reach Parsonage Lane, a fairly busy road, where you turn right. After the traffic lights, take the next turning left into Churchbury Lane and follow it for about 700 metres (770 yd). After passing Chase Community School on the left, take the second right (Canonbury Road). Follow the road round the bend to the left into Inverness Avenue.

2. At the end of Inverness Avenue turn left and immediate right, walking across the pavement into Hallside Road. Cross Russell Road into Old Forge Road, following the signpost for Forty Hall. At the end, turn half-right into Forty Hill. About 500 metres (550 yd) further along on your left you come to the entrance to **Forty Hall**.

3. Built in the 17th century in Jacobean style for Sir Nicholas Rainton, Forty Hall was later owned by the Bowles family. Its 273 acres of land include ornamental gardens and the hall now houses a local history museum

LOCAL INFO

Local Cycle Guide: 2
Start point: Enfield Chase station
Length: 21 km (13 m)
Time: 3–4 hours depending on stops
Type of ride: Medium. Mixture of low-traffic paved roads and off-road tracks; three relatively short stretches of busy road. Knobbly tyres recommended

Sights and places to visit
- Forty Hall, Forty Hill, Enfield EN2 9HA
  Tel 020 8363 8196
- Myddelton House, Bulls Cross, EN2 9HG
  Tel 08456 770 600
- Capel Manor, Bullsmoor Lane, EN1 4RQ
  Tel 0845 612 2122
- Trent Park, Cockfosters Road, EN4 0PS
  Tel 020 8449 1359

Eating and drinking
- Crown and Horseshoes
  12–15 Horseshoe Lane, EN2 6PZ
  Tel 020 8363 1371
- Courtyard café, see Forty Hall, above
- King and Tinker, Whitewebbs Lane
  EN2 9HJ. Tel 020 8363 6411
- Whitewebbs House, Whitewebbs Lane
  EN2 9JW. Tel 020 8363 0542
- Trent Park café, see Trent Park, above

Rail stations: Enfield Chase, Grange Park
Underground stations: Oakwood (non-folding bikes carried only to Cockfosters)

Above: *A sunny autumnal ride down Snakes Lane, which is the entrance to Trent Park.*

(Summer: Tues. – Fri., 11 am – 5 pm, Sat. and Sun., 12 pm – 5 pm; Winter: Tues. – Fri., 11 am – 4 pm, Sat. and Sun., 12 pm – 4 pm, free admission). The **Courtyard café** is open daily (there are some convenient bike stands outside the courtyard).

4. Returning to Forty Hill you pedal northwards (it becomes Bull's Cross) and can visit **Myddelton House and gardens** (19th century). There is a café and a small museum, and cycle parking in the car park to the right of the buildings. A little further north on the right, **Capel Manor**, which is now an agricultural college. Tickets are required.

5. Turn left out of Bull's Cross and beware of fast traffic in Whitewebbs Lane, which leads past the convenient **King and Tinker pub** (serves food) directly opposite Guy Lodge.

6. About 200 metres (220 yd) past the pub, watch out for the sign to Whitewebbs Park and Golf Course on the left.

7. As you approach **Whitewebbs House**, a white, castle-like 19th-century building, you have a choice of stopping off at what is now a pub and restaurant, or continuing the ride by bearing left down a private road just before reaching the house. An enjoyable descent and short hill takes you pass a small café and on to Clay Hill, where you turn right. Where the road bends right by a church, turn left into Strayfield Road. Follow the direction signs for Cycle Route 12, turning left after about 600 metres. Pass under the railway

51

and follow the road left at Rectory Farm. On reaching the main road (the Ridgeway, A1005), turn right and immediately left into Oak Avenue. At the bottom, turn right into Hadley Road.

8. About 2 km (1.2 m) along Hadley Road on the left is the entrance to **Trent Country Park** – once a royal deer park and an interrogation centre during WWII. The park was given to King George III's doctor after he'd saved the life of the king's brother at Trento, then Austria, from where the park derives its name. Entering the park, bear right along a track taking you down a hill. Bear right again past the ponds and, after a short uphill, you'll arrive at a handsome, tree-lined drive where families come to walk. Pedalling west (to the right) along the path brings you to the **Trent Park café**, patronized by both Barnet and Enfield LCC groups .

9. Turning left at the drive you pass a column and road barriers leading into the grounds of **Trent Place**. Visitors to the Georgian-style mansion furthest from the entrance barriers included Charlie Chaplin and Winston Churchill. Returning to the barriers bear left into Snakes Lane, which, after another pleasant downhill and short climb, brings you to the busy Bramley Road, where you turn left.

10. A bike track on the pavement takes you most of the way to Enfield Chase station, although the final stretch has to be done on the busy carriageway.

11. To avoid some traffic, go down Prince George Avenue (opposite Snakes Lane, to the left of Oakwood station) past Oakwood Park. At the triangular junction with Everseley Park Road turn left, then right at the roundabout, down Green Dragon Lane and to the pleasant Arts and Crafts-style suburb of Grange Park. Turning left after the railway bridge into Old Park Ridings and left again into The Chine brings you to Grange Park station.

Right: *Forty Hall, a 17th-century Jacobean mansion, is set in 273 acres of ornamental gardens and lakes.*

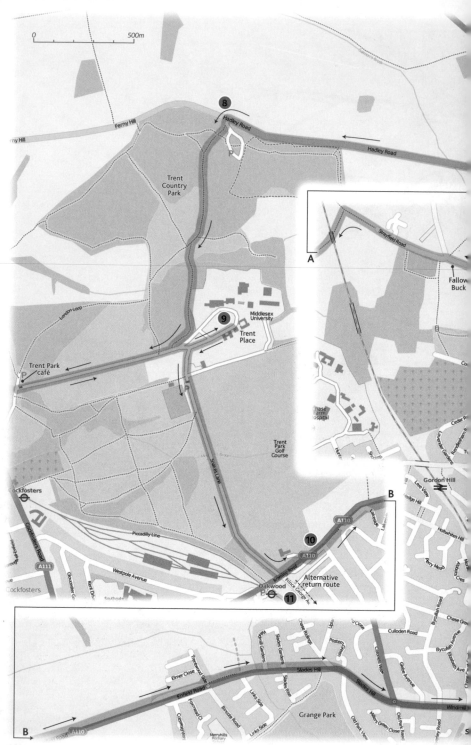

Epping Forest

Epping Forest is the essential London destination for anyone with a taste for mountain biking. With some exceptions for conservation areas, cycling is permitted on the paths in the forest and there are plenty of ups and downs to enjoy. You'll see horses, longhorn cattle and a variety of wildlife. Give way to walkers and steer clear of any areas marked 'no cycling'. It's easy to get lost in the forest, so this ride takes a clear route along broad bridleways. You should take a compass or GPS and a map (OS 174 or the Epping Forest map sold at the visitor centre at High Beach). The use of mountain bikes is strongly advised.

1. Turning right out of **Chingford station** ride (or walk) 100 metres (110 yd) down the busy road to the first junction, where Epping Forest starts at **Chingford Plain**. A well-worn track, with a free car park on the left and the Epping Forest sign just before it, takes you 200 metres (220 yd) to a crossing over a stream on your left (with some wooden barriers). Don't cross it, but bear right down the wide green bridleway with a wooden marker post up ahead.

2. There are two paths to the right leading uphill to 'The View' the visitor's centre, **Queen Elizabeth's Hunting Lodge** and **Butlers Retreat** which is now a fully functional café.

3. The route, however, follows the wide grassy bridleway (up and down) to another small stream where you enter the forest along a wide track. This track (heading northwards) was named **Centenary Walk** to mark the 100th anniversary of the Act of Parliament (1878) that preserved the forest for public use (it's also known as the **Green Ride**).

4. Follow the main path northeastwards, ignoring the left and right turn-offs. If in doubt ask a passer-by for directions to the Visitor Centre or the King's Oak pub. You'll have to walk across one minor road (passing the barrier on the other side) before a series of steep ups and downs. When crossing the minor road you will see a Tea Hut, popular with motorcyclists, a short distance to the right.

5. After 1 km (3/4 m) from the minor road, take a left at the fork just before arriving at another road. You'll see a sign pointing left to the **Epping Forest Visitor Centre**, which you

LOCAL INFO

Local Cycle Guide: Part of map 2 and OS map 174

Start point: Chingford station

Length: 17 km (10.5 m)

Time: 3 hours

Type of ride: Medium, all off-road, some busy roads to cross on foot. Not recommended for bikes with narrow road tyres as it can be rough and muddy in winter and rutted in summer.

Sights and places to visit
- Queen Elizabeth's Hunting Lodge
  8 Rangers Rd, E4 7QH. Tel 020 8529 6681
- Epping Forest Visitor Centre, Nursery Rd
  High Beech, Loughton, IG10 4AE
  Tel 020 8508 0028
- High Beach and Big View

Eating and drinking
- Butler's Retreat, Rangers Road
  E4 7QH. Tel 020 8524 2976
- King's Oak, Nursery Rd, High Beech
  Loughton, Essex, IG10 4AE
  Tel 020 8508 5000
- Foresters Arms, 15 Baldwins Hill,
  Loughton, Essex, IG10 1SF. Tel 020 8508 1313
- Gardners Arms, 103 York Hill, Loughton,
  Essex, IG10 1RX. Tel 020 8508 1655

Rail stations: Chingford

Underground stations: Loughton

can reach by road (left and left again as the signs indicate) or by following the off-road path that runs parallel to the road. The centre offers maps and information (10 am–4 pm winter,

10 am–5 pm summer). Just north of it, fronting onto the open space of **High Beach**, is the popular **King's Oak pub**.

6. The ride continues back at the point where you emerged from the forest bridleway. You cross the road and head for a gate over to the right that will take you back into the forest. About 500 metres (550 yd) up the bridleway you cross a road (Claypit Hill) and continue northeast. When you cross the road there is a Tea Hut in sight a short distance to the left. The major road visible in the middle distance at the 'Big View' is the M25, the London Orbital Motorway.

7. The bridleway meets a very busy road (the A121) – cross with great care. Rejoin the bridleway on the other side and follow it to the right (east) with fields on your left. Stay close to the road as you pass the back of the **Old Orleans restaurant** at Wake Arms roundabout. The path dips to cross a small stream and then

Above: Mountain bikers on a spring ride in Epping Forest, which has miles and miles of suitable off-road trails for cyclists.

crosses a minor road – stay on the path, now running parallel to the B1393, until you come to the busy road which you cross, keeping to the track.

8. After 200 metres (220 yd) you arrive at a junction of paths in a part-open area; turn right to arrive at a car park. Cross the road (the B172) to another car park and go past a barrier to follow the wide bridleway into the forest.

9. At a fork in the path, about 600 metres (650 yd) from the car park and just past two tall silver birches on the left, turn right (southwest) and continue steeply down, then up for another 500 metres (550 yd) to a small car park where you again cross a road (the A121, Golding's Hill). Be careful not to miss the right turn at the

Silver Birches especially if going at speed.

10. Another steep hill brings you to a point where a path comes in from the right (west), but you carry straight on and enter a small clearing about 20 metres (25 yd) on.

11. From the clearing you have the option to make a detour to the **Foresters Arms pub** (or the nearby **Gardners Arms**) before continuing the ride. To make the detour, turn off left (east) and descend the very steep hill that brings you to **Baldwin's Pond**. Ride around the pond to the left and at its far corner you'll see the pub at the top of the hill. Riding time to the pub and back to the clearing is about 25 minutes.

12. To continue the ride, carry on past the clearing, passing **Loughton Camp** on the right and then **Loughton Brook Valley** on the left at the bottom of the downhill (no cycling allowed at either of these places).

13. An uphill brings you to a car park and another road crossing (Earl's Path).

14. You pass two ponds, turning right just before the second (much larger) pond. Follow the path (no longer the wide bridleway but a clear and much rutted cycle/foot path) around the pond and, where the pond ends, bear right at the fork in the path to follow the rutted track to a very busy road (the A104). Cross with care and go through the wooden gate opposite to follow the wide track. After about 200 metres you cross a minor road and go past a barrier to join a wide bridleway.

15. At a fork in the path, about 100 metres (110 yd) on, bear left.

16. At the next fork, about 800 metres (870 yd) further, you will see a large single tree on your right. Follow the bridleway to the right around the tree. You then come to a crossroads in the paths, where you turn left (south) to rejoin the bridleway that took you north to the Epping Forest Visitor Centre.

17. You emerge from the forest onto **Chingford Plain** just as you cross a stream and return the way you came; that is, straight up the wide grassy path (don't turn left down the track). There's the option of tea at the **Butler's Retreat** on the left. Crossing the road at the Hunting Lodge and continuing straight on allows you to continue the ride into the southern half of the forest should you so wish.

Below: *This well-used trail near Baldwin's Pond is very close to both the Foresters Arms and the Gardners Arms.*

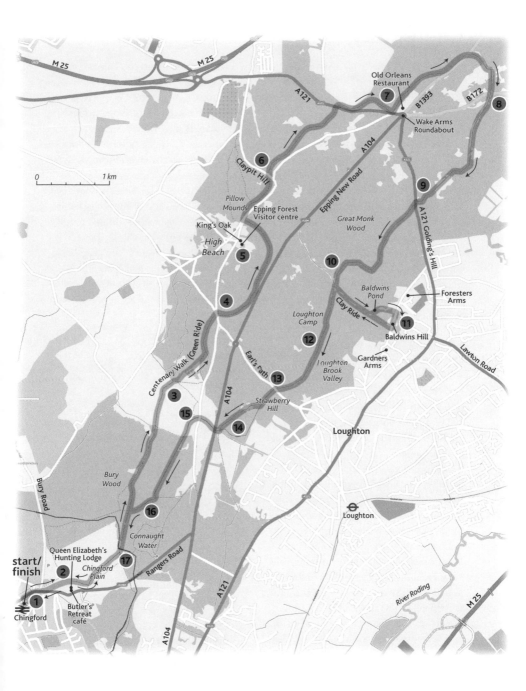

M 25

M 25

A121

Old Orleans
Restaurant

⑦

B1393

B172

⑧

Wake Arms
Roundabout

⑥

Claypit Hill

A104

Epping New Road

⑨

A121 Golding's Hill

Pillow
Mounds

Epping Forest
Visitor centre

Great Monk
Wood

King's Oak

High
Beach

⑤

④

Baldwins
Pond

Foresters
Arms

⑩

Clay Ride

⑪

Baldwins Hill

Lawton Road

Centenary Walk (Green Ride)

Earl's Path

Loughton
Camp

⑫

Gardners
Arms

③

A104

Loughton
Brook
Valley

Loughton

⑮

⑬

Strawberry
Hill

⑭

Bury Road

Bury
Wood

Loughton

⑯

Connaught
Water

Rangers Road

A121

**start/
finish**

Queen Elizabeth's
Hunting Lodge

⑰

River Roding

M 25

②

Chingford
Plain

①

Chingford

Butler's
Retreat
café

A104

0   1 km

Lee Valley

If you ask anyone in east London about bike rides they'll mention the Lee (or Lea – both are correct) Valley. Tower Hamlets Wheelers, the local cycling group, ride up the Lee on their social rides and local doctors send patients there for exercise. The river towpath can take you all the way to Amwell in Hertfordshire but the ride described here is a little less ambitious, reaching as far as Stonebridge Lock before returning via Hackney Marshes and the Queen Elizabeth Olympic Park, offering the opportunity to see part of the park including the Velodrome and road circuit up close. The towpath can get busy on summer days so be prepared to ride slowly and give way to walkers. You'll be rewarded with some fine views across Hackney Marshes and opportunities to see dozens of painted house-boats, as well as a selection of natural habitats, old sluice gates and a variety of wildlife including herons, swans and geese. Cyclists often stop off at the Springfield Marina café or the one in Springfield Park.

The most convenient station is Hackney Wick, which is a bit desolate but it's only a short distance from the Lee. An alternative is to ride to the Lee Valley along Regent's Canal from Islington or up from the Thames. There is car parking near the north end of the route (Marsh Lane), where an on-pavement path takes you to a pedestrian island from which an off-road path leads to Stonebridge Locks. You can then ride the route north to south and back – cycle hire is available at Stonebridge Lock.

1. Starting at **Hackney Wick station** turn left and left again into White Post Lane, which brings you to a bridge over the **River Lee**. Cross the bridge and go down to the river towpath, then go beneath the bridge and head north alongside the perimeter of the **Olympic Park** (marked NCN1 – National Cycle Network).

2. You go under one railway bridge and then under the road bridge carrying the Eastway and A12 (bridge marked 14).

3. Just past the next bridge (under the B112) you see the wide expanse of **Hackney Marshes**, which once provided 100 football pitches. Famous footballers who played there include Terry Venables, Paul Ince and David Beckham.

4. Follow the gravel path by the football pitches to avoid the narrow stretch of canal path.

5. Just before the red changing rooms go back onto to the canal path (via a small gate). This section of the towpath can get very busy, so you may have to walk this short stretch.

6. The **Middlesex Filter Beds Nature Reserve** (open 8 am–5:30 pm), whose entrance is just before the footbridge across the canal, has some interesting old sluice gates as well as a variety

LOCAL INFO

Local Cycle Guide: 4
Start point: Hackney Wick station
Length: 16 km (10 m)
Time: 2.5 hours
Type of ride: Easy. All off-road aside from crossing the A12 and access from Hackney Wick, which can be walked. Suitable for children

Sights and places to visit
- Hackney Marshes
- Middlesex Filter Beds Nature Reserve
- Springfield Marina
- Stonebridge Locks (0774 787 3831 for canoe and cycle hire)
- White Lodge House, Springfield Park E5 9EF. Tel 020 8806 0444
- Velodrome, Queen Elizabeth Olympic Park

Eating and drinking
- Princess of Wales, 146 Lea Bridge Road E5 9RB. Tel 020 853 33463
- Spark café, see White Lodge House, above
- Timber Lodge Café, Olympic Park

Rail stations: Hackney Wick, Tottenham Hale, Northumberland Park, Stratford International station (High Speed from St Pancras/Kent), Stratford Regional

Underground stations: Tottenham Hale, Stratford (tube and DLR)

of frogs and toads. The filter beds were built in 1852 after a cholera outbreak to provide pure water for the local area. They were replaced in 1960 by the Copper Mills treatment works in Walthamstow.

7. Return to the towpath, cross the footbridge and continue on the other side of the river past the **Princess of Wales pub**, which offers food and outside seating by the **Lea Bridge weir**.

8. Crossing beneath the Lea Bridge Road continue to the next footbridge. This takes you back over to the east bank where you follow the wide gravel path until you see the footbridge by **Springfield Marina**.

Above: *Ever-changing giant grafitti along the Lee Valley route. This route is suitable for children since most of it is off-road.*

9. Cross the footbridge and turn left to visit Springfield Park and the café inside White Lodge House, or go right to head further up the Lee Valley.

10. You enter **Springfield Park** about 30 metres (32 yd) south of the footbridge. Pedal up the hill to arrive at a beautifully set café inside **White Lodge House**, an elegant Victorian house (open daily, 10 am–4 pm winter, 10 am–6 pm summer). There are more than 230 species of plants

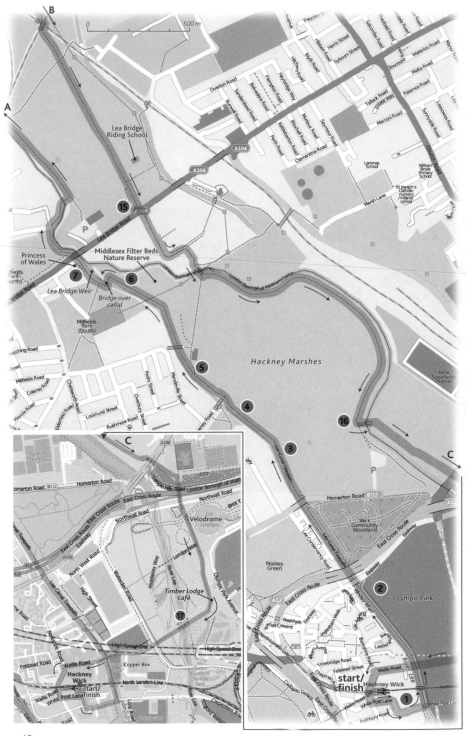

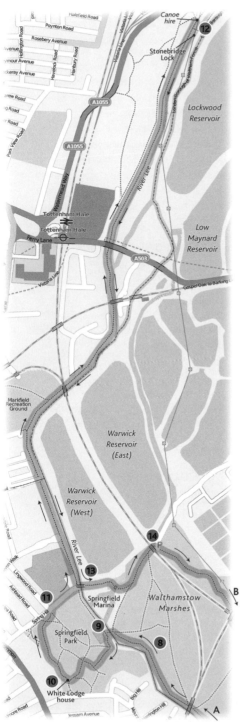

in the park and it is visited by some 56 different bird species.

11. Pedal past the café to exit the park through the north entrance nearest the river (**Spring Hill**), which brings you back to the towpath. Heading north, a pleasant 20-minute ride takes you to **Stonebridge Lock** where there is a permaculture project, and canoe hire.

12. If you are feeling energetic you can continue the ride as far as Waltham Abbey (following NCN1). Alternatively, retrace your route back to Springfield Marina and cross the first footbridge at the point where you exited the park.

13. Go past the boatyard and follow NCN1 towards **Waltham Nature Reserve**. Take care under a very low bridge.

14. Take a sharp right into **Walthamstow Marshes**, passing a barrier. Keep right by the railway track and you'll pass a second barrier just before a railway bridge which has a chicane cycle path beneath it. Follow the wide path past a riding school on the left.

15. Pass under a bridge and follow the signs for Three Mills and Hackney Marshes. As you come back to the river you cross the red (**Friendship**) bridge bringing you back to Hackney Marshes. Keep to the left following the river with the playing fields on your right.

16. Turn left and cross the river Lee, then take the wide path going up a long ramp to reach two bridges over roads and arrive at the **Velodrome** (you can go inside free of charge most days).

17. Continue ahead to the **Timber Lodge** café and then turn right across a bridge to reach a main road. Cross over, leaving the **Copper Box** arena to your left, then cross the canal on a footbridge with steps/lift down to Wallis Road, and turn left to return to Hackney Wick. Alternatively descend to the towpath before the bridge to follow the canal right down to the Thames. To avoid steps, take the alternative route via Clarnico Lane and White Post Lane to Hackney Wick.

Queen Elizabeth Olympic Park

The Olympic Games of 2012 were held in London and have left a legacy of award winning sports structures and the capital's largest modern expanse of parkland. For cyclists, the star attraction has to be the Velodrome, designed by Hopkins Architects to reflect externally the high-speed racing on the oval circuit inside. Visitors can see the Siberian pine track at any time (free) except when events are taking place. You can book to ride on the track (cycle hire is provided), the road circuit or the off-road and BMX tracks. Winner of even more awards is the London Aquatics Centre by Zaha Hadid, which looks like a giant Manta Ray and features a cathedral-like 50m main pool – worth using the plentiful parking stands and taking a dip. The main Olympic stadium is more functional than spectacular and has been converted to a football ground for local club West Ham. Surrounding the venues is parkland with the River Lea flowing through the middle – there are also two outstanding playgrounds for children. Largely off-road, the ride is suitable for children with supervision on the very short road section.

1. Arriving at **Stratford International station** or on London Overground head for the main entrance to Westfield shopping centre in Montfitchet Road (named after local landowners). If you arrive at **Stratford Regional station** you have to cross the wide footbridge (lifts under the steps) to Montfitchet Road.
2. Follow the cycle track southwards on the opposite side to Westfield's towards the car parking board bizarrely located in the centre of the track. Continue downhill until you reach a set of traffic lights where you turn right following the signs for the **Aquatics Centre**, one of the masterworks of the Egyptian architect Zaha Hadid. If you have the gear and time for a swim the bike stands and entrance are on the lower level of the Centre (lifts from the upper level).
3. If not entering the Aquatics Centre turn left just as you approach it following a footpath towards the unmistakable red **Arcelor Mittal Orbit** (the name refers to its steel industry funder) by British sculptor Anish Kapoor. You can go up to the top (open 10am – 6pm April – Sept., 11pm – 5pm Oct. – March) for great views of London.
4. Ride up to the **Stadium**, designed by HOK (also responsible for the nearby Arsenal

LOCAL INFO

Local Cycle Guide: 7 and 4
Start point: Stratford stations
Length: 14 km (9 m)
Time: 2 hours
Type of ride: Easy. Mostly off-road; a few stretches of busy road that can be walked

Sights and places to visit
- London Aquatic Centre, Olympic Park, E20 2ZQ. Tel 020 8536 3150
- Olympic Stadium, Queen Elizabeth Olympic Park, E20 2ST. Tel 0800 072 2110
- Fish Island
- Victoria Park
- Velodrome, Queen Elizabeth Olympic Park, Abercrombie Rd, E20 3AB. Tel 0300 003 0613

Eating and drinking
- Stour Space, 7 Roach Rd, Tower Hamlets, E3 2PA. Tel 020 8985 7827
- Pavilion Café, Corner Old Ford Road, Victoria Park, E9 7DE. Tel 020 8980 0030
- The Crate, 7, The White Building, Queen's Yard, E9 5EN. Tel 020 8533 3331
- Hackney Pearl, 11 Prince Edward Rd, E9 5LX. Tel 020 8510 3605
- Natura Pizzeria, 30 Felstead St, E9 5LG. Tel 020 8533 2264
- Timber Lodge Café, 1A Honour Lea Avenue, E20 3BB Tel 020 7241 9076

Rail stations: Stratford International, Hackney Wick, Stratford Regional
Underground stations: Stratford, Stratford DLR, Pudding Mill Lane DLR

stadium, and take the zig-zag path down to the river along where you head to the right (north) crossing underneath a bridge.

5. Pass a popular climbing wall and, staying by the waterside, keep to the right which path takes you up in a loop to the level of the stadium at a cleverly designed children's park. The fountains (where the noise is) are a delight in the summer. From the children's park head right (north) towards the tall copper-coloured power station that uses biofuel and biomass.

6. At a wide paving area bear left aiming for the Shard (London's tallest building) which is visible in the distance. You pass a decorative garden on the left and head for a pink building advertising **H Foreman & Sons**, a salmon smoking factory and fine fish restaurant visited by celebs. Bear left down towards the canal and once on it turn left (south) to reach **Old Ford Lock** where you cross over the canal onto **Fish Island** and then turn first right (Bream St) and follow the road back towards the canal.

7. The Victorian warehouses on Fish Island,

Above: *Six Day racing at the QE Olympic Park Velodrome.*

surrounded by two canals and a motorway, house dozens of artist studios – you can see some of their work at **Stour Space** which is also a pleasant cafe with a canal terrace (9 am – 5 pm daily)

8. Continuing up Roach Road you pass a lone Victorian chimney and a footbridge back to the Lea Navigation canal (for a shorter ride). The main route, however, carries straight on, to another footbridge that takes you across the Hertford Union canal where you turn left and, after passing the ever changing graffiti walls, exit the canal just before the next bridge. To your right you will see the entrance to Victoria Park (St Mark's Gate).

9. Enjoy a ride clockwise around Victoria Park (connection to Limehouse Cut ride, page 188) with an optional stop at the **Pavilion Café** (public WCs outside) open 9 am – 3 pm winter, 9 am – 5 pm summer.

10. Having rounded most of the Park look out for a path towards an old post office on the Park's eastern side (Cadogan Terrace). This takes you to a pedestrian bridge across the A12 motorway. Follow Wallis Road past Hackney Wick station near which there is a choice of trendy eateries (Hackney Pearl in Prince Edward Road; The Crate in White Post Lane and Natura Pizzeria in Felstead Street) as well as the vintage style Skinny Eric's bike shop (Felstead Street).

11. Once watered and fed, follow Wallis Road which turns left and right to cross the canal bridge (lift access) and loop round onto the canal heading northwards. After passing under three road bridges the canal bears to the left at which point you turn right (east) onto a narrow path across **Hackney Marshes** football grounds (where David Beckham trained as a lad). The path leads to a bridge across the River Lea where it turns right.

12. Don't follow the fork to the river but head left up the ramped path to cross a red bridge over the Eastway and then another over the A12.

13. As you cross the second bridge you are treated to a great view of the **Velodrome**, an outstanding structure, inside and out, by Hopkins Architects. It's worth circumnavigating it – turn off left just before the building – to see the road,

off-road and BMX circuits (all open to visiting riders for a charge). You can visit the interior of the Velodrome for free (except during events) and bike stands are plentiful. You have to book training sessions on the track in advance (9am –10pm most days—bike hire included in the price) and they come highly recommended.

14. Return to the path leading off the bridge and turn left passing the ingenious **Tumbling Bay children's playground** followed by the convenient **Timber Lodge café** with its plentiful cycle stands.

15. Just after the café turn right (west) to cross the River Lea enjoying the fine views then turn left before reaching the main road, and cross over at the traffic light and turn left on the cycle track to head for Westfield Shopping Centre.

16. At the bottom of the hill, riding straight on will take you to Stratford International, or you can turn right on the cycle track and follow it round (left at Montfitchet Road) to Stratford regional station, or walk through the shopping centre at the wide boulevard.

Below: *The Aquatics Centre designed by the Iraqi-born British architect Zaha Hadid.*
Right: *Arcelor Mittal Orbit by Anish Kapoor offers great views from the top.*

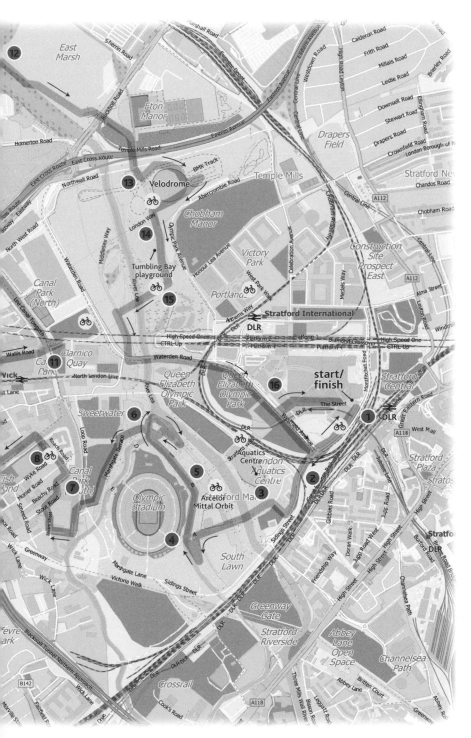

Royal Docks and the Greenway

The capital's rapid growth is very evident throughout this ride: City Airport, modern hotels, the Excel exhibition halls, new rail stations, giant modern sculptures plus the Olympic Stadium all compete for your attention alongside 18th-century mills and Victorian pumping stations. The ride takes you to London's only lighthouse, the Royal Docks and to little-known Beckton Alp, which offers spectacular views of London. Most of the ride is off-road, including the elevated Greenway, although there are a few short sections of fairly busy road that can be walked. Give way to pedestrians on all shared paths. Continuing construction works can mean you may have to use diversions on this route.

1. Starting at **Stratford station**, walk southwards (right as you exit the station) past the buses and cycle down a no-through road leading to Farthingale Walk on the left. This brings you to the busy A118, which you can cross (by the spiky sculpture) and ride westwards (right) along the blue cycle track up to a bridge crossing the Waterworks River. Just before the bridge turn left down the path marked towpath to House Mill.

2. Behind you is the **Olympic Stadium** designed by Peter Cook of HOK architects for London's 2012 Olympic Games, and across the river, as you ride down the path, is a tall metal sculpture of an Olympic torch, marking a residential development by furniture retailer IKEA.

3. Crossing a small bridge you continue southwards to reach **Three Mills**, believed to be the largest tidal mill still in existence (see Limehouse Cut ride, page 188). A café (Miller's House) opens weekends May – Oct (11 am – 4 pm). Turn left (south) staying on the eastern side of the River Lea, after passing the mills complex, and pass under the railway bridge.

4. You have to walk up and down a ramp over a white bridge to cross Bow Locks after which stay to the right to join a floating towpath leading to the Limehouse Cut – a straight wide canal (built 1760s), overlooked by new housing developments, that takes you to Limehouse Basin, a buzzing hub of dockside activity in the 19th century, now a sedate marina by the Thames River.

5. Arriving at the marina, marked by a metal foot-bridge across the canal, you need to turn

LOCAL INFO

Local Cycle Guide: 7
Start point: Stratford station
Length: 20 km (12.5 m)
Time: 4 hours
Type of ride: Easy. Mostly off-road; a few stretches of busy road that can be walked

Sights and places to visit
- Olympic Stadium view
- Millennium Dome view
- The Miller's House, Three Mill Lane, E3 3DU. Tel 020 8980 4626
- London Docklands Museum, No.1 Warehouse, W India Dock Rd, E14 4AL. Tel 020 7001 9844
- Royal Docks
- Thames Barrier Park, North Woolwich Road, E16 2HP. Tel 020 7511 4111
- Beckton Alp viewpoint
- Abbey Mills Pumping Station

Eating and drinking
- Miller's House café (see above)
- London Docklands Museum café (see above)
- Fatboy's Diner, Trinity Buoy Wharf, 64 Orchard Place, E14 0JW. Tel 020 79874334
- Thames Barrier Park café (see above)

Rail stations: Stratford, Canning Town, West Ham, Excel

Underground stations: Bromley-by-Bow, West Ham, East India DLR, City Airport DLR, Beckton DLR

off to the left, up a ramp into a small park, Ropemakers Field, which you cross, passing the bandstand, to arrive at Narrow St featuring a marked cycle route (CS3). Follow the route to the left (eastwards) unless you want to visit Canary Wharf which is accessed via a narrow passageway, in between the columns on the right side of Narrow St, at Dunbar Wharf.

6. When you reach the rail bridge stay on the blue marked cycle route which follows the Docklands Light Railway (DLR) on its south side and then crosses underneath the DLR. Just to the right, south of the bridge, is the Georgian **Dockmasters House** and, across Hertsmere Road, you can visit the (signposted) **London Docklands Museum** (free and open daily 10am – 6pm, café on ground floor). The route however follows the CS3 blue markings, signposted for Poplar High St, across the busy highway.

7. The blue route brings you to a hole in the wall on the left which you enter and follow discreet blue squares across the square leading to Saffron Avenue.

Above: View of the Dome, Bell Sculpture and London skyline from Trinity Buoy Wharf.

8. Where Saffron Avenue reaches a small roundabout, stop following CS3 and cross onto the right-hand side cycle path leading to a much larger roundabout. Here you stay on the pavement and ride anti-clockwise, with care, crossing first Aspen Way and then Blackwall Way as you aim for a gated entrance to East India Dock Basin (open daytime – if closed, follow signs marked for Trinity Buoy Wharf).

9. From East India Dock Basin there is an amazing view of the Millennium Dome (architect Sir Norman Foster) now a concert venue. Follow the basin around to leave by its eastern gate and head right to **Trinity Buoy Wharf**.

10. The wharf includes London's only lighthouse, now an art installation (open Sat and Sun 10 am–4 pm), and the legendary **Fatboy's Diner** (open 10 am–4 pm daily except Mondays and Bank Holiday weekends). There are public WCs just behind the diner.

11. Exiting Trinity Buoy Wharf via Orchard Place you turn left (west) on the cycle path, just before the dual carriageway (A 1020) and, after 20 metres (25 yd), cross over, doubling back on yourself, to turn right onto the two-way eastward cycle track alongside the A1020 across the bridge over the River Lea.

12. At the roundabout, turn right down Dock Road. Follow the road until it meets the DLR, by Waterfront Studios, where you cross (left) under the flyover to enter the impressive expanse of **Royal Victoria Dock**.

13. Going north around the dock you pass the **Emirates Airline cable car** which can take you and your cycle (included in ticket price) on a spectacular trip to the Dome and the Greenwich Palaces ride (page 86). Beyond the cable car in Royal Victoria Dock is the colourful pumping station designed by Sir Richard Rogers, architect of the Lloyd's Building. Continuing eastwards around the north side of the dock

Above: *Strand East Olympic torch sculpture by ARC-ML architects.*

you reach a high bridge, which is accessible via a lift. From the bridge there are very fine views of **Canary Wharf** (tallest tower by Cesar Pelli). You can cycle around the south side of the dock if you don't like heights or the lift is closed.

14. Heading south down Rayleigh Road you then have to walk across the busy North Woolwich Road to reach the cycle track on the south side and turn left (east) to the **Thames Barrier Park**, just past Pontoon Dock station. It has a pleasant café (open 7 am–dusk, bike stands outside) WCs, and great views of the Thames Flood Barrier.

15. Returning to the shared use pavement head east, cross beneath the DLR, and follow the cycle track under it northwards (some on pavement sections) until you reach a small roundabout which you circumnavigate using

the shared pavement anti-clockwise turning off at the one o'clock position down a shared path just before the turn onto the bridge. The path leads to the Travelodge Hotel, which you exit via the car park and cross over the road and ride left (east) on the shared use pavement to just before the roundabout where you turn right onto a shared use path that is on the right (east) side of the dual carriageway, then go underneath the road to arrive at Royal Albert Dock.

16. Cross a short iron footbridge leading towards the Ramada Hotel and turn right, following signs for the Royal Albert/Regatta Centre. While building works obstruct the waterfront path heading east, follow Dockside Road eastwards until you pass the Holiday Inn where you turn left onto a wide cycle and footpath which takes you over the A1020 and turns right along Jake Russell Walk. This pleasant path through **Beckton Park**, where horses

Left: *Giant sculpture by the Three Mills Wall River.*
Below: *View from Beckton Alps, once a dry-ski slope on the site of a gasworks.*

graze, leads you to Beckton DLR station. When you see the station just across the road, you turn left and follow the cycle path north, past Asda, and around the mini-roundabout to cross underneath the road by a short tunnel. After the tunnel, a left turn on the cycle path brings you out onto a road (Alpine Way) opposite **Beckton Alp**.

17. A gate in the fence opposite leads to a path up the 'Alp', which is made of slag from the old Beckton gasworks. The peak is sometimes closed, but even from the path the views across London are superb.

18. Descend the Alp by following the path back the way you came but at the T-junction where the road can be seen, turn right and exit via a gate to go under the flyover, using several crossings, heading for a sign marked Greenway on your far left.

19. The Greenway is a shared use path built on top of the Northern Outflow Sewer (designed

Above: *Fatboy's Diner at Trinity Buoy Wharf.*
Right: *London's only lighthouse at Trinity Buoy Wharf.*

by Joseph Bazalgette in 1853) hence the slight whiff. Passing great views, you can enjoy a relaxed ride (with some road crossings) for 4 km (2 1/2 m).

20. After crossing the railway tracks look out for the 150 year old **Abbey Mills Pumping Station** on the left. The ornate neo-Gothic building, designed by Joseph Bazalgette, has been described as a 'cathedral of sewage'. It was built on former abbey lands.

21. When you reach Stratford High Street (A118) cross over and turn right to retrace your steps towards Stratford station via the blue cycle track remembering to turn off left at Farthingale Walk. Alternatively you can turn off at Warton Road to join the QE Olympic Park ride (see page 64).

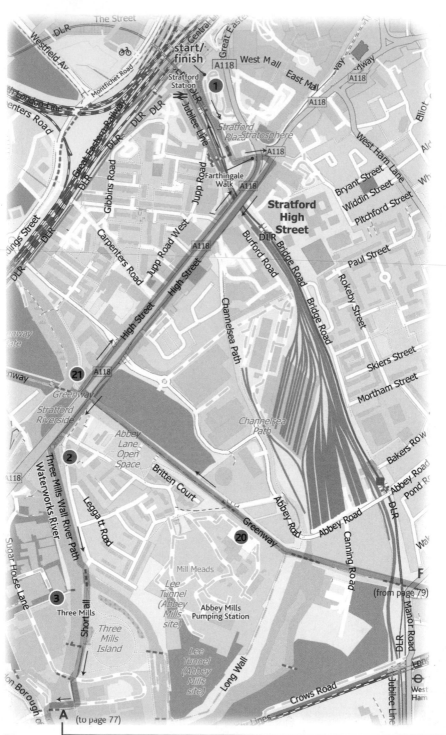

(from page 76)

(to page 78)

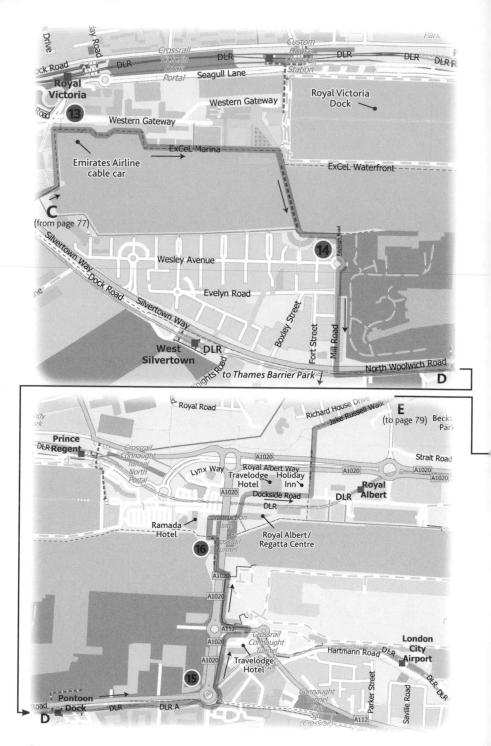

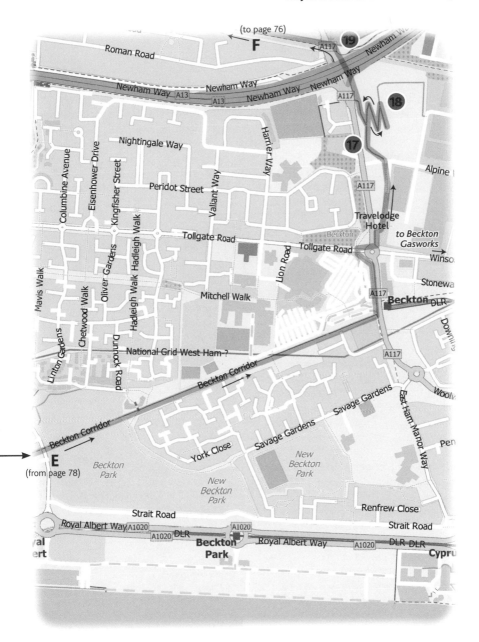

(to page 76)

F

19

18

17

Roman Road

Newham Way A13

Newham Way

A13

Newham Way

Newham Way

A117

A117

Nightingale Way

Harrier Way

Alpine

Columbine Avenue

Eisenhower Drive

Kingfisher Street

Peridot Street

Valiant Way

A117

Travelodge Hotel

to Beckton Gasworks

Mavis Walk

Oliver Gardens

Hadleigh Walk Hadleigh Walk

Tollgate Road

Beckton

Tollgate Road

Lion Road

Winso

Chetwood Walk

Mitchell Walk

Stonewa

A117

Beckton DLR

Linton Gardens

Dunnock Road

National Grid West Ham ?

Beckton Corridor

A117

Dow

Beckton Corridor

York Close

Savage Gardens

Savage Gardens

Woolv

East Ham Manor Way

Pen

E

(from page 78)

Beckton Park

New Beckton Park

New Beckton Park

Renfrew Close

Strait Road

Strait Road

val
ert

Royal Albert Way A1020

A1020 DLR

Beckton Park

A1020

Royal Albert Way

A1020

DLR DLR

Cypru

Thames Estuary

Riding eastwards along the Thames Estuary, you may forget that you are still in one of the world's biggest cities and surrounded by almost eight million people. The peace and quiet enables you to hear the seabirds as you ride past unusual examples of old and new industrial architecture. This ride was developed by Bexley Cyclists to go beyond the standard riverside route (NCN1) and takes you to the ruins of Lesnes Abbey, giving a glimpse of what this part of England looked like in the Middle Ages, and further east there is the curiously named Franks Park. At the start or end of the ride you can visit the museum at the Royal Arsenal, and if you can plan ahead, it's worth riding on a day when the Victorian Crossness pumping station is open. Being desolate at times, it's a route that's best done in company.

1. From **Woolwich Arsenal station**, turn right into Woolwich New Road, and bear left into the street market. You will need to walk with your bike through the street market. Cross over the road at the crossing. This brings you to the entrance of Woolwich Arsenal, whose military role in weapons storage and manufacture dates back to the 17th century. Some of the barracks and buildings remain but have been converted to office and residential use. You can visit the Firepower Museum and the Gun Pit café (open daily, 9.30 am–5 pm), which is a favourite with cyclists from the Bexhill, Greenwich and Southwark groups. Cycling past the museum you encounter a curious sculpture called *Assembly* by Peter Burke.

2. Keep heading for the river where a paved and signed path, National Cycle Route 1 (NCN1) takes you eastwards.

3. After 4 km (2¹⁄₂ m), just before the riverside development of Thamesmead, is a small lake. The extensive housing development was planned as a model town in the 1960s and 70s.

4. About 500 metres (550 yd) after the lake, near the end of the row of houses, look out for a signpost to Lesnes Abbey, which takes you away from the Thames path and onto an off-road cycle path through Thamesmead. You now head directly south for 1 km (³⁄₄ m) until you meet the dual carriageway.

5. En route you pedal through **Manor Way Green** and under a footbridge. Don't follow the Green Chain Walk (GCW) at this point, although you will do so later on, but follow the path next to the water channel.

LOCAL INFO

Local Cycling Guide: 8
Start point: Woolwich Arsenal
Length: 20 km (12½ m)
Time: 4 hours
Type of ride: Easy. Almost entirely off-road, with short road sections that can be walked, two sections which could be muddy if wet – alternative routes possible.

Sights and places to visit
- Firepower Museum, Royal Arsenal SE18 6ST. Tel 020 8855 7755
- Lesnes Abbey, Bexley
- Franks Park, Erith Road, Bexley
- St John the Baptist, West St Erith, Kent. Tel 01322 332555
- Crossness Pumping Station, Belvedere Road, SE2 9AQ. Tel 020 8311 3711

Eating and drinking
- Unity Kitchen, Royal Arsenal see Firepower Museum, above.
- Crossness Pumping Station café (on open days only) see Crossness Pumping Station, above
- Lesnes Lodge at Lesnes Abbey – refreshment kiosk/toilets
- Dial Arch, The Dial Arch Buildings, Major Draper Street, Royal Arsenal, Woolwich, London SE18 6GH. Tel 020 3130 0700

Rail stations: Woolwich Arsenal, Erith, Belvedere. Woolwich Arsenal DLR

6. A sign marked for Abbey Wood and Belvedere via Southmere Park takes you under a road.

7. The path continues past the backs of houses

Above: *Riding through Peter Burke's sculpture, which is close to the Firepower Museum at the Woolwich Arsenal.*

until you reach a dual carriageway, where you go up the ramp to a bridge that crosses the A2016. On the other side of the bridge, don't follow the Ridgeway but go down the ramp and turn left, following the sign for the Green Chain Walk (GCW) via Southmere Park.

8. Stay on the quiet road until the end of the lake, at which point you enter the park and follow the route around the lake, and head directly south on the off-road path (still marked GCW) to Lesnes Abbey.

9. En route you cross a blue bridge, then another blue bridge over the railway tracks and another road and barrier.

10. Lesnes Abbey was founded in 1178 by Richard de Luci, reputedly as a penance for participating in the murder of St Thomas à Beckett. There is a refreshment kiosk (Lesnes Lodge), and a WC, or it's an ideal place for a picnic.

11. Heading eastwards there is a short road section (Abbey Road), or you can walk across Lesnes Abbey park and, at the end of the park, turn right up Leather Bottle Lane (signed 'Byway 7'), a bumpy track running behind the houses on Abbey Road. If wet, this will be very muddy. You may prefer to use Elstree Gardens, leading to Kingswood Ave (next right). At the end of the lane (or Kingswood Ave) turn right uphill, then immediately left.

12. Follow CGW signs and continue into Upper Abbey Road, and keep heading east along Halt Robin Road until you come to the entrance to Franks Park.

13. Franks Park, while very lovely, can be hard going after wet weather. (If wet, you can avoid most of the park by continuing on Halt Robin Road.) Birdlife ranges from owls to woodpeckers, and the woods take you to a children's playground and then on to a green barrier/gate at Valley Road.

Above: *Sailing on the boating lake at Southmere Park.*

14. At the end of Valley Road turn left and, after about 30 metres (33 yd) 6, on the right hand side you'll see a path up some shallow steps that let you to walk across a bridge over the A2016.

15. On the other side of the bridge is the church of **St John the Baptist**, parts of which date back to the 12th century. Passing the church, cross the road and turn left, staying on the pavement, follow cycle route signs to the river (about 100 metres/110 yd). If you need supplies there is a supermarket at no. 174 going east down West Street.

16. Follow the path to the left and stay by the river all the way back to Woolwich.

17. There are interesting examples of industrial architecture en route, notably the old and new cathedrals of sewage at Crossness.

18. The **new Crossness sewage treatment** works

(2008) looks like a steel bird and derives 20 percent of its energy from sludge – a wind turbine supplies additional power. Next to it is a **nature reserve**, and on the other side of the river you can glimpse Ford's Dagenham car plant.

19. A little further on, the Victorian **Crossness Pumping Station**, designed by Joseph Bazalgette and opened in 1865, is worth visiting, although it is only open on certain days. It still has its original beam pumping engines and a richly decorated interior.

20. You then ride 5 km (3 m) until you come to a black staircase, which you avoid by taking the ramp just before it.

21. After returning to the Arsenal you can either head back to Woolwich Arsenal station or continue along the river to **Greenwich** to take the Greenwich Palaces ride (see page 86).

Right: *The ruins of Lesnes Abbey are extensive and provide a good spot for a picnic.*

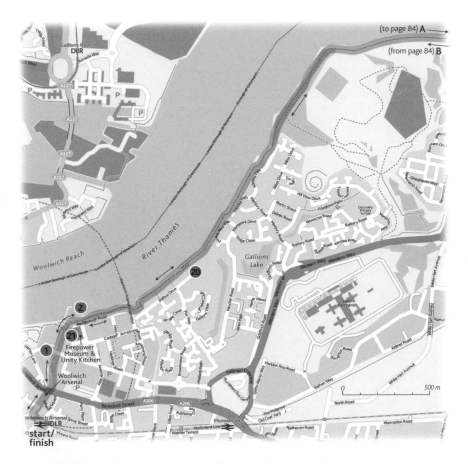

0   500 m

River Thames

London Borough of Bexley

London Borough of Havering

(17)

Crossness
ewage works

(18) New Crossness sewage
treatment works

Eastern Way

A2016

Eastern Way

Eastern Way

Wodong Way

P

Halley Road

Halley Road

Halley Road

P

A2016

Brook Age Way

A2016

(16)

Church Manorway

Yarnton Way   Yarnton Way   Yarnton Way

Way

Sutherland Road   Caldy Road

Viking Way

Norman Road

Maida Road

Belvedere

Dylan Rd   Dylan   ead

North Kent Line - Woolwich Branch

A2016

Picardy Street

P

Gilbert Road

Brook Age Way

B213

Ambrooke Road

Lower Road

St John the
Baptist church

Gyproc Business Park

Picardy Street

Ripley Road

Coleman Road

Edwards Road

Sheridan Road

Gertrude Road

Lower Road

Lower Road

Gordon Road

Stanmore Road

Bostall Road

Lower Road

Wood Avenue

St Augustines Avenue

Upper Abbey Road

Abbey Crescent

Picardy Hill

Bowen's Hill

Halt Robin Road

Parkside Mount

Pelwood Road

B. Allan's Road

Mayfield Road

Parkside Road

(11)

(12)

(14)

(15)

Raglan Road

Heron Hill

Orchard Close

Chieftan

Ruskin Road

Main Road

Kentish Road

Picardy Road

Jackson Road

Heron's Drive

Reade Square

Ebourne

Upper Park Road

Franks Park

(13)

Valley Road

Barnhill Crn

Hillside

Bexley Close

A2016

Gilbert Road

Abbey Road

Lessness Park

Pembroke Road

Church Road

St John's Road

Nelson Road

Bethelton Road

Eardley Road

A206   Erith Road

Hurst Road

Church Road

Sandpit Road

Woolwich Road

Holly Hill Road

Holly Hill Road

Riverdale Road

De Luci Road

Alford Road

Victoria Street

Bexwell Road

Chapman Road

Stapley Road

Roberts Road

Salmon Road

Chapman Road

Riverdale Road

A206   Frazer Road

85

Greenwich Palaces

Once a fishing village, Greenwich became a favoured royal location in the 15th century. Henry VIII extended the Tudor palace and Sir Walter Raleigh allegedly threw his cloak on the ground in front of Queen Elizabeth I at Dover Road gate. The Greenwich Cyclists group uses this ride to introduce the many grand residences in the borough. The Queen's House is a masterpiece of the English Renaissance, Charlton House is a rare example of a Jacobean house in London, and the Old Royal Naval College, Royal Observatory and Morden College showcase the work of Sir Christopher Wren. Icons of modern architecture are represented by the Dome and the Thames Barrier. In between you will discover delightful parks and paths. Construction and variations in permissions can mean that some sections of the ride by the river have to be walked or diverted.

1. You can arrive at **Cutty Sark Gardens** by boat (bikes permitted), bike, train (Greenwich rail station) or on foot via the Greenwich Tunnel under the Thames. The *Cutty Sark*, the world's last tea clipper, was damaged by fire in 2007 having survived numerous sea voyages since its launch in 1869, but has now been restored.
2. Negotiating the one-way system (or walking south down King William Walk) takes you past the Village Market and along King William Walk into **Greenwich Park** (open 6 am till dusk), laid out by Louis XIV's gardener Le Notre. The Palladian-style **Queen's House** (reached on foot), designed by Inigo Jones in 1616, was a key influence on English classical architecture. It houses the **National Maritime Museum** (bike stands in the museum car park in Park Row).
3. Retracing your steps to the park entrance and pedalling up the hill inside the park to the **Royal Observatory** (built by Wren in 1675) enables you to enjoy a spectacular view across the river to Canary Wharf and beyond. Within the observatory you can see the **Greenwich Meridian** line and a collection of telescopes.
4. Turning your back on the view, head towards Blackheath and bear left at the fork in the path after crossing the busy Shooters Hill (route marked to Kidbrooke). Passing the Georgian Paragon you reach **Morden College**. You have to walk along the path past this building, attributed to Wren, or cycle down Kidbrooke Gardens. About 200 metres (220 yd) down Rochester Way is a convenient footbridge across the A2.

LOCAL INFO

Local Cycle Guide: 7
Start point: Cutty Sark, Greenwich
Length: 18 km (11 m)
Time: 3 hours
Type of ride: Easy. Paved roads with little traffic, short stretch through parks. Thames path is traffic-free. Crosses a few busy roads.

Sights and places to visit
- Queen's House and Royal Observatory, National Maritime Museum, Romney Road SE10 9NF. Tel 020 8312 6712
- Old Royal Naval College, University of Greenwich, 2 Cutty Sark Gardens SE10 9LW. Tel 020 8269 4747
- Charlton House, Charlton Road SE7 8RE. Tel 020 8856 3951
- Thames Barrier Visitors Centre 1 Unity Way, SE18 5JN. Tel 020 8305 4188

Eating and drinking
- Mulberry Tea Rooms, Charlton House
- Anchor and Hope, 2 Riverside Walk, Anchor and Hope Lane SE7 7SS. Tel 020 8858 0382
- Cutty Sark Tavern, 4–7 Ballast Quay SE10 9PD. Tel 020 8858 3146
- The Yacht, 5 Crane St SE10 9NP. Tel 020 8858 0175
- The Trafalgar, 6 Park Row SE10 9NW. Tel 020 8858 2437

Rail stations: Blackheath, Greenwich DLR, Maze Hill
Underground stations: North Greenwich

5. Turn left after the bridge into Eastbrook Road then right into Hervey Road. Take care not to miss the sharp right turn into Begbie Road then turn left and second left. Cross over Shooters Hill again (right and immediate left). Another right and left bring you into Hornfair Road where you'll see a sign for Charlton House.
6. Only slightly older than Jones's Queen's House, **Charlton House** (1607–12) is elaborately ornamented – typical of Jacobean mansions. It now houses a public library. You can visit the **Mulberry Tea Rooms** inside.
7. Turning right out of Charlton House you pass **St Luke's Church** (1630). The **Bugle Horn** pub in the Village has bike stands across the road but is busy on match days.
8. Turn left into **Maryon Wilson Park** just after the long school wall ends. Bearing right at the children's zoo will take you up a steep hill with shallow steps. Turn right into Woodland Terrace and left into Maryon Road to re-enter the north side of the park next to a tower block.

Above: *Pedalling past the 18th-century Cutty Sark tavern, named after the last tea clipper that sits in Cutty Sark Gardens.*

Go left around the playing fields and cross the railway track by the bridge. Then bear left to cross the busy Woolwich Road at the pedestrian crossing.
9. Follow the shared-use footpath, with signs for Thames Cycle Route no. 1.
10. The route goes around the **Thames Barrier buildings** (on your right is the Visitors' Centre) and you emerge by the river to see the gleaming steel flood gates erected in the 1970s and 80s to control floods at high tide. It's been used defensively more than 100 times. There is a café here with views of the Barrier. As this is about halfway, it is a good place to stop.
11. You can now follow the Thames path all the way back to the *Cutty Sark*, barring any construction works and diversions – you may have to walk along some sections. A couple of

Above: *A river view of the Queen's House by Inigo Jones between the Baroque facades of Sir Christopher Wren's Royal Naval College.*

hundred metres from the Barrier, the **Anchor and Hope** pub offers food and great views. A little further is the UMA aggregate plant with its impressive array of cranes and giant conveyor belts.

12. Just past the Greenwich Yacht Club the path is generously wide and a display describes the history of the Thames from 8000 bc to the present day and the advent of the Dome. You also pass the Emirates AirLine Terminal, a cable car on which bikes are accepted, which takes you across the river to Royal Victoria Dock and the Excel Exhibition Centre and connects with the Docklands Light Railway (DLR). There is a café by the terminal building.

13. Built to mark the Millennium, the **Dome** was designed by leading British architect Norman Foster as a temporary structure. Like so many grand projects it overran on costs, but

has now become a popular concert venue.

14. You have to walk a short section just past Pelton Road (or cycle around) to reach the **Cutty Sark Tavern** (dated 1795). A little further is **The Yacht** – both have fine views. The final potential stop is the well-established **Trafalgar** pub next to Wren's **Royal Naval College**.

15. Although Wren gave the Old Royal Naval College its Baroque character, the complex of buildings also includes the work of John Webb, Vanburgh and other architects and was originally the Royal Naval Hospital. The Royal Naval College took over the complex in 1873. It is now part of the University of Greenwich. Between 8 am and 6 pm you can now cycle through the college (accessed via a gate in Park Row to the left of the Trafalgar Pub) along a cycle path to arrive back at the *Cutty Sark* – at other times you have walk along the narrow riverbank path.

Right: *Charlton House – a rare Jacobean building in London.*

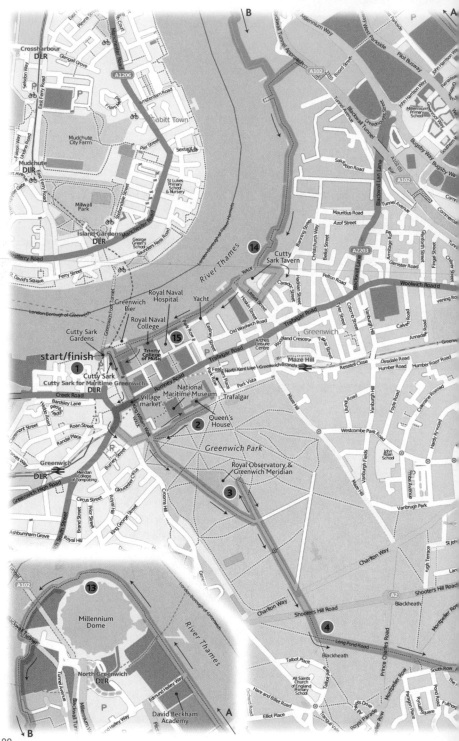

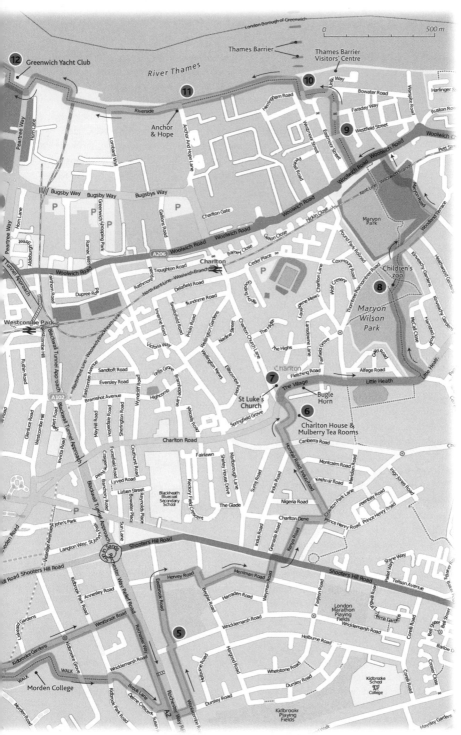

Waterlink Way

Flowing through the heart of southeast London, the Pool and Ravensbourne rivers are virtually unknown except to locals. Following these rivers is the Waterlink Way, a fascinating cycle route revealing a variety of landscapes. From beautiful country parks to post-Industrial landscapes, this has some hidden gems. Sustrans, a sustainable transport organization, developed the route as National Cycle Network (NCN) with help from LCC members. Following the route from south to north means you don't get the sun in your eyes and you end up nearer central London for transport links and amenities. When you reach the Thames you can catch the train home or link up with the Thames Cycle Path (NCN4), or go via the Greenwich Foot Tunnel to NCN1 northwards (see also the Thames Banks ride, page 98).

1. At **Elmers End station** (northbound side) cycle down the access road straight ahead, out onto the road then turn in immediately to your left. Alternatively go through the car park to your left and walk your bike down the path to your right to join the route from there.

2. Pedal southwards to follow the path until you reach the tram tracks, where you turn right and then right again and come to the **Environmental Gardens**. Passing the car park and swings, you see one of the Sustrans marked signs that look like a mini-totem pole; follow the shared-use path northwards again.

3. When back on the north side of the park, the signs point left for Beck Lane. However, bearing right using the crossing then left down Ancaster Road takes you to a park trail. Keep following the trail north until you get to a school entrance, then turn right down Churchfields Road.

4. Follow the cycle path on the pavement to cross the busy Beckenham Road, which takes you over the crossing and under the bridge. Turn immediately right at the petrol station and go down the tree-lined **Barnmead Road**, a place of unique character with its unsurfaced roads and fine porches outside the Victorian houses. Turn left, and on your right after about 200 metres (220 yd) go through **Kent House station** to the other side. Turn right down Kings Hall Road, but look out for the concealed entrance to **Cator Park**, which is another 200 metres (220 yd) on your left.

5. Cator Park has some spectacular firs and

LOCAL INFO

Local Cycling Guides: 11, 7
Start point: Elmers End station
Length: 12 km (7½ m)
Time: 3 Hours
Type of ride: Easy. Mostly off-road and quiet streets. Busy junctions can be walked

Sights and places to visit
• Norwood Country Park
• Cator Park
• Pool River
• Ladywell Fields
• St Mary's Church, 346 Lewisham High St SE13 6LE. Tel 07836 384 229
• Ravensbourne River
• Greenwich

Eating and drinking
• Ladywell Fields café, Ladywell Road, SE4
• Le Delice, 38 Ladywell Road, SE13 7UZ. Tel 020 8314 0314
• The Bird's Nest, 32 Deptford Church St SE8 4RZ. Tel 020 8692 1928

Rail stations and DLR: Elmers End, Kent House, Sydenham, Catford, Ladywell, Lewisham (NR and DLR), Deptford Bridge DLR, Greenwich

pines and is ideal for a picnic. The **Pool River** runs through the park, and then continues alongside the bike route to eventually meet the **Ravensbourne** in Catford.

6. Cross Lennard Road and keep heading

Above: Beautiful specimen firs and pines line the path that runs through Cator Park and along the Pool River.

north, following the river to your right. The dense weeping willows are impressive along this stretch. Stay by the river all the way to a small bridge; left then right gets you to Kangley Bridge Road and through an industrial estate. Keep looking out for the no. 21 route signs.

7. Look for the right turn for **Lower Sydenham station**. The area's famous residents have included Rolling Stone Bill Wyman and Karl Marx's daughter Eleanor. The rough ground just after the station with the milepost might look unkempt but that's a deliberate attempt to nurture a wild habitat.

8. Across the next main road is **Riverview Walk**, where an old gasworks has been landscaped and the river channelled to create a linear park. A spiky gas pipe by one bridge and the two gasometers further up by the next bridge are remnants of the area's rich industrial past.

9. Follow the river and the cycle route signs for Catford, over a couple of small bridges. As you approach **Catford railway station** you go

through a retail centre. It's better to bear right here using Halfords car park to access the route as it goes under the road bridge, because the formal route involves facing vehicles coming into the car park. There is no dropped kerb in Halfords car park. You may also wish to use footpath to your right which links to the route at the top.

10. Going up Adenmore Road, turn second left under the railway bridge, heading for Ladywell and Lewisham, to enter **Ladywell Fields** to your right. There is not a dropped kerb to access route under the railway bridge.

11. Midway through this park you come to a remarkable spiral bridge that spans the railway tracks, a cyclists' favourite.

12. As you come to the end of Ladywell Fields there is a convenient café on the left. As you

Above: *From the end of the route you can follow the Thames to Tower Bridge and carry on along the Thames Banks ride (see page 98).*

turn left, over the hump bridge, you pass **Le Delice**, a bar and restaurant. You may wish to walk this section until the crossing.

13. Take the first right after the hump bridge and go right again to head down Algernon Road and Marsala Road. Follow route signs that should bring you back by the **Ravensbourne River** with a right turn from Elmira Street into Pine Tree Way.

14. Follow the river 100 metres (110 yd) north and then bear left down the wide pavement – do not go underneath the arches in front of you – and cross the major road (Loampit Vale, the A20) to go up Thurston Road following

the cycle path. Retail units should be to your
left. Use the informal crossing to turn right, go
through a tunnel under the railway track and
through a housing estate (stick with it) until
you reach a red wall, where you turn left, and
then take a right after 100 metres (110 yd).

15. Stay on the west side of the river and follow
the NCN21 signs through **Brookmill Park**. You
then cross the river again to arrive at **Deptford
Bridge** with the Docklands Light Railway (DLR)
overhead. The route uses a cycle track on the
pavement to cross the busy road; keep to the
cycle track on the other side as it turns right
around the corner into Deptford Church Street.
Where the pavement section ends by a roundabout you can stop at the **Bird's Nest pub**,
where cycles are often parked outside.

16. Creekside leads through a fascinating area
with its mixture of social housing, industrial
buildings and trendy art galleries, one of which
has an impressive mural just underneath the
arches.

17. Just before the end of Creekside turn right
into Copperas Street, where you will find the
unusual iridescent building of the Laban Dance
Centre.

18. Across the main road (Creek Road) NCN4
signs take you along the pavement and over to
the river – where you can pedal left to **Tower
Bridge** via a pleasant river route (part of the
Thames Banks ride, see page 98) or cycle
right (east) to visit the heart of Greenwich.
Alternatively, by walking along Creek Road
and turning right at Haddo Street you can go
to Greenwich station and catch a train to your
destination.

Right: *A mural underneath the arches along
Creekside (top) and a contained stretch of the
Pool River (bottom) that runs through Cator
Park and meets the Ravensbourne.*

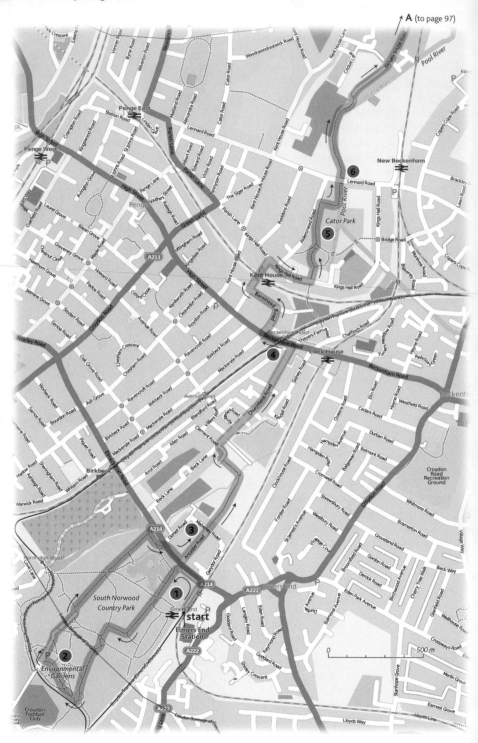

A (to page 97)

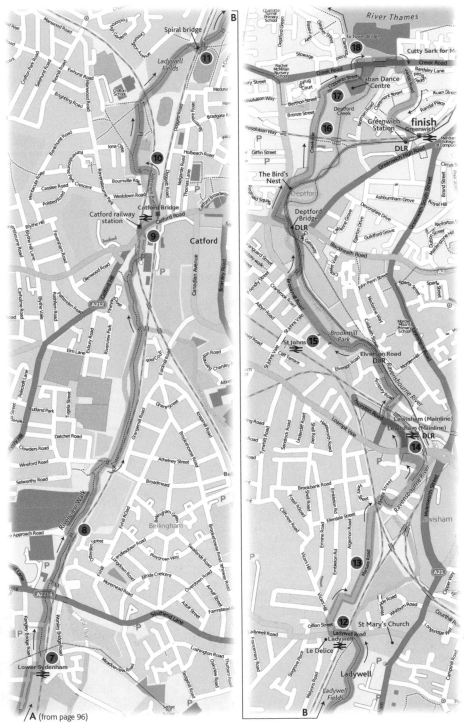

Thames Banks

You're not a true London cyclist until you've experienced the ride from Tower Bridge to Greenwich along the Thames. Once a run-down area of disused warehouses, the riverbank has become a sought-after residential zone and dozens of the warehouses have been converted into swanky flats. Southwark Cyclists have all but branded this ride, though their colleagues in Greenwich and Lewisham are also enthusiasts. There are views, pubs, churches and museums along the route, including the Mayflower Inn from which the Pilgrim Fathers departed for America, Brunel's museum and the little-known Ornamental canal. Permissions to ride can vary along this route and sections may have to be walked. There is also construction along the riverfront which can mean diversions. Please respect the signs.

You can start this ride either with a walk to Bermondsey Wall from City Hall, the egg-shaped Norman Foster building a stone's throw from Tower Bridge, or by riding to Bermondsey Wall from London Bridge station.

1. To start this ride from **City Hall**, first walk there from **London Bridge station** along the river (cycling is not permitted). From City Hall, walking under **Tower Bridge** brings you to the Dickensian **Shad Thames**, which is now a popular shopping and eating destination. On foot you can return to the riverbank by going through the arch 100 metres (110 yd) on the left (next to Le Pont de La Tour restaurant) or at the street 20 metres (21 yd) further on. Then walk across the suspended footbridge over a small dock at Bermondsey Wall.

2. To ride from **London Bridge** turn right (east) into Tooley St, bear left by Tower Bridge (but don't go onto the bridge) and go straight over (eastwards), using the cycling crossing, into Queen Elizabeth St. Turn right at the T-junction, then left for 20 metres (21 yd) along the pavement of the busy Jamaica Road and left again into Mill St, heading for the river at Bermondsey Wall.

3. Follow Bermondsey Wall eastwards, following the intermittent signs for National Cycle Network NCN4. There is virtually no traffic as you continue down Rotherhithe Street.

4. As you reach 18th-century **St Mary's church**, there is an enclave that evokes the past. The **Mayflower Inn** (once the **Shippe**) is located where the Pilgrim Fathers sailed for America (1620), and the **Brunel Engine House**, which once housed the steam pump for the first tunnel under the Thames, is now a museum (open 10 am–5 pm daily).

5. Stay close to the river ignoring routes to the right. As you pass the Hilton Doubletree there is an opportunity to cross the river to **Canary Wharf** on a ferry that takes bikes. Walk through the hotel to access the pier – there are boats every 10 minutes (peak) 20 minutes (off-peak) – cost £3.90.

6. You can cycle through **Surrey Docks Farm** when it is open and on weekends (visiting

times: Tue–Sun, 10 am–5 pm, cycle parking provided). At other times, go around the farm.

7. You also have to go around Convoy's Wharf. Ignore NCN4 signs into Dacca St and turn down the next left, Prince St, to head back towards the river passing Greenwich Cyclists' frequent meeting place, the **Dog and Bell** (with bike stands). Cross the 'new swing' bridge at Deptford Creek.

8. You arrive at Greenwich where you can link to the Greenwich Palaces ride (see page 86) to see several historic palaces and homes.

Left: *The 'Cutty Sark' clipper ship at Greenwich.*

Above: *The Mayflower Inn marks the departure point of the Pilgrim Fathers to America in 1620.*

9. Cross the river by the **Greenwich Foot Tunnel**, or check for alternatives if the tunnel is closed (note – if the lifts aren't working you have to carry your bike down steep steps to the tunnel). One option is to take the *Thames Clipper* riverboat from Greenwich Pier to Masthouse Terrace Pier on the other side of the Thames (every 20 minutes), and follow West-ferry Road eastwards to rejoin the route.

10. From the Foot Tunnel, exit Island Gardens and turn left, continuing straight on into Ferry Street. A right turn at the Ferry House pub takes you across Westferry Road, after which you should look out for a small sign directing you onto a cycle path that goes under the Docklands Light Railway (DLR) via a tunnel.

11. You come out into the calm **Millwall Dock**. Cross the small bridge, round a barrier and continue to the road, then through the gap opposite into Tiller Road. After 200 m (219 yd), turn right into Alpha Grove, following it as far as possible (across a final short stretch of path) then turn left into Byng Street, then almost immediately right into Manilla Street. Turn right along Westferry Road for a short distance, then left into Cuba Street, bringing you back to the Thames.

12. Follow NCN1 signs along the riverside path. Bear right through bollards into Three Colt Street. Here you can take a break at **Vesuvio Caffé** (cycle parking available) before continuing.

13. Turn left at the end of Three Colt Street into Narrow Street, and passing the well-established and pleasant **Grapes pub** (bike stands opposite).

14. Near the end of Narrow St you can follow a path, on foot, through the flats and walk westwards by the river through the **King Edward VII Memorial Park** (open 8 am to dusk). When you leave the park, turn left down Glamis Road and into Wapping Wall. If the park is closed, turn right from Narrow St into Spert St.

15. After 20 metres (25 yd) cross onto the pavement to your left, follow the ramp up and cross a bridge over the busy A1203 (the Highway). Then turn left though a small park to the busy Butcher Row. Cross over it on foot, turn right on the pavement and then turn first left to join the segregated bike lane going west along Cable St. Continue until you see a church, where you turn left off the blue CS3 down Glamis Road to cross back over the Highway. Carry on down Glamis Road into Wapping Wall.

16. In Wapping Wall you can stop for refreshment at the historic **Prospect of Whitby** (dated

Right: *Once an area of warehouses and shipping offices, Shad Thames is now filled with smart flats, shops and restaurants.*

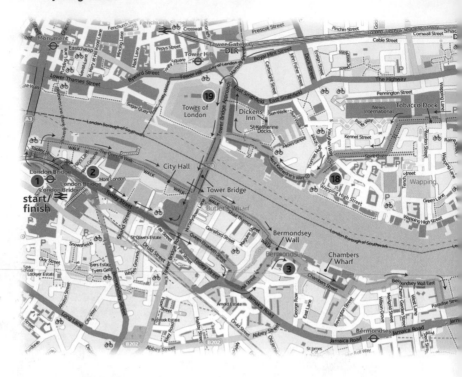

1520). For the final stretch of this route, head back up to Glamis Road and turn left after crossing the red bascule bridge to enter **Shadwell Basin**.

17. Follow Shadwell Basin around, past **St Paul's church**, until you see the **Ornamental Canal**, which passes through a park (follow the red brick path across the park) and leads to two sailing ships – replicas of 18th-century vessels – moored at **Tobacco Dock**.

18. The canal continues up a ramp to Wapping High St (on the left as you come out). Walk straight over to the river to see the great views from the small park, and then continue westwards down St Katherine's Way to **St Katherine Docks**. Entering the marina there you can have a final break at the **Dickens Inn** before following the road, on foot, across a slippery bridge and past a hotel to emerge at the **Tower of London** (no bikes allowed in).

19. To return to London Bridge, ride up to Tower Bridge (right and then left onto the bridge itself). After riding over the bridge with care, turn right using the cycle crossing on the south side of the bridge and follow Tooley St back to London Bridge.

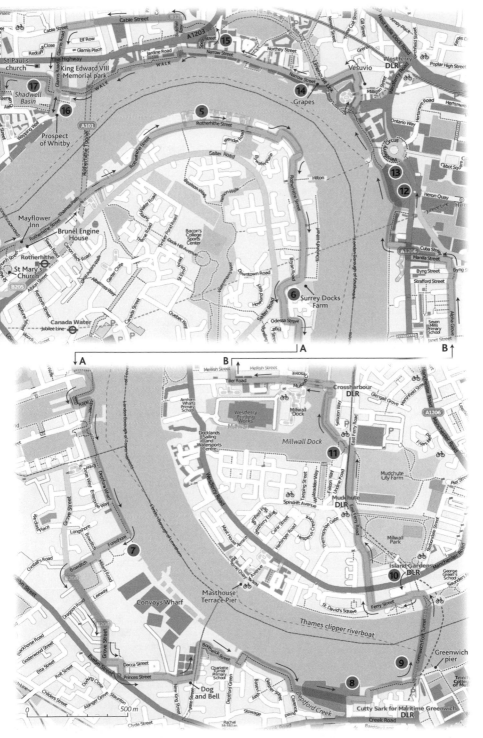

Lambeth and Dulwich Parks

South London was the rough side of town in Shakespeare's day, and some North Londoners still prefer to stay north of the river. What they're missing out on are some lovely parks such as Dulwich and Peckham, beautiful Georgian houses in Camberwell, and streets such as Rye Lane that rival Morocco with their colour and vitality. This ride is a Southwark Cyclists' creation with some Westminster Cyclists' input and features Herne Hill Stadium, where many Olympic cycling medallists have trained, and Burgess Park where adults and children can take up BMX riding.

1. Starting at **Waterloo station**, take a right out of the main ticket hall to leave the back way down the taxi road, following it left at the roundabout to end up opposite the classical portico of the **Old Vic Theatre**. Walk across Baylis Road and follow the bike lane going right.

2. At the complex junction 200 metres (220 yd) on, by a church, walk across to Hercules Road. Follow the signed cycle route that crosses the next busy road (Lambeth Road) and stays by the railway tracks until you see the **Queens Head pub**, where you turn left.

3. Don't follow cycle route 3 down Vauxhall St but go straight on (Black Prince Road/Newberry St/Cardigan St) past an estate opened by Edward, Prince of Wales, in 1914 for elderly residents from the Duchy of Cornwall. In the charming **Courtney Square** you can spot the Prince of Wales's feathers emblem above one of the terraces.

4. The bike route takes you conveniently across the busy Kennington Road (A23). If you fancy a break at the Edwardian **Prince of Wales pub** in handsome **Cleaver Square**, loop round via Kennington Park Road. Otherwise take care crossing this road (walking is easier) and turn left at the traffic lights.

5. Take care turning right, then left at the next junction. Bethwin Road leads to the attractive **Addington Square** and its flower garden. On the left, the changing rooms by the tennis courts have a WC (when open).

6. Cross Addington Square and head south past a splendid Edwardian mansion built in 1900, following cycle route 23, which takes you across the busy Camberwell Church Street. Take care turning right, and then go sharp left

LOCAL INFO

Local Cycle Guide: 14
Start point: Waterloo station
Length: 24 km (15 m)
Time: 3 hours
Type of ride: Easy, mostly quiet streets with a few junctions to negotiate

Sights and places to visit

- Herne Hill Velodrome, Burbage Road SE24 9HE. www.hernehillvelodrome.com
- Brockwell, Dulwich, Burgess parks
- Dulwich Picture Gallery, Gallery Road SE21 7AD. Tel 020 8693 5254
- Khans Bargain, 135 Rye Lane, Peckham SE15 4ST. Tel 020 77328680
- Burgess Hill BMX Track, 285 Albany Rd SE5 0AH. Tel 020 7252 1101
- Red Cross Garden, Redcross Way SE1 1HA. Tel 020 7403 3393

Eating and drinking

- Prince of Wales, 43 Cleaver Square SE11 4EA. Tel 020 77359916
- Au Ciel café, 1a Calton Avenue, Dulwich SE21 7DE. Tel 020 8488 1111
- Mimosa, 16 Half Moon Lane, Dulwich SE24 9HU. Tel 020 7733 8838
- Brockwell Park café
- Dulwich Park café
- Peckham Rye Park café
- The Cut Bar, Young Vic Theatre 66 The Cut, SE1 8LZ. Tel 020 7928 4400

Rail stations: Waterloo, Denmark Hill, Herne Hill, Peckham Rye, Elephant and Castle

Underground stations: Waterloo, Oval, Elephant and Castle

to pass the impressive Georgian terraces of **Camberwell Grove**.

7. There are some Arts and Crafts houses from 1907 in **Champion Hill**, at the end of which you go straight on to the shared-use path and turn left down the hill to Dulwich.

8. Keep following route 23 toward Dulwich Park. At the Dulwich Village junction is the cosy **Au Ciel café**.

9. Go straight on then turn right into Burbage Road, and look out for a concealed entrance on the right to **Herne Hill Velodrome**. Budding Olympic hopefuls train there and you can join a beginners' session on Saturday.

10. Turn left after the rail bridge, right, and left again into Half Moon Lane. There's another café opportunity at **Mimosa**, with bike stands opposite.

11. Going under the bridge take care at the junction that takes you over into **Brockwell Park**, which has a lido and the Georgian **Brockwell Hall** with a café (open daily) and WC.

12. Enjoy the ride around the park, exiting near the Hall (just before the pale green and black hut) and going straight across into Rosendale

Above: *On your marks at the Burgess Park BMX track. Adults and children alike can try their skills at BMX riding here.*

Road, which takes you back to Dulwich via quiet streets – don't miss the sharp left into Turney Road at the roundabout.

13. In addition to the fine art collection at **Dulwich Picture Gallery** you can also see, at the Gallery Road entrance to the right, the inspiration for the London phone box on top of the mausoleum designed by Sir John Soane (bike stands provided).

14. Turning right at the roundabout, turn immediate left into **Dulwich Park**, where **London Recumbents** has a cycle hire facility (open daily).

15. After circling the park, exit via Court Lane Gate, go straight across the road and follow the bike route 25 to Peckham Rye (the left turn into Friern Road is not signed).

16. When you reach **Peckham Rye Park**, follow route 25 across the traffic lights and turn half-right into the park on a cycle path. The park has an ornamental garden as well as a café and

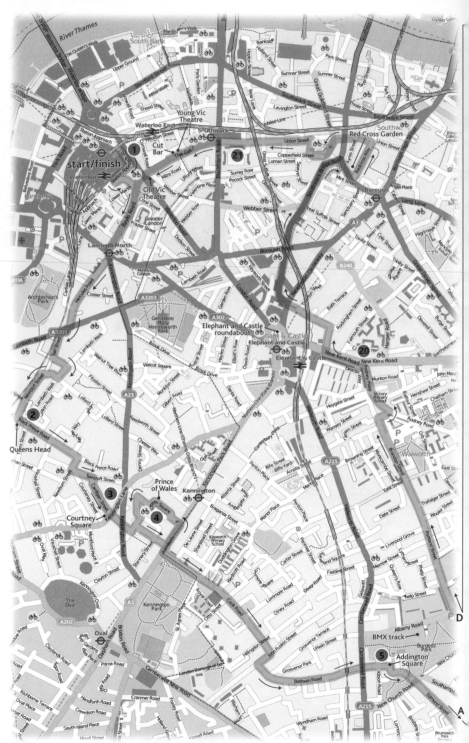

B (to page 109)

C (from page 109)

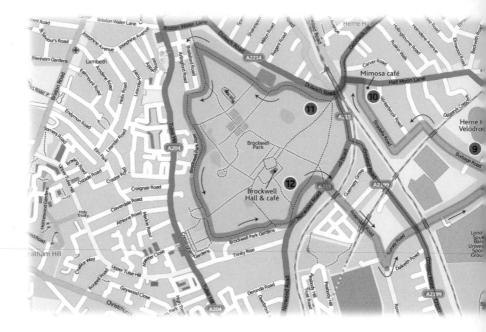

WCs. Follow the path across the park and turn left. At the bottom of the slight hill you have to negotiate a difficult junction, ultimately turning right but doing this by bearing left and then turning sharp right. Then bear left along the cycle lane into Rye Lane.

17. The bustling Rye Lane reveals the delights of multicultural London, with colourful shops offering products from around the world. **Khans Bargain** is perhaps the largest corner shop you'll ever see.

18. At the end of Rye Lane you cross over on foot to the Surrey Canal shared-use path following cycle route 22, which passes the award-winning **Peckham Library** designed by Alsop & Stormer and opened in 2000.

19. At the end of the path cross left into **Burgess Park**. Just after going through the short tunnel turn right by a lime kiln to leave the park. Take care crossing Albany Road, where you'll find the entrance to the **BMX track**. Follow the bike route 23 north up Portland Street, continue into Brandon Street, then use the cycle cut-through to the right and turn left into Rodney Road.

20. About 100 metres (110 yd) along take care at the difficult right turn into Rodney Place and then continue on route 23, turning left, using the pavement track along New Kent Road and cross before the bridge to bypass the Elephant and Castle roundabout. Follow the marked bike route 23 under two railway bridges.

21. A short detour from Marshalsea Road via Quilp Street takes you to **Red Cross Garden** (open daily, 9 am–dusk), which was created in 1887 by Octavia Hill, co-founder of the National Trust. Then turn left down Union St, cross the busy road using the cycle crossing, and turn left and right to see the **almshouses** in Copperfield Gardens. Turning right then left after the almshouses brings you back to Union Street. Continuing straight on, pass the original Evans Cycles, just before the Old Vic in The Cut, and return to Waterloo station the way you arrived. **The Cut Bar** at the Young Vic is patronized by Lambeth Cyclists and TfL's cycling experts (bike stands provided).

Right: *Once a canal basin, Burgess Park now has avenues of trees and green open spaces, making it popular with joggers and cyclists.*

B (from page 107)

C (to page 107)

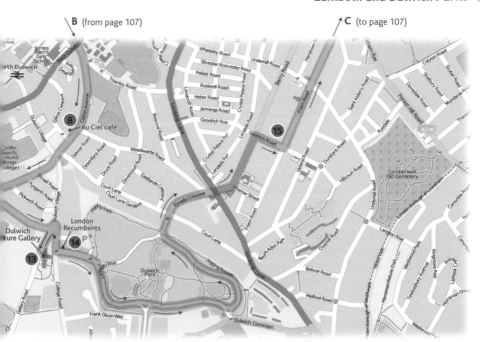

South London Commons

Discovering that you can cycle through most of south London's commons is an eye-opener for many locals, let alone visitors to the boroughs of Wandsworth and Lambeth. The other great discovery is the variety of fine churches, Georgian mansions, and Arts and Crafts houses as well as pleasant streets and parks. South London used to be a run-down area before it became fashionable in the 1980s and 90s, but revitalization has transformed once-dull streets into places full of cafés, elegant shops and even bicycle stands. The improved cycle routes that this ride benefits from are a credit to the Wandsworth and Lambeth Cycling Campaigns which have worked tirelessly to make their boroughs more cycle-friendly.

1. Ornately decorated **Battersea Park station** opens into busy Battersea Park Road. Turn right and walk up to Queenstown Road, where you turn right again and cycle 20 metres (25 yd) to the roundabout – circumnavigate on the pavement, following the cycle track. The entrance to **Battersea Park** is directly opposite. The park, created a century ago, was a popular destination for Victorian cyclists. It has a large lake, bicycle hire on weekends (next to the sports centre), a café, public WCs and a small children's zoo (entrance fee). The park is open daily from 8 am till dusk.

2. Pedal to the left, as you enter the park, to see the **Barbara Hepworth sculpture** with its trademark hole. A walk, clockwise, around the lake (no cycling permitted) reveals **Henry Moore's sculpture** of three standing figures.

3. Return to the park entrance (or walk past the Henry Moore sculpture and head for the east side of the lake), and cycle northwards past the café and running track (bike stands outside) towards the Thames. The road turns left at the river and passes the **Peace Pagoda**, as well as WCs and the children's zoo, before arriving at a park gate.

4. Leave through the gate and cross over into Parkgate Road with the popular **Prince Albert pub** on your right. There is a friendly bike shop a little further down the road.

5. At the traffic lights at the junction with Battersea Bridge Road, turn right with care and then immediate left at the next traffic lights into Battersea Church Road. This brings you to the classically styled Victorian church of **St Mary's**, by the river.

LOCAL INFO

Local Cycle Guide: 14
Start point: Battersea Park station
Length: 16 km (10 m)
Time: 2 hours
Type of ride: Easy. Quiet roads and parks with a few busy roads that can be walked

Sights and places to visit
- Battersea Park sculptures and pagoda
- Villas by Charles Voysey
- The Priory in Wimborne Court
- Windmill, Clapham Common
- Clapham Old Town

Eating and drinking
- La Gondola, Battersea Park SW11 4NJ. Tel 020 7978 1655
- The Prince Albert, 85 Albert Bridge Rd SW11 4PF. Tel 020 7228 0923
- Mazar, 11–12 Battersea Square SW11 3RA. Tel 020 7978 5374
- Skylark café, Wandsworth Common, SW18 3RT. Tel 020 8879 9386
- Windmill on the Common, Windmill Drive SW4 9DE. Tel 020 86734578
- The Sun, 47 Old Town SW4 0JL. Tel 020 7622 4980
- The Prince of Wales, 38 Old Town SW4 0LB. Tel 0871 258 9746
- La Baita Café, Clapham Common, Windmill Drive, SW4 0QW.
- Tooting Bec Common Café, SW16 1RT

Rail stations: Battersea Park, Clapham Junction, Wandsworth Common, Queenstown Road
Underground stations: Tooting Bec, Clapham Common

Above: *Cycling has been popular in Battersea Park since the 1890s.*

6. Following the road to the left brings you to the renovated **Battersea Square** with its outside cafés and bike stands. To see some fine Georgian mansions you can turn right and ride around the busy **Vicarage Crescent**, staying left all the way to Battersea High Street. Otherwise, cycle straight across the square, passing the **Mazar Lebanese restaurant** on your left.

7. Just past the square on your right is **Thomas's School**, formerly Sir Walter St John's School, a 19th-century Gothic Revival design by William Butterfield.

8. Continuing down Battersea High St, pass under a railway bridge and 20 metres (25 yd) further on, bear left through the cycle cut-through. Then turn right at the fork immediately afterwards into the local market street (outdoor stalls on Saturdays).

9. At the traffic lights head straight on down Falcon Road, where traffic can be heavy. Take care under the bridges at Clapham Junction, Britain's busiest rail interchange.

10. Beyond the bridges stands the grand Edwardian **Arding & Hobbs** department store (now Debenhams). Go straight on, with the store on your left, down a bus-and-cycle road packed with shops. Continue straight into Northcote Road, which is equally packed with restaurants. After 200 metres (220 yd), turn

Above: *The Peace Pagoda in Battersea Park; the park is an excellent place for children to cycle in safety.*

right into Mallinson Road to reach **Wandsworth Common**, where you turn left.

11. Just past the pond, turn right into the park along a marked cycle path, opposite Honeywell Road, which leads to a small footbridge. After crossing the bridge you can take the marked cycle path to the right to visit the **Skylark café** (open daily, 9 am–5 pm; WCs) or take the path to the left that takes you to a pedestrian crossing over the busy Trinity Road. Cross and continue through the park to quiet Lyford Road with its Arts and Crafts houses, where you turn left. At no. 68 the distinctive white house, with medieval-style windows, is by influential architect **Charles Voysey**.

12. Going straight on takes you though a section of park on a cycle path then back to the road, arriving at a T-junction where you turn right and, at the mini-roundabout, left into Beechcroft Road.

13. After 1 km (3/4 m), at the traffic lights, turn right and immediate left into Brudenell Road. You pass the large neo-Gothic church of **All Saints** and, at the end of the road, turn left then, just before a roundabout, cross onto a shared-use path to your right (over a small green area), cross the next street (Rectory Lane) and bear left on into Birchwood Road. Two left turns, Daleside and Parklands roads, take you to Clairview Road where you turn right.

14. At the T-junction turn left, and then right and left at the mini-roundabout into **West Drive** with its grand mansions. The finest is around the corner in **North Drive** at no. 8, Dixcote, a house designed by Voysey and built for Lord Essex by Walter Cave.

15. Go back down North Drive and turn right where it turns onto the busy Tooting Bec Road, walk up to the traffic lights, where you cross over to the right and follow the well-marked cycle path northwards across **Tooting Bec Common**.

16. Cross the major road (Bedford Hill), walk 50 metres (55 yd) to the left, and enter Wimborne Court to see a restored 19th-century castle-like folly, the **Priory**. Return to the cycle path you were on and continue straight through the common until it ends just after a railway bridge.

17. Continue straight ahead, down Cavendish Road, until you come to traffic lights. There, using the cycle crossing, cross the road to a cycle track on the right-hand-side pavement, which then follows the main road, curving to the left. After 50 metres (55 yd) on pavement turn right, following the bike route sign down Abbeville Road, a street of bars and cafés.

18. Turn left off Abbeville Road, into Narbonne Road. A signal crossing at the end takes you over into **Clapham Common** then to another road. If you ride 100 metres (110 yd) to the right you'll find the legendary **Windmill on the Common** (built in 1790), which overflows with customers throughout the summer because most of the nearby streets were built with no pubs during the late Victorian era of temperance. Across the road are fine Georgian villas at nos. 53 and 54.

19. Unless you're visiting the Windmill the route continues to the left for 50 metres (55 yd) on the road, then turn right, back into the park, along a cycle path heading north.

20. At the traffic lights turn right and bear left into North Side, passing surviving early 18th-century Georgian villas just before the bus depot in the centre of Clapham Old

Town. The **Sun** and the **Prince of Wales** offer refreshments, and there are bike stands near the buses.

21. At the mini-roundabout beyond the bus depot, turn left down North Street and take care on the busier road. The downhill road crosses one set of traffic lights and, at the end, by some workers' cottages, you are forced left.

22. At the next lights, at the junction with Queenstown Road, you turn right and follow the road, using the pavement under the bridge, to reach Battersea Park Road and the station on the right.

Below: *The Windmill on the Common at Clapham Common is one of the busiest pubs in London.*

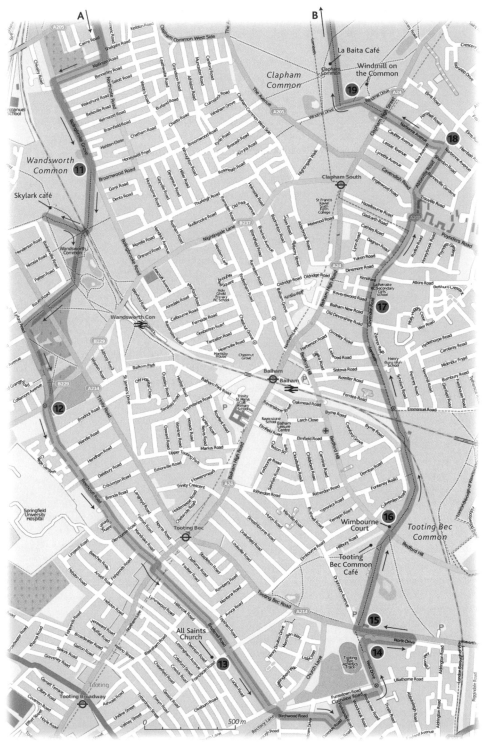

Wandle Mills

The River Wandle was once London's hardest-working river, with mills along it that ground corn and produced paper, oil, calico and snuff. Some 50 mill sites have been identified but very few survive. The river and the parks along it make an ideal leisure ride, which is being constantly improved by the work of local councils, Sustrans, and Merton and Wandsworth LCC members. The route starts at East Croydon station and ends at Wandsworth Town station. It follows the Wandle River throughout, with some minor diversions where the river bank is not accessible. Much of the route is well marked as National Cycle Network NCN20 but there are gaps in signage and, on occasion, two choices are marked – here the better options are presented. A weekend ride in the summer will enable you to see the stalls and music at Merton Mills.

1. Turn right out of **East Croydon station** down George St and cross the busy dual carriageway to the pedestrian and tram zone (watch out for the tram tracks).

2. Pass the Tudor almshouses, the **Hospital of the Holy Trinity**, continue through the shared use area and follow the bicycle signs turning right and then left.

3. The neo-Gothic buildings on your left conceal 'one of the best surviving examples of a medieval archbishop's palace in England' (Croydon Palace, open occasionally). Continue past **Croydon Minster**, the medieval parish church reconstructed after a fire in 1867, to find (behind a wall) a toucan crossing over a dual carriageway.

4. Bike signs marked on the road itself direct you down Waddon Road and Mill Lane until you reach the source of the river **Wandle** at Waddon Ponds, from where you follow a bridle path.

5. At the corner of Wandle Road is the first mill building on the route (marked **Wandle Mill**) built as a flour mill and bakery. Dismount to follow the narrow path beside the river.

6. At the busy Hilliers Lane (the B272) cross into Guy Road, then go a little way uphill and turn right into Church Lane. A shared-use path takes you to the medieval church of **St Mary's**, which has a fine Norman font. Next door is **Carew Manor** and its large brick dovecote. Return to the marked cycle path with signs for NCN20, which leaves the park at a car park.

7. You turn left across the bridge, using the pavement, to follow the cycle route across the busy London Road, heading for the **Rose and Crown** (with bike stands). There you can take the

Above right: *The Snuff Mill on the Wandle at Morden Hall Park is a National Trust property.*

shorter Butter Hill route or the more winding NCN20 route via Westcroft Road and a housing estate behind the Westcroft Leisure Centre.

8. From Butter Hill the route stays close to the river, passing the **Wilderness Island nature reserve** to Hackbridge Road from where you follow cycle route signs for Morden.

9. Don't cross the cream bridge but stay on the east side of the river to go past a housing estate. At Culver Avenue, cross and go through a bike gate on the other side and stay by the river. You then bear left at two path junctions, coming to a wooden bridge. Cross and stay by the river heading north.

10. You come out at a road and follow NCN20 left and right. At the end of **Poulter Park** you turn right, and have a 400-metre (440 yd) stretch of busy road (do not follow the bike route signs down Seddon Road) until you cross the Wandle again and rejoin the path on the left to enter **Ravensbury Park**. Do not cross the bridge in the centre of the park, but continue on the same side of the river until you pass some grindstones and exit onto a busy road where you use the pavement. Cross at the signal crossing and enter **Morden Hall Park** through a wooden gate, just before the Surrey Arms.

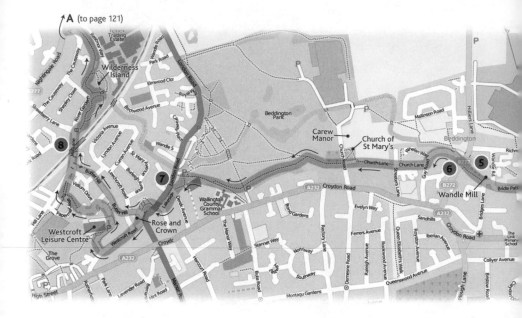

↑A (to page 121)

11. A wide path in the park brings you to a decorative bridge where you turn left to visit the National Trust's **Snuff Mill** and its mill wheels. Behind the mill is a garden, a walled garden and a café (open daily, 8 am–5 pm). Next to the Snuff Mill, over a second iron bridge, is the 18th-century **Morden Hall**.

12. Return to the bike route by the first bridge and follow signs for Colliers Wood. You cross tram tracks as you leave the park and soon arrive at **Merton Abbey Mills market**.

13. The waterwheel (19th-century) at Merton Mills has been restored and currently powers a potter's wheel. The area is popular with herons as well as tourists, who are treated to live music and a range of arts and crafts on weekends (WCs and bike stands). There are a range of cafes and restaurants. Both Liberty's and William Morris used to have textile workshops nearby.

14. You pass several superstores, cross two major roads, go through an arch and follow a signed section (NCN20 to Wandsworth) on quiet streets to **Wandle Meadow Nature Park**.

15. The route comes out on Summerley Road just before Earlsfield station, near a bike shop,

Right: *Break time in Morden Hall Park, with its mill, gardens and café.*

and there's a choice of **Café Nero**, **Carluccios** and the **Halfway House pub**.

16. Take care at Earlsfield and, after turning off left, follow the NCN20 signs via Ravensbury Rd.

17. Turn right into Acuba Road and then ride though **King George's Park**, heading for the tower block where you have to join busy Garratt Lane. The **Spread Eagle**, on the right at the junction, has lovely etched glass and is a Wandsworth Cyclists' favourite.

18. Riding down the contra-flow bus lane opposite brings you to Armoury Way, where you cross at the lights, turn left along the pavement on the north side and turn very sharply right for the final bit of the Wandle that takes you to the Thames.

19. Smugglers Way brings you to a junction where you cross using the cycle crossing and turn right into Old York Road. **Wandsworth Town station** connects to Waterloo, while the Alma Tavern and Pizza Express offer final refreshment possibilities.

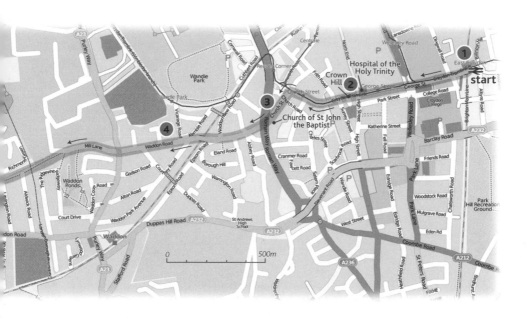

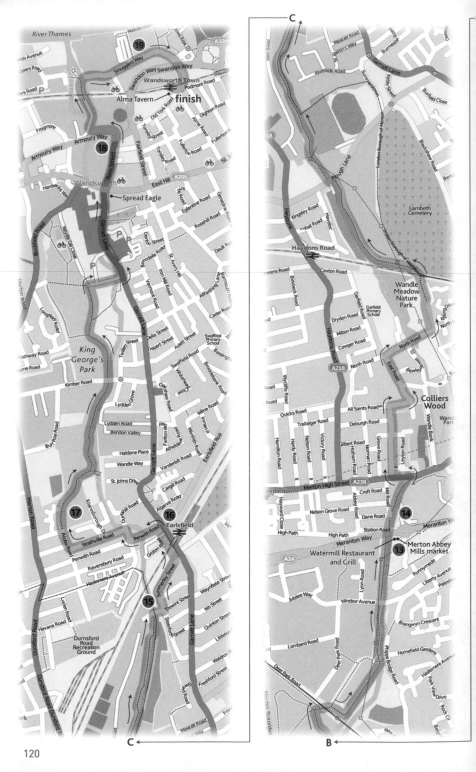

B

12

National Trust
Snuff Mill

Morden
Hall

11

*Morden Hall
Park*

Surrey
Arms

Belgrave Walk

Morden Hall Road

A239

*Ravensbury
Park*

Ravensbury Grove

Bristol Road

Brisch Road

Arras Avenue

The Drive

Edward Avenue

Milner Road

Wandle Road

Morton Road

Pollard Road

Seddon Road

St. Helier Avenue

Ravensbury Avenue

Leonard Avenue

Florence Avenue

Langdon Road

Johns Lane

Leominster Road

Llanthony Road

Liskeard Road

Merevale Crescent

Malmesbury Road

Montacute Road

Newminster Road

Mulholland Road

Bishopsford
Community
College

Benedict Road

Bishopsford Road

Botton Drive

Robertsbridge Road

St. Benet's Grove
St. Benet's Grove

Standdale Road

Keats Road

Paisley Road

Twyford Road

Thornton Road

Titchfield Road

Wigmore Road

Whitford Road

Travelock Road

Tintern Road

Wyche Lane

P

*Rose
Hill Park*

B278

Wendling Road

Whitby Road

Westminster Road

Greenshaw
High
School

Aultone Way

Batsworth Road

Miles Road

Edward Road

Phipps Bridge Road

New Close

Belgrave Walk

Haslemere Way

Church Road

Rossal Road

Green West

London Road

A217

Baron Grove

Mitcham Park

Mitcham

Tramway Path

Brookfield Avenue

Riverside Drive

Rawnsley Avenue

Ravensbury Road

Hillsid Road

London Borough of Merton

River Wandle

*Poulter
Park*

Ripewell Road

Penshore Grove

Quen Road

Rewley Road

Revelby Road

Green Wynne Lane

Shaftesbury Road

Stoneleigh Road

Sherborne Crescent

Winchcombe Roe

Middleton Road

Thornbourne Road

Theobalds Road

Assembly Walk

New Walk

Green Wynne Lane

Winchcombe Road

Brambewood Close

Wickham Road

Groveside Close

Bakers Gardens

Cricket Green

London Road

Micham Park

Barncote Avenue

Dewson Crescent

The Close

Wandle Way

Willow Lane

Willow Centre

Watery Way

Wade Way

Elis Road

P

10

Middleton Road

Budge Lane

Peterborough Road

Tull Stripe

McRae Lane

Wandle Trail

Newort Close

Buckhurst Avenue

Elm Close

Lime Avenue

Durand Close

Culvers Avenue

Culvers Avenue

Langstoke Avenue

Commonside

Whitford Gardens

Albert Road

Cold Blowlows

Madeira Road

Cranmer Road

Commonside West

Hilary Avenue

Casens Walk

Mitcham Garden Villa

Aspen

Micklethorn Road

Wandle
Trading
Estate

Wood Street

Spencer Road

York Road

Seymour

Mill Green Brnch

Orchard Av

New

Mullards Close

Wandle Trail

East
Wood Drive

Culvers Avenue

Corbet Close

Mill Bridge Rd.

9

0   500m

(from page 118) **A**

Sutton Villages and Parks

Tucked away among the suburban homes of Sutton are delightful parks, medieval churches and Tudor houses. The Westminster Cyclists' parks and gardens expert Colin Wing has devised this ride, utilizing the network of cycle routes in Sutton that conveniently link the grounds of Nonsuch Palace in Cheam with the Tudor-period Carew Manor in Beddington, via the Sutton Ecology Centre in Carshalton. In Beddington you can, if you wish, extend your expedition by linking up with the Wandle Mills ride (see page 116) that follows the Wandle River all the way to Wandsworth. Otherwise, the ride starts at Cheam station and ends at Hackbridge station near Beddington Park.

1. If arriving at **Cheam station** from the north, leave by its south exit and turn right and right again under the railway bridge into Station Way. If arriving from the south, a left turn out of the station takes you on to Station Way, where you turn right.

2. About 100 metres (110 yd) from the rail bridge turn left into Kingsway Road then right into Anne Boleyn's Walk. Walk across the busy Ewell Road onto the opposite pavement, and ride to the left (west) on the cycle path. This brings you to the entrance of **Nonsuch Park** (open dawn till dusk).

3. When you come to a barrier about 250 metres (270 yd) inside the park, turn right towards **Nonsuch Mansion. Nonsuch Palace**, built for King Henry VIII, is long gone but the early 19th-century Gothic-style mansion creates a hub for the pleasant park with a convenient café, bike stands and WCs.

4. The ride continues past the front of the mansion along a path that curves back towards the avenue you arrived on. When you reach it turn right (west) to see the site of the original Nonsuch Palace, marked by stone obelisks just after the avenue bends to the right. Return back along the tree-lined avenue to the park entrance and cycle alongside Ewell Road to the junction with Park Lane. There you turn left, following cycle route signs for Sutton and passing a lodge at the entrance to **Cheam Park**.

5. Park Lane curves to the right up a hill to meet Malden Road. On your left as you come to Malden Road is **Whitehall**, a rare timber-framed Tudor house. The house has a tearoom, and is open Wed, Thurs and Fri, 2 pm – 5 pm; Sat 10 am – 5 pm; Sun and Bank Holiday Mondays,

LOCAL INFO

Local Cycle Guide: 12
Start point: Cheam station
Length: 13 km (8 m)
Time: 2 hours
Type of ride: Easy. Quiet streets and parks, with a few busy sections of road

Sights and places to visit
- Nonsuch Mansion, Nonsuch Park, Ewell Road, Cheam, SM3 8AL. Tel 020 8393 2676
- Whitehall, 1 Malden Road, Cheam SM3 8QD. Tel 020 8643 1236
- Carshalton Water Tower, 136 West Street, Carshalton, SM5 2NR. Tel 0208 647 0984
- Sutton Ecology Centre, The Old Rectory Festival Walk, Carshalton SM5 3NY. Tel 020 8770 5820
- Honeywood Museum (Heritage Centre) Honeywood Walk, Carshalton SM5 3NX. Tel 020 8770 4297
- St Mary's Church, Church Road, Beddington SM6 7NJ. Tel 020 8647 1973
- Carew Manor and Beddington Park Church Road, SM6 7NH. Tel 020 8770 4781

Eating and drinking
- Nonsuch Mansion café see Nonsuch Mansion, above
- Whitehall tearoom, see Whitehall, above
- Little Windsor pub, 13 Greyhound Road SM1 4BY. Tel 020 8643 2574
- Honeywood Museum café, see Honeywood Museum, above
- Pavilion café, Beddington Park

Rail stations: Cheam, Sutton, Carshalton, Hackbridge

2 pm – 5 pm (admission is free; audio guide is £1.00).

6. Cross Malden Road using the crossing, cycle to the left on the pavement and then turn right into Park Road. After passing **Ye Olde Red Lion** pub, turn left and right into Love Lane, following cycle route signs for Sutton.

7. Cross the busy A217 on foot and continue walking straight on, along a footpath by the side of Sears Park. After 50 metres (55 yd), turn right by a red brick wall to reach Quarry Park Road, where you turn left, still following the well-signed cycle route to Sutton. It heads west for 1 km (¾m) along Tate and Western roads and includes a cycle contra-flow in Camden Road.

8. At a T-junction, route signs for Carshalton direct you right and left along another contra-flow past the flint-covered church of **St Nicholas**, rebuilt by Edwin Nash in 1862.

9. Cross the main road by the crossing and use the pavement path to ride up the hill to the right along the cycle track. Turn left down Hill Road just before the imposing church of **Holy Trinity**. There's a choice of stops including the

Above: Carew Manor, built in the Tudor period and home to the Carew family, is now a school. It is open for a limited time each year.

Moon on the Hill and All Bar One (there are bike stands just past the pubs).

10. Crossing the pedestrian precinct, go straight on up Throwley Road to meet Throwley Way, where you turn left along the pavement and cross over to the right side at the first traffic lights. Go a few metres to the left on the pavement and then turn right down Greyhound Road. Carry on down Greyhound Road, past the **Little Windsor** pub, and at the end turn right into Lind Road. Turn immediately left into Vernon Road, then take the third left into St Barnabas Road.

11. At the bottom of the slight downhill turn right into the busy Westmead Road, heading for Carshalton. Then turn left just before the railway bridge along the tree-lined Colston Avenue.

12. At the mini-roundabout turn right into the fairly busy West St. Stop when you see the tall brick **Carshalton Water Tower** on the right. The tower, which was part of the 18th-century

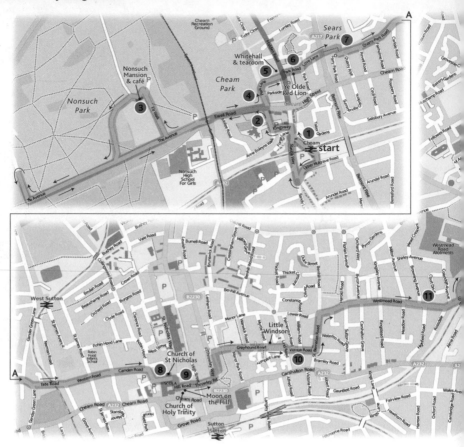

Carshalton House (now a girls' school), can be visited on Sunday afternoons in the summer. There are WCs and refreshments.

13. Directly opposite the tower is Festival Walk, down which is the **Sutton Ecology Centre** on the left (open every day from 9 am to sunset).

14. Leaving the Ecology Centre continue eastwards along Honeywood Walk to Carshalton Ponds. **All Saints' Church**, which you can see across the ponds, has medieval origins. Also by the ponds (opposite the Greyhound Hotel) is **Honeywood Museum** (Heritage Centre), open Wed–Sun, 11 am–5 pm, with café and WCs.

15. Continue straight ahead along Honeywood Walk, with the pond on your right, to the junction with North Street. Turn right with care, cross the bridge over the ponds and then turn left into Carshalton High Street in front of All Saints' Church. Alternatively, cross the road, turn left

and enter the Grove through a gate in the wall, then follow the edge of the pond on foot round to the right, turning left on leaving the park.

16. Just after the **Fox and Hounds** pub, turn left into Westcroft Road and pass through the road closure on the right – do not follow the bike route to the left. You come out to the busy London Road, which you avoid riding on by staying on the pavement to the left, crossing over Butter Hill and onto a cycle track by the little lake. The track takes you past the lake to a crossing over London Road and along the south side of another small lake (Lakeside) to Derek Avenue, which you cross (don't turn right following the bike route) and then stay on the pavement going left and then right, following London Road northwards for 50 metres (55 yd). Turn right into a car park and head for its right (south-east) corner.

17. A narrow cycle path leads you into

Beddington Park, where you follow the cycle path markings to the medieval **St Mary's Church**, which has a fine Norman font.
18. Next door is the Tudor-period **Carew Manor**, once owned by the Carew family. It is now a school, but is open to the public on four Sundays a year. Further on, the road forks to the right past an **octagonal dovecote**.
19. Taking the left fork, the route continues along the cycle path, over a terracotta bridge, past the **Pavilion café** (last chance to stop for tea) and continues northwest to the park exit.
20. Turn right along the busy road and **Hackbridge station** is 200 metres (220 yd) away just over the bridge – if you prefer to walk, stay on the right-hand pavement.

Right: *The 18th-century dovecote at Carew once housed over 1300 nesting boxes.*

125

Richmond Park and Wimbledon Common

Richmond is the largest Royal Park, covering 1,000 hectares, with Royal connections that date back to Edward I who brought the court down to the Manor House at Sheen (Richmond's earlier name) in 1299. Queen Elizabeth I went stag hunting in Richmond Park and died at Richmond Palace, of which little remains (see the West London Palaces ride, page 144). The park remains Crown property and is unique in having a purpose-designed cycling and walking trail all around it – the Tamsin Trail. There are brooks and ponds to see as well as thousands of ancient trees, more than 600 fallow deer and gardens with exotic azaleas, irises and rhododendrons. While you can limit your ride to Richmond Park and stay off-road throughout (useful with children) it's worth following a route recommended by LCC groups in Richmond and Kingston to the Windmill Museum on Wimbledon Common and returning to Richmond on mostly quiet roads. Knobbly tyres are useful for Wimbledon Common. Richmond Park is open from 7 am–dusk in summer and 7.30 am–dusk in winter. Cycle hire is available April–September at the Roehampton Gate car park, daily from 9 am till 4 pm. This ride can be linked to the West London Palaces and the Hampton Court, Bushy Park and Ham House ride (see page 132). There are several car parks in the park (see map for details).

1. Leaving **Richmond station** walk to the right, around the corner into Church Road. Head uphill until you pass the tall Victorian church of **St Matthias** on the left, where you turn right and immediate left into Marlborough Road.

2. Use the zebra crossing on the left to cross busy Queen's Road, and turn right and left into Cambrian Road. This brings you to Cambrian Gate through which you enter **Richmond Park**.

3. Ride to the right along the wide, hard-surfaced yellowish track, which you will continue to follow around the park.

4. As you reach a road by **Richmond Gate** (WCs), stay close to the park entrance and bypass the roundabout using a cycle crossing.

5. After about 300 metres (330 yd), next to a small hut, you'll see a fenced-off area with a gate into **Pembroke Gardens**. Lock your bike and walk to **King Henry's Mound**, from where there is a spectacular view across the river. Opposite the view, though a hole in the vegetation, you can see St Paul's Cathedral.

6. About 300 metres (330 yd) beyond Pembroke Gardens is **Pembroke Lodge**, a Georgian mansion where philosopher

LOCAL INFO

Local Cycle Guide: 9
Start point: Richmond station
Length: 19 km (12 m)
Time: 3–4 hours
Type of ride: Easy. Richmond Park is off-road. Wimbledon section can be muddy and includes 1.5 km (1 m) of road. Knobbly tyres are advised

Sights and places to visit
• King Henry's Mound
• Pembroke Lodge
• Isabella Plantation
• Wimbledon Windmill, Windmill Rd SW19 5NR. Tel 020 8947 2825

Eating and drinking
• Pembroke Lodge café, Richmond Park TW10 5HX. Tel 020 8940 8207
• Park Tavern, 19 New Road, Kingston upon Thames, KT2 6AR. Tel 020 8546 8411
• Windmill café, Windmill Road SW19 5NQ. Tel 020 8788 2910
• Roebuck pub, 130 Richmond Hill TW10 6RN. Tel 020 8948 2329

Rail stations: Richmond, Kingston
Underground stations: Richmond

Bertrand Russell lived. It is now a café with superb views, and WCs and bike stands.

7. At the next road crossing, Ham Gate, turn left (east) to follow the road for about 300 metres (330 yd) to the **Isabella Plantation** on the right-hand side – you can lock your bike outside and admire the azaleas if you happen to be there at the right time of year.

8. Returning to the turn-off point, ride westwards towards Ham Gate along the trail on the north side of the road until just before Ham Gate itself. There you turn left (south) to continue along the Tamsin Trail until the next road crossing at Kingston Gate. A local resident recommends the **Park Tavern** just outside Kingston Gate in New Road.

9. The **Tamsin Trail** heads northeast along the perimeter of the park. As you come to a steep slope there are fine views.

10. At a road crossing near a car park (Robin

Above: Give way to fallow deer in Richmond Park. The ride around Richmond is traffic-free, making it suitable for cycling with children.

Hood Gate), you can either cross the road and continue around the park on the traffic-free Tamsin Trail to rejoin the route at Roehampton Gate (skip to No. 20) where there are WCs and bike hire, or exit the park at Robin Hood Gate and ride through Wimbledon Common. It can get muddy and includes an on-road stretch for 1.5 km (1 m).

11. Leave the park following the cycle route signs for Wimbledon, using the two-stage, light controlled Pegasus crossing (which allows pedestrians, cyclists and horse riders to cross the road at the same time) to the banks of the pretty **Beverley Brook**. Non-cycling paths are clearly marked.

127

Above: *The Windmill Museum on Wimbledon Common has a very handy café attached to it.*

12. You pass a parish boundary marker, and then arrive at another bridge before which you turn left (east) along a straight tree-lined path.
13. Go through the car park at the end of the track and ride down a tarmac road for about 20 metres (25 yd). Stay left on a wide track that brings you to a gate (part of the golf course), which you pass through, and continue straight along the track towards another wooded area.
14. After 1.5 km (1 m) you come to the **Windmill Museum and café** (bike stands, WCs). The museum is open weekends (2–5 pm Sat, 11 am–5 pm Sun); the café is open daily 9 am–5.30 pm.
15. Leaving the café head north and, after 100 metres (110 yd), bear left at the fork in

the path. You go through a tunnel under Kingston Road and cycle route signs direct you to Putney.

16. Bear left at the fork just past the pond.

17. At the main road turn left, following cycle route signs to Roehampton. About 250 metres (270 yd) later turn right, on foot if you prefer, at the T-junction with Roehampton Lane. You leave this busy road almost immediately by turning left into Danebury Avenue at the traffic lights.

18. You follow Danebury Avenue, which curves right past the row of shops and then passes through the **Alton Estate** which, when it was built in the Fifties, was considered a radical development in social housing based on the Modernist principles of French architect Le Corbusier.

19. At the junction with Priory Lane turn left following the Thames Cycle Route sign taking you back into Richmond Park through Roehampton Gate.

20. In the park turn right (west) along the Tamsin Trail. Stay on the track for 3 km (2 m), crossing one road, until you reach Richmond Gate where you exit carefully and head straight across the mini-roundabout and down Richmond Hill.

21. After 300 metres (330 yd) you'll see the **Roebuck**, where LCC groups gather during Bike Week and enjoy the best pub view in London. Turning right further down the hill brings you back to Church Road (bear left at the church) and Richmond station.

Below: Yellow irises fringe a pond at Isabella Plantation in Richmond Park. The azaleas here are spectacular in the spring.

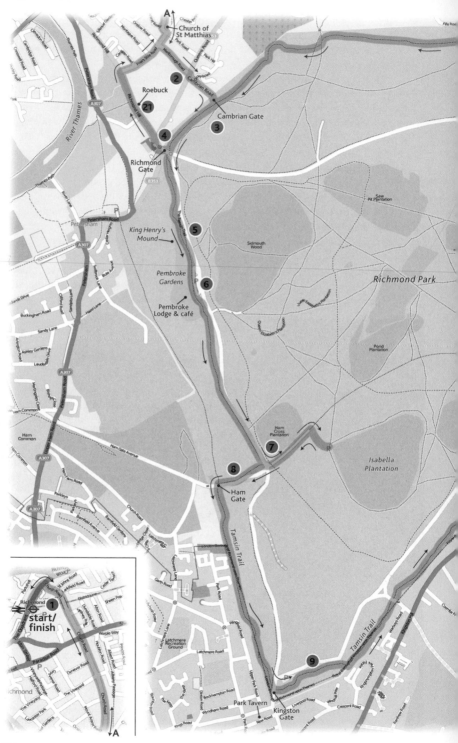

Church of St Matthias

2

Roebuck

21

4

Richmond Gate

Cambrian Gate

3

River Thames

Petersham

Petersham Road

King Henry's Mound

5

Pembroke Gardens

6

Pembroke Lodge & café

Sidmouth Wood

Saw Pit Plantation

Richmond Park

Pond Plantation

Ham Common

Ham Gate Avenue

Ham Cross Plantation

7

8

Ham Gate

Isabella Plantation

Tamsin Trail

Tamsin Trail

Richmond start/finish **1**

Sheen Park

Latchmere Recreation Ground

Latchmere Road

9

Park Tavern

Kingston Gate

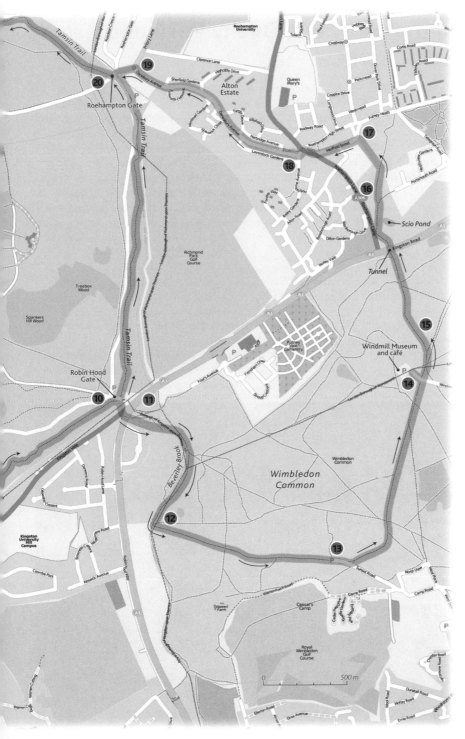

Hampton Court, Bushy Park and Ham House

Several centuries ago west London was a royal playground – its stately homes and hunting grounds attracted kings and queens over many generations. Today, the Kingston LCC group attracts cycling visitors to the same destinations. This ride includes Hampton Court, described as Britain's Tudor masterpiece; the relaxed spaces and paths of Bushy Park; Ham House with its elegant Jacobean lines; and a long, beautiful stretch of the Thames. Most of the ride is off-road and knobbly tyres are advisable but not essential. The ride is designed as a figure-of-eight starting at Kingston station, but you can make it a loop from Richmond station by following the riverside towpath from Richmond to Ham House (see the map for how to reach the river from Richmond station) and returning the same way. At Richmond Park's Kingston Gate the ride links to the Richmond Park and Wimbledon Common ride (see page 126).

1. Coming out of **Kingston station** turn immediately left along the segregated cycle track going underneath the railway bridge. Just after the bridge you are aiming to turn right – you do this by using the crossings straight across then right and finally by turning left into Canbury Park Road.

2. Turn left 200 metres (220 yd) down the road into Elm Road, which leads to the fairly busy Queen's Road. (**Park Tavern** in nearby New Road comes highly recommended by a local resident). Turn left and enter **Richmond**

Below: *The Gothic facade of Hampton Court Palace. It was first built by Cardinal Wolsey, who felt compelled to give it to Henry VIII.*

LOCAL INFO

Local Cycle Guide: 9
Start point: Kingston station
Length: 19 km (12 m)
Time: 3 hours

Type of ride: Easy. Almost all off-road. A few busy junctions and roads that can be walked Sights and places to visit
- Ham House, Ham Street, Ham, Richmond-upon-Thames
  TW10 7RS. Tel 020 8940 1950
- Teddington Lock, Teddington
- Bushy Park, East Molesey, Surrey
- Hampton Court Palace, East Molesey Surrey, KT8 9AU. Tel 020 3166 6000

Eating and drinking
- Park Tavern, 19 New Road, Kingston upon Thames, KT2 6AP. Tel 020 8546 8411
- Ham House café, see Ham House, above
- Boaters Inn, Lower Ham Road
  Kingston upon Thames
  KT2 5AU. Tel 020 8541 4672
- Hampton Court café, see Hampton Court Palace, above

Rail stations: Kingston, Richmond, Hampton Court
Underground stations: Richmond

Park after 100 metres (110 yd). You can join the off-road **Tamsin Trail** immediately on the left. The yellowish walking and cycling trail follows the perimeter of the park – please give way to pedestrians.

3. When you reach Ham Gate Avenue, turn left and proceed along it until you can turn off to use the shared path parallel to the road. Follow the path westwards to leave the park.

4. After 1 km (3/4 m) you cross Petersham Road to a quiet road around the north side of **Ham Common**. You turn off down the second right (just before the pond) between two gatekeepers' cottages into a very wide track called Ham Avenue. This leads all the way to **Ham House**, which you will see on your left.

5. Now a National Trust property, 17th-century Ham House was originally designed by Sir Thomas Vavasour to a Jacobean H-shaped plan but has been much altered over the following centuries. Noted for having much of its original 17th-century furniture and contents, the house is open Sat–Wed, 12–4 pm (entrance fee). The gardens and café open an hour earlier.

6. Leaving Ham House, make your way to the Thames and follow it to the left (west) through

Left: A short hill by the Thames at Hampton Court. The Thames path provides London cyclists with great access to the river.

a tunnel of trees that takes you past a nature reserve, and then to **Teddington Lock**, built in 1810. For a better view of the lock and the river, you can go up onto the footbridge there. The towpath is rough and muddy in places, so as an alternative you can turn left out of the car park into Ham Street, then turn right into Riverside Drive for approximately 1 km (3/4 m), and then turn right onto a path that leads to Teddington footbridge.

7. The ride continues along the river where you have a choice of the upper path for shade or the lower path for better views.

8. Just past a short section of quiet road along the river is the **Boaters Inn**, recommended by the Kingston Cycling Campaign.

9. As you approach the stone **Kingston Bridge**, it is simplest to walk a very short section under the bridge and turn immediately left up a ramp leading onto the bridge itself, where you then join a segregated cycle path across the bridge.

10. Stay to the left at the end of the bridge and cross the busy road using the zebra crossing. Walk left along the pavement and turn right into Church Grove.

11. Just after the tennis courts, opposite a church, is a gate to a path leading to **Bushy Park** along which you may need to walk. An alternative is to cycle further up Church Grove, then turn left into the park just before the **Thatched Cottage** as the road bears to the right. A wide path then takes you across the park, along Cobblers Walk, to **Chestnut Avenue** where you turn left.

12. If you've taken the path past the tennis courts, you enter Bushy Park through a gated barrier. Now follow a wide path past the **Royal Paddocks** until you reach Chestnut Avenue just south of the **Diana Fountain** (in fact a statue of Arethusa, a mythical nymph who became a fountain).

13. Turning left down the often busy Chestnut Avenue takes you to the Lion Gate exit from Bushy Park.

14. You might find it better to cross the very busy road and walk through the grounds of **Hampton Court gardens** (no charge) to the front of **Hampton Court Palace**. The on-road alternative is to turn right then left along the busy road, which takes you to the palace entrance.

15. Hampton Court Palace was originally built for Cardinal Wolsey in the 16th century. In its day it was one of the greatest houses in Britain, and it continues to be one of Britain's most popular visitor attractions. Wolsey's standing with Henry VIII took a turn for the worse after it was completed, and he felt compelled to give the house to the king in 1528, shortly before he died. Henry expanded it in the same style. There are bike stands to the left of the main entrance along with a café, gardens and the famous maze. The café and informal gardens (gardens open 7 am–dusk) are free to visit, but there is an entrance fee for the palace and the formal gardens (open daily, 10 am–4.30 pm in winter and 10 am–6 pm in summer).

16. You join the river path by walking through a small gate to the right of the main palace entrance.

17. Turn left and cycle around the back of the palace where you get a superb view of **Sir Christopher Wren's Baroque facade** at the rear of the palace.

18. The river path leads all the way back to Kingston Bridge.

19. After crossing Kingston Bridge on the right (south) side, carry on straight down a buses-and cycles-only road and bear left (before the pedestrian zone) around the big John Lewis store, using the signed cycle track. As you come to the busy Wood Street, stay on the cycle track on the right-hand pavement until a signalled crossing. Your aim now is the footbridge that you can see over to the right – so cross the road using the crossing and walk to the right to the footbridge. This leads to Kingston station, which is less than 200 metres (220 yd) away on the same side of the road.

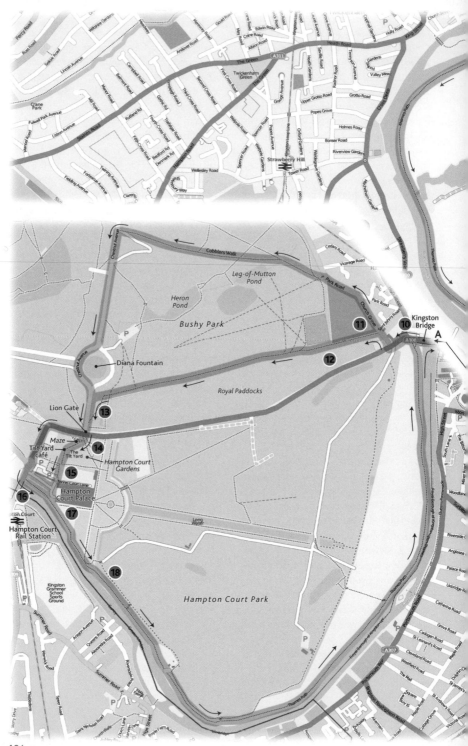

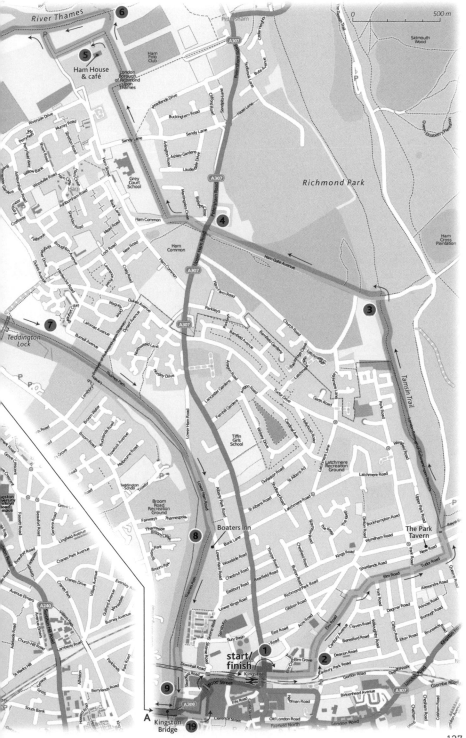

Crane River

On this route, you can ride through the heart of urban Richmond along the banks of the Crane, a river that appears to flow through a forest. This 'forest', Crane Park, remained undeveloped while Richmond grew because it was the site of a large gunpowder factory that used the river for motive power; the factory blew up at regular intervals with devastating effects. Paul Luton of the Richmond Cycling Campaign has combined Crane Park with the wide green spaces of Bushy Park to create this perfect afternoon bike ride. The ride features in the Richmond Cycling Campaign's annual events if you want to ride in company. After enjoying the Crane River ride, you have the option of a detour to Bedfont Lakes, created by flooding old gravel pits, although this requires cycling through some housing estates and along a very busy road.

1. Strawberry Hill station is on a loop line from Waterloo via either Richmond or Kingston. The suburb of Strawberry Hill is most notable for the fanciful 'plaything house' built by Horace Walpole, the 18th-century writer and politician. The building created a fashion for an architectural style known as '**Strawberry Hill Gothick**'. Now run by an independent trust it is open regularly and has a café. You can take a look at the exterior by cycling eastwards down Tower Road and Waldegrave Gardens. The ride, however, heads in the opposite direction, along Wellesley Road.

2. At the T-junction take a left (with care) then turn first right into Fifth Cross Road, following the London Cycle Network signs.

3. At the end of the road a toucan crossing and cycle track leads to Mill Road, which takes you into **Crane Park**. As you enter the park you cross two parts of the River Crane that were used in centuries past to drive mill wheels.

4. Turn left alongside the main stream onto a tarmac path that leads you upstream under two road bridges and across a cross path.

5. You soon come to the **Shot Tower**, an 18th-century building with an alarm bell in case fire was seen at the local gunpowder works. You may want to leave your bike at the bike stands provided and visit the **Crane Park Island Nature Reserve**, home to the now rare water vole.

6. Continuing through the park, along a tarmac path, turn left at the exit – using the pavement is permitted. Then turn right near the zebra crossing to enter Pevensey Road.

7. Turn left into Meadow Road then cross into Woodlawn Drive, which leads to a toucan crossing that will take you across the A312 to The Hounslow Airparks Leisure centre (cafe and WC).

8. Cycle right on a shared use path past the

tennis courts and then bear left diagonally across Hanworth Park. On your left you will see the Longford River, a canal built by Charles I to bring water from the Colne to Hampton Court. On emerging at a roundabout, bear right.
9. At the roundabout with a propeller sculpture commemorating the local aircraft works, keep straight on into Air Park Way then into Browell's

Above: *The 18th-century Shot Tower in Crane Park housed an alarm bell at one time.*

Lane. This arrives at **Feltham Green** with a small lake on one side and the convenient **Red Lion pub** on the other. Turn left for the main ride or follow route points 10–14 for a visit to **Bedfont Lakes**.

Above: *If you make the extended ride to Bedfont Lakes, this spiral bridge for cyclists and pedestrians takes you safely over the busy A316.*

10. Follow the road across the main junction, after which go left into Highfield Way and Orchard Road. Where this meets the railway, take the cycle track that leads left beside it and then walk the short section that passes under the tracks.

11. Continue along a succession of tracks westward with open ground on your left (some walking involved). You emerge by Fairholme Primary School and turn right and left into Dudley Road.

12. After about 50 metres (55 yd), go through an alleyway on your left and bear right on a shared-use gravel path through a green space.

13. Turn left at a path junction and continue to reach Bedfont Lakes entrance.

14. After visiting the country park, cycle east along Bedfont Road, passing Feltham Young Offenders Institution, and then left up Feltham High Street.

15. Opposite 'Carpet Right' store pass through a closure into Elmwood Avenue, follow it as it mutates into Castle Way, where after a picturesque Victorian church you can see the 18th - century gothick stables which remain from the Tudor hunting lodge where Elizabeth I was brought up.

16. At Country Way (A316) you cross by an **unusual spiral bridge** and continue straight on past allotments to Main Street, Hanworth.

17. At the crossroads turn right into Green Lane (later Oak Avenue) and, at the end, left into Broad Lane.

18. Where this runs into Uxbridge Road turn right and immediately right and left into Howard's Close. Follow this through to a closure into Warwick Close, emerging onto Hampton High Street near a crossing.

19. Continue in the same direction past the open air baths for 100 metres (110 yd), then, at the **Dukes Head**, cross over to the left and take a track through a gate by the pub into **Cobblers Walk** (this was named after a shoemaker who fought for the right of way through Bushy Park).

20. You re-cross the **Longford River**, and enter **Bushy Park**, where considerate cycling is permitted. The park has 320 free-roaming deer. **Companion Cycling**, based at the southwest corner of the park, lends cycles for all ability use (Sat and Sun mornings, must book).

21. Turn right along a tarmac track, staying by the north side of the woodland garden enclosures within the park. You will come to the **visitor centre** with kiosk and WCs.

22. Continue along the (now tarmac) path to a T-junction where you turn left, passing the 17th-century **Bushy House**. After about 1.5 km (1 m) you pass the recently restored 18th-century **water gardens** accessed by a track on your left.

23. Where the main path bends to the left, go straight ahead along a narrow path (give way to pedestrians) to a gate out of the park.

24. Continue straight ahead across a main road (A313) to a T-junction with Princes Road. Turn right then left into the busy Stanley Road, on part of which you can use the right-side pavement.

25. Wellesley Road, a turning on the right off Hampton Road, gets you back to **Strawberry Hill station**. Just past the right turn, in Hampton Road, is the **Prince of Wales** pub, recommended by Richmond Cyclists.

Below: *Former gravel pits were flooded to create Bedfont Lakes, now home to waterfowl, bats and other wildlife species.*

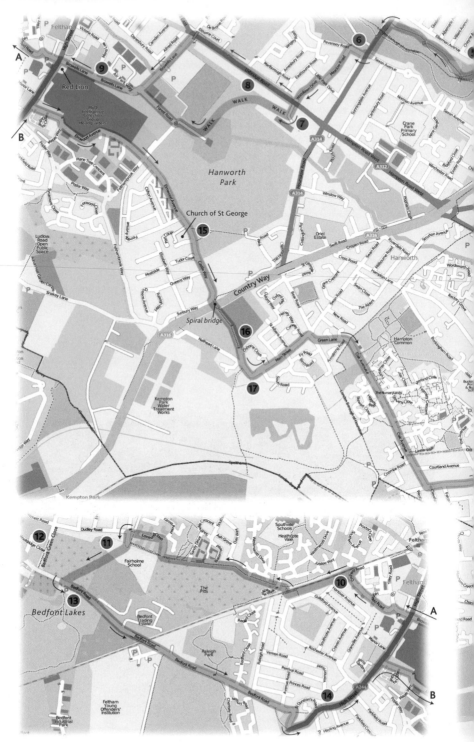

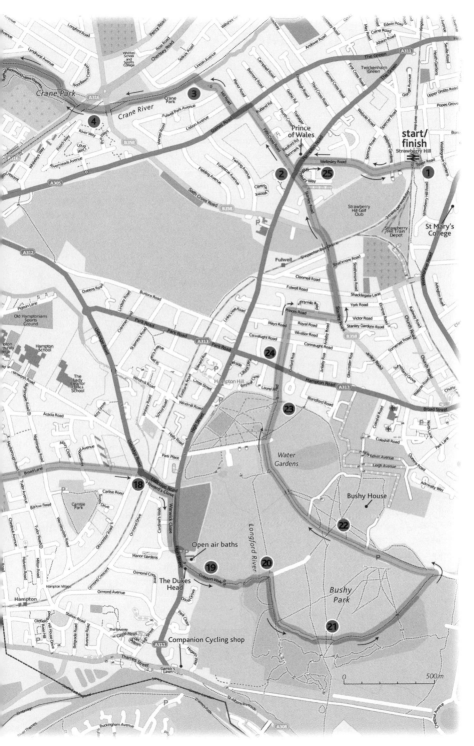

West London Palaces

West London's palaces are a delight to visit and ideal destinations for cycle rides. The area around Syon House and Osterley, the two great 18th-century works of Robert Adam includes many quiet roads and bike routes that take you through parks and along canals. In the 19th century most of the area was rural and there are moments on this ride where you might think you are still in the countryside. Adam's two houses are surprising in their different styles, even though they were built at roughly the same time. En route to the palaces there is the riverside at Richmond, which strives to look as though it too, is a piece of Georgian architecture. Although criticized as a pastiche, there is little doubt that it attracts tourists and locals in the summer. This delightful ride, drawn up independently by both Westminster and Richmond Cyclists, includes some canal paths and a few short stretches of busy road. You can combine it with a ride around Richmond Park (see page 126), a ride along the Thames Path (see page 132) or the ride around the West London Waterways (see page 154).

1. Starting at **Richmond station** (NR and Underground), you cross the road and walk down the small passageway opposite, next to Barnard Marcus estate agents, to reach Parkshot where you turn left and ride to **Richmond Green**.
2. Riding around the green you pass the Edwardian splendour of the **Richmond Theatre** and then, just after turning right around the square, you can see the gatehouse of the medieval **Richmond Palace**, whose first incarnation was built in the 13th century for Edward I. Very little remains of the palace where Queen Elizabeth I used to stay while on stag hunts in Richmond Park.
3. The charming Old Palace Lane takes you past the recommended **White Swan pub** down to the riverside, where you have to walk to the left along the often-busy section of riverfront. There you pass Quinlan Terry's **neo-Georgian riverside complex**. After going under the bridge, turn left to follow the ramp (around the café) up to the bridge itself.
4. There are fine views as you cross the bridge. Take care as you turn right just at the end of the bridge into Willoughby Road.
5. Continue along the river under Twickenham Bridge and past the ornate footbridge until you are forced to leave the river and ride a short section of busy Richmond Road (to the right).
6. Turn off right down Lion Wharf Road when you come to a mini-roundabout. This takes

LOCAL INFO

Local Cycle Guide: 6, 9
Start point: Richmond station
Length: 21 km (13 m)
Time: 3 hours
Type of ride: Easy. Quiet streets and parks with some short sections of busy road

Sights and places to visit
• Richmond riverfront
• Grand Union Canal
• Osterley House, Jersey Road TW7 4RB. Tel 020 8232 5050
• Syon House, Brentford TW8 8JF. Tel 020 8560 0882
Eating and drinking
• The White Swan, Old Palace Lane TW9 1PG. Tel 020 8940 0959
• Osterley House café, see Osterley House, above
• Syon House café, see Syon House, above
• The London Apprentice, 62 Church St TW7 6BG. Tel 020 8560 1915
Rail stations: Richmond, Brentford, Isleworth
Underground stations: Richmond, Osterley, Boston Manor

you back to the river and then up Town Wharf Road, left into Swan Street and then right past the classically styled buildings in Lower Square and into Church Street.
7. Just after crossing a stream, a left down Mill

Above: Syon House, designed by Robert Adam for the Duke of Northumberland in 1761.

Platt path takes you to Twickenham Road, where you turn carefully right and first left into Linkfield Road.

8. At the end you reach London Road, where you turn left, ride past **Isleworth station** and then turn right into The Grove, following cycle route signs for Osterley. After turning right at a triangular junction into Osterley Road, you will turn left into Church Road and right into Thornbury Road. After crossing the A4 and the railway, cross Jersey Road into **Osterley Park**. Cycle around the lake to reach the house.

9. Osterley House, now a National Trust property, was built in the 16th century but was extensively remodelled, starting in 1761, by Robert Adam (architect of Syon House and Kenwood in Hampstead) in neo-Classical style, adding a grand portico with six Ionic columns. The interior is considered to be one of Adams' best works, and is worth a visit. There is a **café** in the converted stables and separate WCs conveniently located on the bike route, just past the main house on the left-hand side after passing the lake. The park is open daily, 7 am – 7:30 pm from April to October, and 7 am – 6 pm from November to March. The house is open Tues to Sunday in the summer, 11 am – 5 pm. There are

wooden cycle parking stands. You cannot cycle through when the park is closed.

10. Beyond the WCs take the path half-left to leave the park via a gate, then turn left into Osterley Lane.

11. You'll be pleasantly surprised as a small bridge takes you over the M4 motorway and you continue down a quiet country lane.

12. At the end of Osterley Lane at Norwood Green turn right into Tentelow Lane. At a mini-roundabout turn left into Minterne Avenue and right into Melbury Avenue to arrive at abridge across the **Grand Union Canal**. Turn left to reach the towpath and turn left onto the path, passing under the bridge.

13. Shortly after the first of the six **Hanwell locks** pass under **Windmill Bridge**, designed by Isambard Kingdom Brunel to handle a road, rail and canal junction. Behind the wall along the canal is **St Bernard's Hospital**.

14. The path continues, passing Jubilee meadows, Elthorne Rough, Boston Manor playing fields and park.

15. Reaching Brentford Princess Moorings, a

145

large marina full of houseboats, you bear right
and come off the canal and turn right along
a 50 metre (55 yd) stretch of busy road before
turning left after the signal-controlled pedestrian crossing, into Syon Park.

16. Syon House is another fine work of
remodelling and grand interiors by Robert
Adam. There is a pleasant café and WCs
through the garden centre and some convenient bike stands. The house is open
11 am–5 pm on Wednesdays, Thursdays and
Sundays from 18 March to 31 October. The café
is open daily.

17. Riding past Syon House, you turn left on
leaving the park, return to the river and have
the opportunity to stop at the justly popular
London Apprentice, which says it was a meeting place for Charles II and Nell Gwynne.

18. Going up Church Street, you are obliged
to fork right into Manor House Way. Turn left
into North Street, left into South Street and
right at the mini-roundabout into Richmond
Road. Just after crossing a bridge, turn left
into Railshead Road, which leads back to the
river. You can now retrace your steps back to
Richmond station or link the ride to a circuit
of Richmond Park and Wimbeldon Common
(see page 126) or a ride along the Thames to
Hampton Court (see page 132).

Left: *One of the six Hanwell Locks on the Grand Union Canal. The towpath is a popular route for west London cyclists.*

Above: *A Westminster Cyclists' ride passes Osterley House and its Ionic portico, extensively remodelled by Robert Adam.*

147

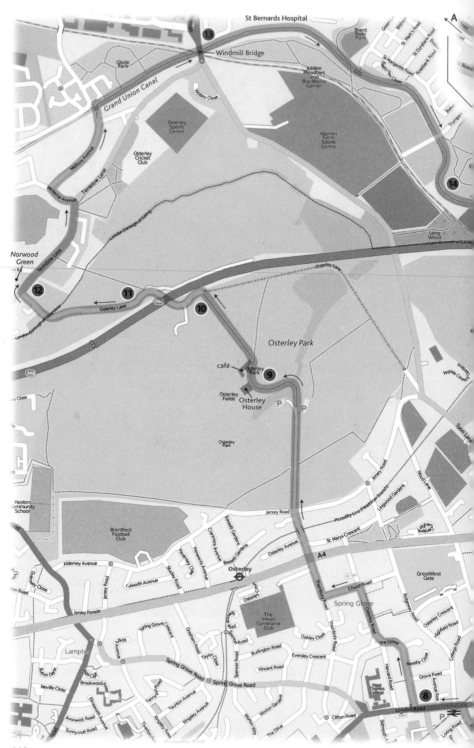

Ealing Garden Suburbs

Ealing's growth as a London suburb in the late 19th and early 20th centuries coincided with the rise of the garden city idea and the popularity of Arts and Crafts architecture. These two factors make it an ideal place for a cycle ride through leafy streets lined with picturesque houses in a range of medieval- and Dutch-influenced styles. There are plenty of parks, cafés and places to take a break. This particular ride was devised by members of the Ealing branch of the London Cycling Campaign and showcases Bedford Park, one of the original garden suburbs, as well as its successors around North Ealing and the former village of Pitshanger. In Bedford Park there are several gems of the Arts and Crafts style, notably Charles Voysey's Tower House and Norman Shaw's houses in Woodstock Road.

1. Leaving **Acton Central station**, head up the contra-flow cycle lane opposite the main side of the station. After passing a street gate, bear left at the fork and follow the road sharp left.
2. Take care crossing the busy A4000 into Hereford Road and take a right and left into **Lynton Road**. Note the white houses on the left which imitate the 'roughcast-concrete' style developed by **Charles Voysey**, one of the great Victorian architects. A little further on are some old Victorian lampposts.
3. After a right into busy Noel Road take the next left (about 400 metres/440 yd) to ride past **West Acton station**, which keeps to the early modern style established by Charles Holden at nearby Acton Town.
4. Turn left again (the road is a continuation of Queen's Drive) and you enter what appears to be a mock-Tudor village lined with nicely maintained half-timbered houses and blocks.
5. Just after crossing a bridge there is a side road on the right to **North Ealing station** which, by contrast to the nearby modern tube stations, looks like a country cottage.
6. Just after the busy Hanger Lane junction the houses take on an ecclesiastical flavour with church-like porches.
7. Just before the Haven Green mini-roundabout the route goes right up Mountfield Rd, but if you fancy a break Haven Green itself has convenient bike stands and a choice of Thai Kitchen, the Gourmet Burger Kitchen and many more.
8. At the top of Mountfield Road, don't follow the road to the left but go straight up the footpath that takes you along West Walk to

LOCAL INFO

Local Cycle Guide: 6
Start point: Acton Central station
Length: 14 km (8¾ m)
Time: 2 hours
Type of ride: Easy. Minor roads with a few stretches of busy road that can be walked

Sights and places to visit
- Bedford Park garden suburb
- Brentham garden suburb
- Pizthanger Manor Gallery & House Walpole Park, Ealing

Eating and drinking
- Gourmet Burger Kitchen, 35 Haven Green Ealing, W5 2NX. Tel 020 8998 0392
- The Duke of Kent, 2 Scotch Common W13 8DL. Tel 020 89917820
- The King's Arms, 55 the Grove W5 5DX. Tel 020 8567 0606
- Acton Park café, East Churchfield Road W3 7LL. Tel 020 8743 2108

Rail stations: Acton Central, South Acton, Ealing Broadway
Underground stations: Acton Town, Ealing Common, North Ealing, Turnham Green

West Road, where you continue for 100 metres (110 yd) to a park.
9. Turn left at the park to follow a shared-use path leading to Mount Avenue. Turn right into Brentham Way to enter the Arts and Crafts style suburb of **Brentham**, designed in the early 20th century by Barry Parker and Raymond Unwin (who had earlier designed Letchworth)

and architects Sutcliffe and Pearson. (Nos. 1–7 in **Winscombe Crescent** are by Parker and Unwin.)

10. Bear right and then head straight on downhill. Turn left at Brunswick Road and then left again as you pass the Brentham Club building into Denison Road.

11. At the end of Denison Rd by St Barnabus church turn right into Pitshanger lane to the **Duke of Kent pub**, which is popular with members of Ealing Cyclists.

12. Just after the pub, turn left into Kent Avenue. Turn left then right into North Avenue then The Avenue. At a mini-roundabout turn left into Gordon Rd. Note the steeply pitched roofs in the Arts and Crafts manner.

13. Along Gordon Road, a right turn marked 'Neighbourhood Recycling' brings you out at the massive **Ealing Town Hall**. You may prefer to walk across this busy junction, taking a right at M&S that will bring you to Walpole Park. Alternatively, cross Uxbridge Road on foot, walk down Barnes Pikle passage and turn left.

14. At **Walpole Park**, which has a snackery and public toilets, the elegant classical building on the right is **Pitzhanger Manor**, once owned and redesigned by Sir John Soane, and now an art gallery and museum.

15. Turn left (east) into the Grove (or walk eastwards over the crossing opposite the Manor), which has a cycle cut-through. You pass the **Café Grove** at no. 65, a pleasant Polish restaurant where Ealing Cyclists meet regularly. Alternatively there's the **Kings Arms** at the end of the road.

16. At **Ealing Common** turn right and then left onto Warwick Rd. Cross the toucan to Leopold Road. A right turn through more garden suburbia takes you to Tring and Carbery avenues. Then take a left into Gunnersbury Lane and sharp right into Bollo Lane past **Acton Town station**, a classic work by Arts and Crafts turned Modern architect Charles Holden.Turn right at the roundabout into Bollo Lane. After two level crossings take the third left into Antrobus Road.

17. The first right takes you to South Parade, where you turn left towards Bedford Park and its many spendid Arts and Crafts houses.

Above: The Tower House built by Charles Voysey in 1889 is one of many interesting houses to be found in Bedford Park.

18. No. 14 South Parade is the classic **Tower House** by Charles Voysey. Built in 1889, it is one of his earliest works and established the white roughcast concrete style that was widely imitated.

19. The streets behind Tower House are strewn with excellent examples of Arts and Crafts work, notably several designs by the first great domestic Arts and Crafts architect Norman Shaw (**nos. 24–34 Woodstock Road**). You turn left into the Orchard, then right at Bedford Road and left at the wider Woodstock Road.

20. At the end of Woodstock Road, follow a shared use path and turn left into Canham Road, then right into Stanley Gardens. This takes you down to the Vale by **Acton Park**, which you can enter near the traffic lights.

21. You are allowed to cycle through Acton Park, heading northwest, and may wish to have a final cup of tea and cake at the café in the centre of the park (open 10 am–4 pm, WC for patrons). Aiming for the top left corner of the park will bring you back to **Acton Central station**.

West London Waterways

West London has always been the more relaxed end of town, without the dense network of narrow streets that characterizes the City of London and its surroundings. Its gradual urbanization was assisted by better rail connections and, in the 1930s, by the growing Tube network. But before those came the canals, in particular the Grand Union Canal and its offshoots. That legacy of waterways makes it possible to cycle around Ealing all day and hardly see a motor vehicle. This delightful ride, devised by members of the Ealing Cycle Campaign, passes nature reserves, lockkeepers' cottages, mosques and superstores. There are a few pleasant canalside pubs where you can take a break and, if you have the energy, there's a spectacular view of London from atop Horsenden Hill. The ride starts at Ealing Broadway station. A bike with strong knobbly tyres is recommended for the rougher stretches.

1. Leaving **Ealing Broadway station**, pedal across Haven Green on the shared-use path and continue down Gordon Road, directly opposite the end of the path. At the T-junction turn right up the Avenue.

2. From **West Ealing station**, turn left and then immediate right into the Avenue at the **Café Onik**. The Avenue is lined with tall trees and semi-detached houses with very steeply pitched roofs. **St Stephen's** neo-Gothic church, like many in London, has been converted into flats. At the junction follow cycle route signs for Perivale.

3. When you reach **Scotch Common**, take care turning right and go past the **Duke of Kent pub** (real ale, food, garden). At the roundabout, turn left down the cul-de-sac and pass through the park gates to ride down a beautiful tree-lined avenue.

4. Take the shared-use path (marked 'Perivale') next to the bowling green. There is a fenced-off golf course on either side of the path. At the top is the charming church of **St Mary the Virgin**, dating from 1135 but with curious rebuilt sections, including a wooden tower.

5. Cross the A40 via the convenient footbridge from which you can see the extravagant **Art-Deco Hoover Building** (Wallis and Gilbert, 1932). It is now a supermarket.

6. Continue northwards along Horsenden Road South until the traffic lights. To see a great view of London, cross at the lights and turn right into Horsenden Woods, where a surfaced shared-use path takes you to a wooden signpost that directs you to the summit of the **Horsenden Hill**. Return

LOCAL INFO

Local Cycle Guide: 6
Start point: Ealing Broadway station
Length: 21 km (13 m)
Time: 4 hours
Type of ride: Easy. Mostly canal towpath, quiet roads, one walkable bit of busy road

Sights and places to visit
- Horsenden Hill
- St Mary the Virgin Church
- Hoover Building
- Hanwell Locks

Eating and drinking
- Café Onik, 1 The Avenue W13 8JP. Tel 020 8248 0580
- Duke of Kent, 2 Scotch Common W13 8DL. Tel 020 89917820
- Brilliant Restaurant, 72–76 Western Road UB2 5DZ. Tel 0871 961 0302
- Fox Inn, Green Lane W7 2PJ. Tel 020 8567 4021
- Drayton Court Hotel, 2 The Avenue W13 8PH. Tel 020 89917970

Rail stations: West Ealing, Ealing Broadway, Greenford

Underground stations: Ealing Broadway, Northolt, Boston Manor

to the traffic lights the way you came and then follow the path onto the canal beneath the bridge.

7. Ride westwards along the canal leaving the colourful houseboats behind. You can peer through the fence at **Perivale Nature Reserve**,

which is famous for its bluebells.

8. At the second road bridge over the canal you have the option of stopping off at the **Black Horse pub** (real ale, garden overlooking the water).

9. Passing more colourful houseboats there is a **mosque** to the right – one of several in the area around Southall, which has a large Asian population and boasts some great curry houses. Historically, Southall was well known for making bricks, which were transported along the canal to London.

10. Spikes Bridge Park was once a farm producing hay for London's horses.

11. Crossing beneath the Uxbridge Road (the A4020) you are a few streets east of the Hillingdon Cycle Circuit where Olympic gold medal winner Bradley Wiggins used to train.

12. The smell of gas marks the local gasworks as you approach **Bull's Bridge canal junction**, which used to be a repair yard for barges. Today it has a number of very domestic-looking houseboats and is flanked by superstores. Turn left down the very wide towpath, keeping to its right side. Pubs begin to be plentiful along the canal/roadside but Ealing cyclists favour the Fox further down.

Above: *The towpath along the Grand Union Canal is ideal for cycling.*

13. For a curry at the much-praised **Brilliant** restaurant (booking advised) veer off down Western Road. As you ride across a bridge in line with the canal you get a good view of a blue gasometer and a golden-domed gurdwara. A long straight stretch brings you to a white bridge and the **Hanwell series of locks**. Just past a large lock with a cottage to the left is the entrance to Green Lanes and the **Fox pub** – a popular Ealing Cycling group watering hole.

14. After 400 metres (440 yd), come off the canal just past the bridge over the canal. Turn right off the path down Trumpers Way, which is flanked by industrial buildings. Cross the junction with Boston Road to enjoy the Arts and Crafts terrace and school, then follow the Cycle Network signs for West Ealing.

15. Leeland Terrace brings you to the busy Uxbridge Road. A right and a left bring you back to West Ealing station and the options of the Café Onik or the large **Drayton Court** pub.

There are several stretches on this ride where the towpath does not have a hard or sealed surface, and are quite narrow and very muddy after rain. The stretches are:
- After 11, approaching 12 – from shortly after Uxbridge Road to Bulls Bridge.
- From Regina Road bridge (next bridge after 13 – Western Road) on page 156 to beyond.
- Norwood Road bridge (approaching 13b) on page 157.

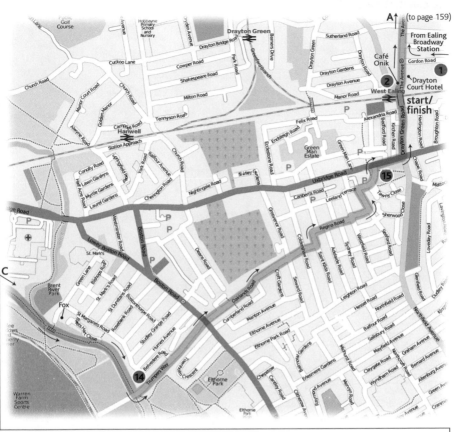

(to page 159)

Islip Manor Road
Northolt
A312
Belvue Road
Castle Road
Oriel Way
Carr Road
Sandringham Road
Belvue Road
Court Farm Road
Summit Road
Grand Union Canal
A312
Church Road
Ealing Road
Belvue Park
Larkspur Rovers FC Clubhouse
Derby Road
Halifax Road
Long Drive
A312
Ealdale Avenue
Rectory Gardens
Bowden Road
Bristol Road
Western Avenue
Field Way
Makepeace Road
Northala Fields
Dolphin Road
Smiths Farm
Western Avenue
A40
Western Avenue
Northolt Golf Course
Farrier Road
Marnham Fields
Greenford Lagoons
Horsen
Union Road
St Crispins
Marsh
Ferrymead Avenue
Rectory Fields
Ferrymead Avenue
Roadene Avenue
Greenway Gardens
Beechwood Avenue
Eastmead Avenue
Ravenor Park
Oldfield Lane South
Croyd
Ruislip Road East
Grand Union Canal
Howdell Road
Ruislip Road
Lynhurst Road
Greenford
Neal Avenue
London Borough of Ea
Hillside Road
Tenderten Road
Avon Road
Avon Road
The Broadway (Ruislip Road)
Margaret Road
Lawson Road
Westbury Ave
Alverton Road
Braund Avenue
Mornington Road
Upper Town Road
Mansell Road
Otter Road
Birkby Road
Rosecroft Road
Bycroft Road
Sunnycroft Aven
Stanhope Road
Greenford Road
Windermere Road
Rutland Road
Ascot Gardens
Windmill Lane
9
Somerset Road
Cornwall Avenue
Alverry Road
Queen's Avenue
Southall
Kings Avenue
10
Spikes Bridge Park
Lady Margaret Road
Osleigh Gardens
Denbigh Road

B (to page 156)

(from page 157)

Ham and High Hills

Hampstead is north London's most desirable residential location for good reason. It has a beautiful heath, lovely Georgian houses, glorious views from the highest point in London, good pubs and restaurants and a network of side streets with little traffic. Camden Cyclists recommends local rides with one note of caution – they include London's steepest hills. But don't be daunted: take it slowly and enjoy breaks at the many cafés and pubs along the way. There is also Kenwood House to visit, with its art collection and pleasant gardens, and many cyclists take picnics to eat there or on the Heath.

This ingenious ride takes you around old Hampstead and Highgate, as well as the early 20th-century Hampstead Garden Suburb, via quiet streets and along some off-road stretches of the Heath (stick to the cycle paths or face a fine). There are a few short stretches of busy road but these are hard to avoid. Unless it's wet, most bikes can tackle the off-road stretches.

1. Starting at **Hampstead Heath** station turn right past the Magdala pub. Bear right at the first fork up Parliament Hill road to reach Parliament Hill itself.

2. Walk up **Parliament Hill** for the superb view of London and watch the kite experts show their skills. Walk back down to the road and ride down the first left, the steep Tanza Road, which brings you to the bottom of Parliament Hill park.

3. You can cycle across the path at the bottom of the park, giving way to walkers. Near the end of the path there is a convenient **café** (open 9 am–4.30 pm) with WCs just the other side of the path. Turn left along the road in front of the park.

4. Turn left again just past **St Anne's church**, into Millfield Lane, which will take you alongside **Highgate ponds** (bathing permitted). On the other side of the road there are grand villas with impressive security. As the road comes to a junction go straight on into **Fitzroy Park**, which is marked 'private property' and 'no through road' but is actually a through route for cyclists.

5. The Grove at the top of the hill has some of Highgate's finest Georgian houses and in Highgate West Hill is the **Flask Tavern**, a well-established pub (bike stands opposite). Head north up West Hill and take the first right into Pond Square, which brings you into the centre of the 18th-century Highgate Village with a choice of eateries.

LOCAL INFO

Local Cycle Guide: 4,7
Start point: Hampstead Heath station
Length: 20 km (12½ m)
Time: 4 hours
Type of ride: Medium. Hilly with off-road sections and short stretches of busy road

Sights and places to visit
- Parliament Hill
- Kenwood House, Hampstead Lane NW3 7JR. Tel 020 8348 1286
- Hampstead Garden Suburb
- Freud's House, 20 Maresfield Gardens NW3 5SX. Tel 020 7435 2002
- Keats' House, Keats Grove, NW3 2RR. Tel 020 7435 2062
- Erno Goldfinger's House, 2 Willow Road NW3 1TH. Tel 020 7435 6166

Eating and drinking
- Parliament Hill café, NW5 1QR
- The Flask, 77 Highgate West Hill N6 6BU. Tel 020 8348 7346
- Kenwood House café, see Kenwood House, above
- Golders Hill Park café, North End Road NW3 7HD, Tel 020 8455 8010

Rail stations: Hampstead Heath, Gospel Oak, Finchley Road, Frognal
Underground stations: Hampstead, Highgate, Swiss Cottage

6. After turning left into Highgate High St take care on two mini-roundabouts, turning right in

both cases. North Road takes you past the two white blocks of **Highpoint**, influential works of early Modern architecture (1936–38) by Russian-born Berthold Lubetkin.

7. Turn left into Broadland Road, which has some large detached houses, many in the Arts and Crafts-ish style typical of this part of Highgate. Don't overshoot the right turn into Denewood Road. Take a left at the end into Sheldon Avenue.

8. Take care turning right into Hampstead Lane and then look out for the left turn 100 metres (110 yd) along to **Kenwood House** (Mon–Sun,

Above: *The spectacular view of London from Parliament Hill.*

11.30 am–4 pm, free) a fine work by 18th-century Scottish architect Robert Adam. If you keep left around the house you'll find the café and bike stands. Exiting Kenwood (left) take care as you take the first right into Winnington Road and carry on for about 500 m (550 yd).

9. Grand villas lead to **Hampstead Garden Suburb**, established by Dame Henrietta Barnett in 1907 in collaboration with architect and planner Sir Raymond Unwin. From

Above: *Kenwood House, by Robert Adam, has a Vermeer painting on display. Kenwood holds outdoor concerts during the summer months.*

Winnington Road, bear left down Linden Lea, right down Kingsley Way, left into Middleway, which brings you to the square.

10. Pedal anticlockwise around the vast central square, which features Henrietta Barnett School and two large churches, all designed by Sir Edwin Lutyens in different styles. Turn right into Thornton Way, which becomes Wildwood Road.

11. Riding past an extension to Hampstead Heath you arrive at the gate to **Golders Hill Park**, which has a pleasant outdoor café with great ice cream. Across from the park, heading uphill, is the **Old Bull and Bush pub**.

12. Directly opposite the pub you'll find Sandy Road, a lovely forest trail leading to Platts Lane.

13. Cross over West Heath Road into Platts Lane. Just before the traffic lights at the end turn left at Kidderpore Avenue, stopping at the corner to see **Annesley Lodge**, an Arts and Crafts masterpiece built by Charles Voysey in 1896 for his father. Every aspect of the house was designed by Voysey, right down to the heart-shaped letter box.

14. Turn left into Oakhill Avenue and keep heading straight along some steep shared-use paths to Branch Hill. Cross over and bear left along Lower Terrace to reach **Whitestone pond**.

15. Take care as you go straight across at the roundabout, and look out for a wooden gate 50 metres (55 yd) down on the right. The clearly marked cycleway heads downhill and across a bridge. Keep right until you reach **Hampstead Ponds**. You have the option of ending the ride here by riding a short distance to **Hampstead Heath station** or carrying on by continuing on to **Hampstead Village**, crossing the road into Downshire Hill.

16. Near Downshire Hill on Keats Grove, is the poet **Keats' House** and, at no. 2 Willow Road, is a 1930s Modernist house by Erno Goldfinger (open for visiting Thu–Sat, 12 pm– 5 pm). The **Freemason's Arms** has a garden and good food.

17. Turn right, with care, into Rosslyn Hill and ride up Hampstead High Street. Turn left at the tube station junction. Just around the corner is the famous **Louis' Patisserie** with lovely cakes.

18. Turn first right (west) into Church Row, which features fine Georgian houses. Past the church turn left then left and right into Langland Gardens.

19. Turning left into Lindfield Gardens you follow the zig-zag marked bike route to Swiss Cottage, passing **Freud's house** (which is now a museum) at no. 20 Maresfield Gardens (Wed–Sun, 12 pm–5 pm). At **Swiss Cottage** turn left across the pavement via the cycle-only access to Eton Avenue (passing a convenient My Sushi) and its grand Edwardian houses. Watch carefully for poor and inconsistent signing of the frequent turns at intersections.

20. Just as you enter Englands Lane on the right, there is another Voysey house – designed for the illustrator Arthur Rackham. Nearby residents have included the likes of actress Helena Bonham Carter and TV presenter Mike Carlson.

21. Cross over Haverstock Hill heading up Parkhill Road. A left into Garnett Road brings you to the final architectural exhibit as you turn right into Lawn Road. The white **Isokon** flats (1934) pioneered Modernism and attracted residents such as writer Agatha Christie and sculptor Henry Moore. A left into Fleet Road brings you back to **Hampstead Heath station**.

Below: Charles Voysey's finest Arts and Crafts house in London is Annesley Lodge, which he built for his father in 1896.

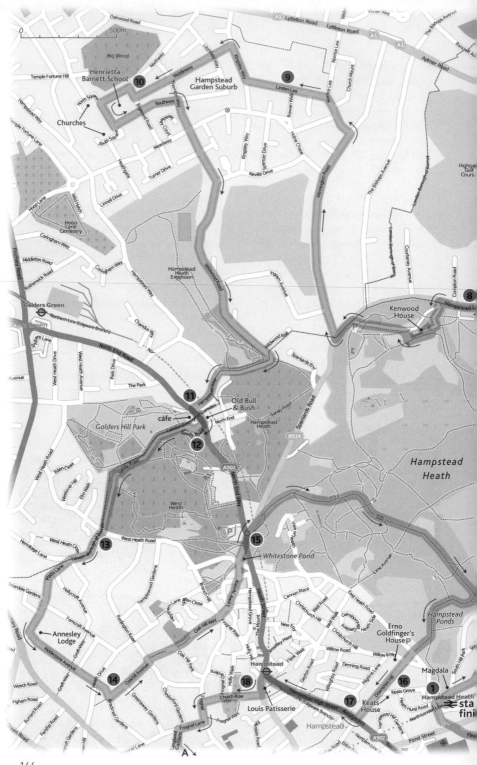

A   B

19

A502   Pond Street

A1000

Langland Gardens   Linstead Gardens

Finchley Road   Frognal

Lithos Road   Rosemont Road

Finchley Road and Frognal

Adamson Road   Maresfield Gardens

Nutley Terrace

Finchley Road ⊖

B519

Law Road   North Hill   Grange Road

Denewood Road

7

Highpoint

Broadlands Road

Aylmer Park   Aylmer Road

George Road   Storey Road

Adderington Road

Freud's house

College Crescent

North London Line (Espinasse Branch)

Thurlow Road   Eton Road

Akenside Road   North London Line

Lyndhurst Road

Wedderburn Road

Lyndhurst Gardens

Lyndhurst Road

Daleham Gardens   Belsize Lane

Belsize Avenue

Glenilla Road   Howitt Road

Belsize Crescent   Belsize Park

Belsize Park Gardens

Buckland Crescent

Lancaster Grove

Swiss Cottage ⊖

Eton Avenue

Fellows Road

Adelaide Road

Finchley Road

Aspern Grove   Garnett Road

Isokon flats

Upper Park Road   Park Hill Road

Belsize Park ⊖

Northern Line (Edgware Branch)

Primrose Gardens   Antrim Road

Lambolle Road   Lambolle Place

Englands Lane

Steeles Road

21

20

West Coast Main Line

King Henry's

South Main Line

London Borough of Camden   North Grove   Southwood Lane

Kingsley Place

Hornsey Lane Gardens

Cornwall Avenue   Hornsey Lane

6

Highgate Village

Highgate High Street   London Borough of Camden

Pond Square

5

The Grove   West Hill   South Grove

Flask Tavern

Fitzroy Park

Millfield Lane

Highgate West Hill   Hill Road   Robin Grove

Merton Lane

Swains Lane

Waterlow Park

Highgate Hill   Waterlow Road

Gresley Road   Dresden Road   Cheverton Road

A1

Harberton Road   Prosper Road   Saint John's Way

Miranda Road   Duncombe Road

The Archway Campus

Magdala Avenue

Archway ⊖

Hargrave Road   Vorley Road

Saint John's Villas   Elthorne Road

Upper Holloway

Upper Holloway ≋

Whittington Park

Oakshott Avenue   Highgate West Hill

Makepeace Avenue

Robin Grove   Hill Road

Highgate Cemetery

Langbourne Avenue

St Anne's church

Brookfield

4

Highgate Ponds

Bisham Gardens   Swains Lane

Raydon Street   Chester Road

Little Angels day nursery

Balmore Street   Bredgar Road

Hargrave Park

St John's Grove

Pemberton Gardens

Bickerton Road

Gordon House Road

Yerbury Primary School

Bush Industrial Estate

Foxham Road   Tytherton Road

Campdale Road

St George's Avenue   Tufnell Park Road

café

Parliament Hill 93m

2

St Albans Road   Croftdown Road   York Rise

Woodsome Road   Laurier Road

Dartmouth Park Avenue   Cathcart Hill

Monnery Road

Dartmouth Park Hill

William Ellis School

Chetwynd Road   Spencer Rise

Twisden Road   Churchill Road

Tufnell Park ⊖

Ingestre Road

3

North London Line

Savernake Road

Mansfield Road

Lissom Road   Roderick Road

Estelle Road   Courthope Road

Shirlock Road

Lisburn Road   Agincourt Road

Gospel Oak ≋

Gordon House Road   Mansfield Road

Oseney Crescent   Ospringe Road   Banking Line

Gospel Oak Primary School

Gospel Oak

Lyn Place

Countess Road

Hugo Road   Corinne Road

Eleanor Palmer Primary School

Hugo Road

Archibald Road   Anson Road

Carleton Road

Dalmeny Road

Cardozo Road   Tufnell Park Road

Torriano Avenue

Camden and Soho

It's hard to imagine more colourful and energetic areas of London than Camden and Soho. Camden's centre throbs with a young clubbing and drinking crowd while nearby streets house some of the wealthiest of London's residents, and Soho has a history as a red-light district despite bordering the most expensive streets on the Monopoly board. Sights on the route are dominated by the architecture of John Nash, planner and architect. This unusual ride takes you through the heart of both districts along mainly little-trafficked roads and through London's best-known parks, but it's essential to follow the route precisely or you may get caught up in complex one-way systems. Note that some sections may be busy at some times of day – so not recommended for children or novice cyclists. Any bike is fine for this flat route.

1. Leaving **Euston station**, walk westwards past the cycle parking to Melton Street. Cross over to Euston St (not Euston Road) then take a right and left into Drummond Street.

2. Drummond Street is well known to fans of Indian cuisine for the large number of curry houses and other delights from the Indian subcontinent. The **Diwana Bel Phoori** house (no. 123) offers great value while **Ambala** (no. 112) specializes in confectionery. Bike stands are plentiful.

3. Turn right into Albany St, taking care, then look for the small turning on the left into Chester Gate and access into **Regent's Park**.

4. The grand terraces around the park are the work of John Nash, the town planner, developer and architect who shaped much of 18th-century London. The park was to be filled with villas but he ran out of funds, and only three of the eight that were built survive.

5. Inside the park, turn right and then soon left and then, 50 metres up (55 yd), turn right onto Broad Walk, the only path in the park where cycling is permitted. Give way to pedestrians as you enjoy the great view of Nash's **Cumberland Terrace** to your right.

6. At the end of Broad Walk you'll see **London Zoo** (bike stands in car park) on the left. Go straight ahead and cross the small bridge over the canal on foot.

7. Follow the route points 8 and 9 below if you want to visit the bustling **Camden Lock Market**, otherwise turn left after the bridge and take care turning right into Albert terrace, then follow edge of **Primrose Hill Park** left into

LOCAL INFO

Local Cycle Guide: 14, 1
Start point: Euston station
Length: 20 km (12.5 m)
Time: Suggest 3–4 hours
Type of ride: Easy. Quiet roads, short busy road on ride extension via Camden Lock

Sights and places to visit

- London Zoo, Outer Circle, Regent's Park NW1 4RY. Tel 020 7722 3333
- Camden Lock Market, Chalk Farm Road NW1 8AF. Tel 020 7485 7963
- Royal Academy of Arts, Burlington House Piccadilly, W1J 0BD. Tel 020 7300 8000
- Sotheby's, 34–35 New Bond St W1A 2AA. Tel 020 7293 5000
- British Museum, Great Russell St WC1B 3DG. Tel 020 7636 1555

Eating and drinking

- Odette's, 130 Regents Park Road NW1 8XL. Tel 020 7586 8569
- Manna, 4 Erskine Road NW3 3AJ T. Tel 020 7722 8028
- The Regent's Bar and Kitchen, NW1 4NU. Tel 020 7935 5729
- Ordnance Arms, 29 Ordnance Hill NW8 6PS. Tel 020 7722 0278
- Bar Italia, 22 Frith St W1D 4RP. Tel 020 7437 4520

Rail stations: Euston, Camden Road, Marylebone
Underground stations: Euston, Camden Town, Marylebone, Marble Arch

Regents Park Road. Continue into fashionable Primrose Hill village. **Odette's** restaurant (bike stands plentiful) is popular as is the vegetarian **Manna** in Erskine Road.

8. For the **Camden Lock Market detour**, after you cross the bridge on foot, walk along the pavement to the right onto the canal towpath (you'll have to walk along it because it's usually busy). Get off the towpath at the well-marked **Pirate Castle** and turn right then left into Jamestown Road (useful bike stands outside Café Nero at no. 3). Optionally just after the Holiday Inn turn left into the back of Ice Wharf, which brings you into the heart of Camden Lock (where it's often too crowded to walk a bike). The bridge across the canal affords nice views of the hustle and bustle below.

9. There is food and drink aplenty at the Lock. From Jamestown Road turn left up the busy

Above: Camden Lock Market throngs with visitors on the weekends; there are many opportunities for eating and shopping.

Chalk Farm Road. Turn left at the lights just before the road forks and then cross the pedestrian bridge into King Henry's Road (see description of Primrose Hill eateries above) and return to the route.

10. Turn right out of Erskine Road into King Henry's Road, then soon left (still King Henry's Road). Route from Camden market joins here. This takes you back to Primrose Hill Park. Turn left and immediate right into Elsworthy Road where, about 100 metres (110 yd) along, Elsworthy Terrace offers secret access to the top of **Primrose Hill** (on foot only, despite a campaign by playwright Alan Bennett) from where you can see one of the finest views of London. On Midsummer

Night, cyclists gather there at 4 am to see the sunrise (see www.lcc.org.uk for ride details).

11. At the end of Elsworthy Road, cross Avenue Road with care, going straight on. At a cross roads turn left into Ordnance Hill. On the right hand side the **Ordnance pub** is conveniently located and has outside benches so that you can keep an eye on your bike. Turn left at the bottom and quickly right.

12. As Charlbert St meets the main road you cross straight over and walk over a footbridge into **Regent's Park**.

13. Turning right when inside the park you pass **Winfield House**, home of the American ambassador. Nearby are some neo-Nash mansions and the dome of the **London Central Mosque**.

14. Turning left into the park's Inner Circle you cross a lake and can stop at the café (cycle stands). The grand mansion on the left, **St John's Lodge**, is considered the most valuable

private house in London and is one of the original park villas. Leave the Inner Circle via Chester Road and then turn right at the Outer Circle. Continue ahead at Marylebone Road into Park Crescent.

15. Turn left into **Portland Place** which was part of Nash's incomplete grand royal route from Regent's Park to Buckingham Palace.

16. Take care when turning right into Devonshire St. At the end turn left then immediately right.

17. Paddington St Gardens offers both WCs and bike stands. Paddington St becomes Crawford St; turn left into Wyndham Place and continue south through Bryanston Square until you hit Marble Arch.

18. At the top of Oxford St use a pedestrian crossing beneath Nash's **Marble Arch** and over to **Speakers' Corner** where free speech is practised loudly every Sunday.

19. A delightful loop around **Hyde Park** and its lake brings you back to a right turn just before Marble Arch – marked as a cycle route to the West End.

Below: *The bright lights of Soho, which is filled with great coffee places and Italian delis.*

20. Cross Park Lane and cycle along Brook Street. The American Embassy building in Grosvenor Square was designed by Finnish architect Eero Saarinen. In 2017, the embassy will move to a new site in Nine Elms.

21. South Molton St, where the well-heeled go to shop, has both bike stands and various coffee places.

22. Turn right at New Bond Street. In between the elegant shops at No 31, is **Sotheby's** auction house, which often has interesting collections of paintings (bike stands at Old Bond St).

23. Diverting from the route you can visit the **Royal Academy** in Piccadilly, which has both a fine outdoor café and cycle parking.

24. To continue on the route, turn left into Burlington Gardens.

25. Crossing Regent St (once a barrier between rich and poor) you enter Soho; take Brewer St to Wardour St, then right and left into Old Compton St. This area is popular with the television and film industry.

Above: The classical facade of the British Museum by Sir Robert Smirke. The Great Court in the museum makes a good coffee stop.

26. Old Compton St is a popular gay meeting place. Just off it in Frith Street is **Bar Italia**, a Southwark Cyclists' favourite stop for coffee.

27. Bear right into Moor St and then take care heading across to Shaftesbury Avenue and when turning into New Oxford St; take the left into Museum St and right into Great Russell St towards the British Museum and turn right in front of it.

28. The **British Museum** has bike stands and a nice café in the Great Court (designed by Norman Foster). Take the first left into Montague St.

29. At **Russell Square** follow the bike-only path in the square's northwest corner and enjoy a pleasant return to Euston station passing some lovely Georgian terraces. (see map for details).

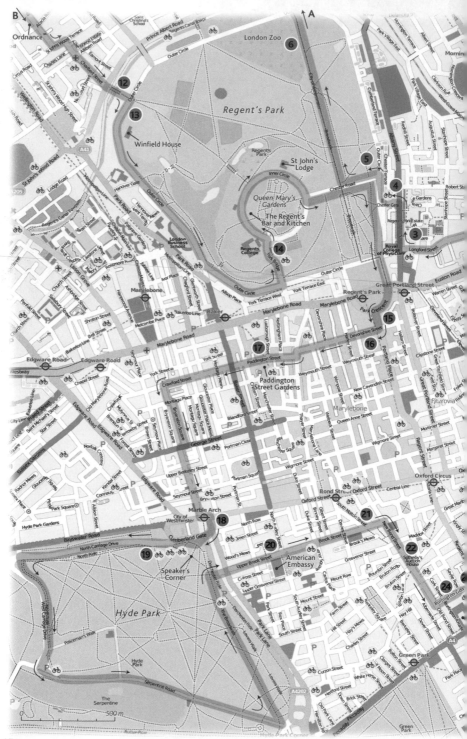

North London Heights

TV broadcasting in Britain was born at Alexandra Palace ('Ally Pally'), where the first high-quality BBC transmissions were made. The commanding height of Alexandra Park over London was the attraction for broadcasters, while the breathtaking views are the attraction for the many cyclists who ride up the hill.

The route to Ally Pally takes advantage of Parkland Walk, a disused railway track that is highly recommended by Haringey Cyclists. You can simply ride up the path to visit Highgate Village – connection via Jackson's Lane and Southwood Lane – and then return to Finsbury Park. But for an exhilarating ride it's worth pedalling up to Alexandra Palace, taking a break, and then following the pleasant descent along quiet streets back to Finsbury Park and its lakeside café. On weekdays, Parkland Walk can be desolate so take care and avoid it after dusk. If you decide to visit Highgate you can link this ride with the Ham and High Hills route (see page 160). Knobbly tyres are advisable following wet weather.

1. Leaving **Finsbury Park station**, head left towards the big bike sign above the cycle parking compound. You enter **Finsbury Park** just behind it. The land for the park was purchased in 1857 and suffragette Sylvia Pankhurst once held rallies there; more recently it has hosted the Sex Pistols, Oasis and Bob Dylan.

2. Keeping to the left (west) side of the park, **Parkland Walk** is accessed via a narrow bridge just north of the tennis courts. Walk your bike across the bridge and turn right onto the path – give way to pedestrians. Parkland Walk follows an old railway track, last used in 1971, to Alexandra Palace. For tasty Italian ice cream divert where the walk starts at Upper Tollington Park, next to the bridge, and ride to **Pappagone** on Stroud Green Road opposite Marquis Road. You can return to Parkland Walk at the bridge across Stapleton Hall Road (the **Micycle** shop nearby (N4 4ED) serves a nice coffee.

3. Exit Parkland Walk when the path disappears as you approach a bridge, and take Holmesdale Road to the busy Highgate Road. There's a café across the road at the friendly **Jackson's Lane** centre (open Tue–Sun). To avoid the busy Archway Road, walk around the corner from Holmesdale into Shepherds Hill, passing the elegant homes, and make a sharp left turn into Priory Gardens.

4. At the bottom of Priory Gardens you reach **Highgate station**, where you walk up a steep path to Wood Lane.

LOCAL INFO

Local Cycle Guide: 14
Start point: Finsbury Park station
Length: 12 km (7½ m)
Time: 3–4 hours
Type of ride: Medium. Hilly ride with long off-road section and quiet roads. Two short busy roads can be walked

Sights and places to visit
• Parkland Walk
• Alexandra Palace
• Hornsey Church tower
• Finsbury Park

Eating and drinking
• Pappagone, 131 Stroud Green Road N4 3PX. Tel 020 7263 2114
• Jackson's Lane Centre, 269a Archway Road, N6 5AA. Tel 020 8340 5226
• Bar and Kitchen, Alexandra Palace, Alexandra Palace Way, N22 7AY. Tel 020 8365 2121
• Weston Park Bakery, 85 Weston Park N8 9PR. Tel 020 8347 7707
• Finsbury Park café, Endymion Road N4 1EE. Tel 020 88802681

Rail stations: Finsbury Park, Crouch Hill, Alexandra Palace, Hornsey, Harringay

5. Queens Wood Road shows off the rich variety of trees in this ancient woodland.

6. Take care descending this steep hill and look

out for a red post box once the road flattens out. At the post box you turn right down a shared-use path with a green railing entrance barrier. This takes you through a sports club to the busy Park Road. Walk or ride down to the junction where you can see the entrance to Alexandra Palace Park.

7. Head into the park (signs for Alexandra Park) through the car park and follow the path around to the left, which eventually brings you back to the road. You are permitted to use the pavement on the right-hand side until the road curves to the right, where you have to get off, cross the road and ride up the final steep section of road to Ally Pally itself.

8. Your hard work will be rewarded with magnificent views. **Alexandra Palace** was originally

Above: *Alexandra Palace has burned down at least twice since being built, but has now been restored to its former Victorian splendour.*

built in 1873 as a Victorian entertainment complex but burned down 14 days after it opened. It was rebuilt within two years, and later served as a TV studio and transmission point for Britain's first high-quality TV broadcasts. It burned down again in 1980, but has been restored and now includes the eponymous **Bar and Kitchen**, which is open seven days a week. It's worth visiting the restored **Palm Court** at the back of the pub. Behind the building are a lake and an ice rink.

9. Go back down the road and the pavement section and turn left on the path, following

signs for Wood Green, then turn right (south) where you see a gravel path, signed for Hornsey, across the flat stretch of parkland. (Going straight on takes you to Alexandra Palace station and a short train ride to Finsbury Park.)

10. As you exit the park turn left along North View Road. This brings you back to the park. Turning left, you follow Newland Road until it reaches a path called Greenways marked for The New River and Wood Green.

11. Just before the New River itself take the wide avenue to the right between the housing blocks (Chadwell Lane). Where you come to a fork bear right, then left (into Cross Lane) at the new development.

12. Cross the road onto the path towards the medieval **Hornsey Church tower**, and take the bike route to the right up the steep Glebe Road and turn left at the top.

13. Cycle route signs take you across a short stretch of busy road – you turn left just before the church and go downhill to Hornsey Vale. At the bottom of the hill, in Weston Park, there is Weston Park bakery and café (open 8 am to 4 pm Mon – Fri).

14. There are fine views of Ally Pally at the top of the climb back towards Finsbury Park.

15. Take care crossing the bridge at the end of Oakfield Road and re-enter **Finsbury Park**. Take a right to enjoy a boating trip, or a cup of tea at the Finsbury Park café (open daily, 9 am–6 pm), or pedal around the park, passing a short stretch of the New River, to return to Finsbury Park station.

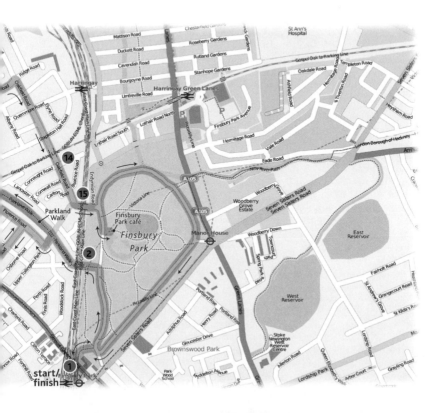

Markets and Squares in North and East London

The once-outlying villages of Islington and Hackney were absorbed into London as developers in the Victorian era built smart squares in the classical style from the borders of 18th-century London out to Islington and beyond. Although World War II bombing and post-war construction in the 1960s destroyed many 19th-century houses, enough squares and terraces remain to make a beautiful weekend afternoon ride. As well as old squares, the route includes local markets that range from the crowded and multicultural Brick Lane to the organic food stalls of Broadway Market and the elegant shops in Spitalfields. Sunday is the best day for most markets, though Broadway Market is active only on Saturdays.

1. Smithfield's Meat Market (follow Cowcross St from **Farringdon station**) stands on the site of a 13th-century cattle market. It's the last major produce market left in central London and is open weekday mornings. By night it becomes clubland, with queues to popular venues. The **Priory Church of St Bartholomew the Great** (open daily £4) is well hidden behind a half-timbered gateway in West Smithfield, near a little roundabout just south of the market. One of London's oldest churches, dating from 1123, this Romanesque building stands next to two timber-framed 17th-century houses in Cloth Fair.

Right: *Fresh food and treats are plentiful at Broadway Market.*

LOCAL INFO

Local Cycle Guide: 7
Start point: Farringdon station/Smithfield Market
Length: 14 km (8¾ m)
Time: 2 hours
Type of ride: Easy. Mostly quiet roads, all surfaced, some cobbles

Sights and places to visit

- Charterhouse: Charterhouse Square, EC1M 6AN. Tel 020 7253 9503
- Priory Church of St Bartholomew the Great, W Smithfield, EC1A 9DS. Tel 020 7600 0440
- St John's Ambulance Museum, St John's Gate, St John St, EC1M 4DA. Tel 020 7324 4005
- Markets: Smithfield Meat Market, Spitalfields, Brick Lane, Columbia Road, Broadway Market, Chapel Market, Exmouth Market
- Squares: Albion, De Beauvoir, Canonbury, Milner, Lonsdale, Cloudesley

Eating and drinking

- Fox and Anchor, 115 Charterhouse Square EC1M 4AA. Tel 020 7250 1300
- Brick Lane Beigel Bakery, 159 Brick Lane E1 6SB. Tel 020 7729 0616
- The Birdcage, 80 Columbia Road, E2 7QB. Tel 020 7739 5509
- Laxerio, 93 Columbia Road E2 7RG. Tel 020 7729 1147
- The Dove, Broadway Market, E8 4QJ. Tel 020 7729 0616
- Pavilion Bread Shop, 18 Broadway Market E8 4QJ
- The Marquess Tavern, 32 Canonbury St N1 2TB. Tel 020 3437 0630
- Hope and Anchor, 207 Upper St N1 1RL. Tel 020 73541312
- Manze's Pie and Mash, 74 Chapel Market N1 9ER. Tel 020 7837 5270
- Bhel Poori, 92 Chapel Market N1 9EX. Tel 020 7837 4607
- Crown Tavern, Clerkenwell Green EC1R 0EG. Tel 020 7253 497

Rail stations: Farringdon, Liverpool Street, London Fields, Highbury & Islington
Underground stations: Farringdon, Barbican, Liverpool Street, Shoreditch, Highbury & Islington

2. Cross on foot (or ride around) to the opposite side of the market to turn right down Charterhouse St, then bear left into the no-entry (for cars) section that takes you past one of London's few Art Nouveau buildings – the **Fox and Anchor pub** (1898) with a façade by WJ Neatby who also designed the food hall at Harrods department store. It serves huge English breakfasts from 7 am on weekdays. Carry on through the gate into **Charterhouse Square** and take a peek at what was founded as a Carthusian monastery in the 14th century and was later visited by Queen Elizabeth I. Today **Charterhouse** is an old people's home which offers guided tours three times a week (Tu–Th) and every other Saturday (must book).

3. You pass the **Barbican Arts Centre** en route to **Spitalfields covered market**, which was saved from demolition and is now an elegant shopping and eating area. The covered market is busy on Sundays, Thursdays and Fridays. There are bike stands in Lamb St.

4. Brick Lane Market sells almost everything and is thronged with people on Sundays.

Below: *Columbia Road flower market is a riot of colour and the bargains are astounding.*

Delicious bagels (beigels) are served 24 hours a day at the two bakeries near Bethnal Green Road, a stopping point for the annual Midsummer Night bike ride. Take care of your bike – the area is a well-known location for stolen bike sales.

5. Columbia Road is the East End's best-known flower market (Sun 8 am till 2 pm) where you can buy plants at knockdown prices. The later you come, the cheaper they are. Local cyclists frequent the **Laxeiro Spanish restaurant** (north end of the road) and the **Birdcage pub** (south end). There are a few rings for bike locking in Ezra St, but beware of theft.

6. Crossing Regent's Canal you reach **Broadway Market**, which has gourmet food stalls every Saturday and a bakery, **Pavilion**, that welcomes bikes inside. The **Dove pub** serves food and is a favourite with the Hackney Cyclists crowd.

7. In **London Fields** there's one of London's finest open-air heated swimming pools (bike stands outside).

8. Then it's squares galore. **Albion Square** features grand Italianate villas, while **De Beauvoir Square** (1838) has a Jacobean flavour.

9. A virtually traffic-free route takes you to busy Essex Road where you cross on foot and follow

Canonbury St, whose nearby residents once included Dame Stella Rimington, former boss of MI5. The **Marquess Tavern**, at the bridge over the New River, is a local favourite.

10. The **Elizabethan Tower** of the Canonbury estate dates back to the 16th century. Next door, **Canonbury House** (c.1780) is a fine example of Georgian architecture.

11. George Orwell, author of *1984*, lived at no. 27b **Canonbury Square**.

12. At the corner of Upper St (whose eateries were favoured by former Prime Minister Tony Blair in the 1990s) stands the **Hope and Anchor**, cradle of punk rock and venue for Madness, Elvis Costello and Blondie.

13. Riding around Milner Square you'll find a secret passage at no. 20 that leads to the popular **Almeida Theatre** and its relaxed café.

14. The Tudor style of **Lonsdale Square** (1838) contrasts sharply with the more classical lines of neighbouring **Cloudesley Square** (1825).

15. **Chapel Market** (reached via a passageway through the car park) has provided Islington-ians with fruit and veg for decades. **Manze's** (no. 74) serves traditional jellied eels as well as pie and mash (closed Mondays), and the

Above: *Beautiful Canonbury Square, where George Orwell once lived.*

all-you-can-eat vegetarian **Bhel Poori** (no. 92) welcomes hungry cyclists.

16. At **Exmouth Market** there are restaurants, bookshops and, at lunchtimes, attractive food stalls. Opposite is the ornate Edwardian **Finsbury Town Hall**.

17. Follow the bike cut-through across the park, aiming for the church steeple, to enter the artisan area of Clerkenwell, once London's Italian quarter.

18. **St James's Church** overlooks Clerkenwell Green and its open air pubs. The 18th-century classical courthouse in now a Freemasons' hall. The original **Clerk's Well** can be seen through the window of Well Court at the corner of Farringdon Lane (nos.14–16).

19. **St John's Gate** (16th-century) is all that remains of the priory of St John of Jerusalem. The **St John Ambulance Museum** is open Mon-Sat 10 am–5 pm.

20. Walk 50 yards southwards from St John's Gate and then cycle back to Farringdon Station.

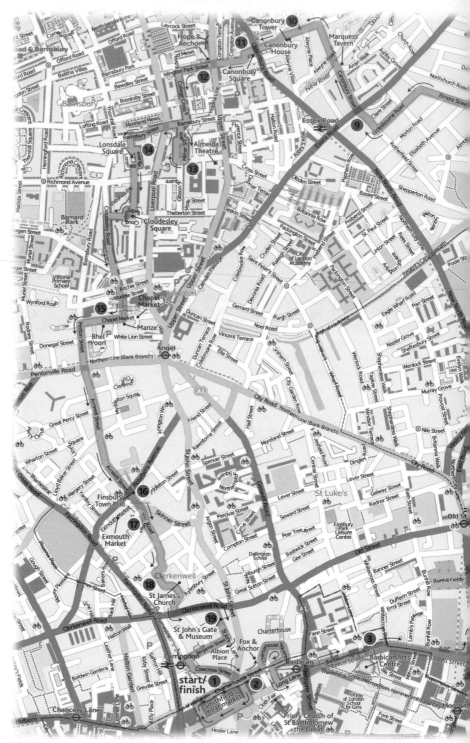

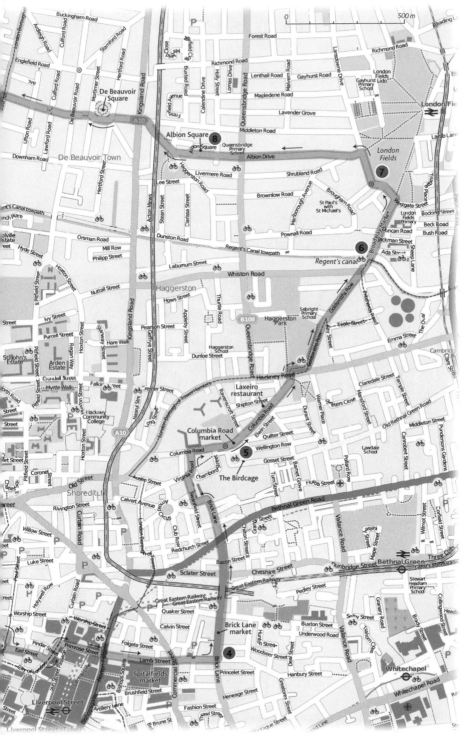

Political Waters in Islington and Hackney

Tony Blair, the former Prime Minister, started his London residency in Hackney before moving to Islington on his way to Downing Street. The two boroughs attract not only well-known politicians but thousands of cyclists with some of the highest levels of cycle use in London. Among the cyclists you might meet in Islington are Boris Johnson, London Mayor from 2008 – 2016; Jeremy Corbyn, the surprise winner of the Labour Party leadership contest in 2015; and Emily Thornberry, MP for Islington South. Cafés and restaurants in the two boroughs have long been a hotbed of politics as well as meeting venues for the very active Islington and Hackney LCC groups. This ride encompasses cycling, politics and the Regent's Canal, which has steadily grown more popular and less desolate.

It's tempting to stop off for many coffees and cakes along this easy ride. You'll see many cyclists and walkers along the canal, so take care and go slowly.

1. Starting at Highbury Corner, you can avoid the busy roundabout (with a precious arboretum in the centre) by walking the few metres to Upper St.
2. On Upper St you may spot actors and politicians, on bikes or off. Juliette Binoche performed at the **Almeida Theatre** in Almeida St, the Sex Pistols played at the Screen on the Green, and two Labour Prime Ministers (Tony Blair and Gordon Brown) conspired at the Granita restaurant, now one of Islington's many estate agents. Just at the start of Upper St it's worth taking a look at the Victorian Gothic **Union Chapel** in the midst of a classical terrace. A little further the Town Hall's many bike stands are a tribute to local cycling activism.
3. If you're hungry or thirsty you can stop off at the acclaimed **King's Head theatre pub** or the justly popular **Oregano** pizzeria (past the cinema).
4. A shared-use path at Islington Green leads to the popular **Camden Passage antiques market** (Wed and Sat am). The ride follows St Peter Street to a short stretch of the New River before turning off to the **Regent's Canal**, which you reach via a bridge on the corner of Danbury St.
5. There is another opportunity for refreshment at the popular **Narrow Boat pub** just past the first bridge on the canal.
6. The first section of canal is packed with houseboats, some large enough to be houses. In the stretch just before Kingsland Basin you will be spoiled for choice of eateries. The best established is **The Proud Archivist**. Further up you'll pass a large red modern building linked to a wooden-clad one shaped like a horseshoe. Home to the Bridge Academy, the horseshoe design is by Keith Papa and BDP.
7. On Saturdays, at an iron bridge across the canal, it's worth exiting briefly onto **Broadway Market** to visit the food and craft stalls.
8. Back on the canal towpath you pass two imposing gasometers.
9. When you arrive at **Victoria Park** (open

Left: *The canal towpath provides an excellent route for both cyclists and walkers, and can become very busy on weekends.*

LOCAL INFO

Local Cycle Guide: 7
Start point: Highbury & Islington station
Length: 19 km (12 m)
Time: 2 hours
Type of ride: Easy. Mostly minor roads and towpaths. Stretch of busy road on Upper St

Sights and places to visit
- Union Chapel, Compton Avenue N1 2XD. Tel 020 7226 3750
- Camden Passage, Islington High St
- Sutton House, 2 & 4 Homerton High St E9 6JQ. Tel 020 8986 2264
- Clissold House, Clissold Park Stoke Newington Church St N16 9HJ. Tel 020 7923 9797
- Emirates Stadium

Eating and drinking
- King's Head, 115 Upper Street N1 1QN. Tel 0844 412 2953
- Oregano, 18–19 St Albans Place N1 0NX. Tel 020 7288 1123
- The Proud Archivist, 2-10 Hertford Road N1 5SH. Tel 020 3598 2626
- Pavilion café, Crown Gate West, Victoria Park, E9 7DE. Tel 020 8980 0030
- Royal Inn on the Park, 111 Lauriston Road E9 7HJ. Tel 020 8985 3321
- Sutton House café, see Sutton House, above
- The Russet, Hackney Downs Studios Amhurst Terrace, E8 2BT. Tel 020 3095 9731
- Clissold House café, see Clissold House, above

Rail stations: Highbury & Islington, Cambridge Heath, Rectory Road
Underground stations: Highbury & Islington, Arsenal

during daylight hours), turn into it via a passage with low walls and cycle parallel to the canal until you pass the **Pavilion café** (bike stands outside). Continue around the lake and exit the park at the next gate into Lauriston Road, or you can stay on the canal for links to the Limehouse Cut ride (see page 188) and the Lee Valley ride (see page 60).

10. Opposite the gate where you leave the park is the **Royal Inn on the Park**, patronized by both Hackney and Tower Hamlets cyclists.

11. Where you see the back of Tesco Metro on Terrace Road, turn left up Elsdale St. At the major road (Morning Lane) cross straight over to the cycle-and-pedestrian path opposite

12. Just after the tunnel under the rail track, turn right for a visit to the Tudor **Sutton House** (open 1 Feb–20 Dec, Thu–Sun, 12 –5 pm, bike railings and a nice café). Returning to the path (turn left out of Sutton House) you pass the 19th-century church of **St John-at-Hackney**.

13. Pretty **Clapton Square** has a mix of Victorian and neo-Georgian houses and leads to **Hackney Downs**, occasional site of bike polo tournaments.

14. Ride across the Downs diagonally passing a play area with an impressive community-made mosaic of animals. Near the end of the park you can turn off left and, through a foot tunnel, reach **The Russet café/restaurant** and directly opposite the **Hackney Peddler bike shop**.

15. Otherwise continuing to the end of the park, turn left into Farleigh Road and go straight across the main road into Brighton Road.

16. Left and sharp right out of Brighton Road takes you into Allen Road and past the local **Shakespeare pub**, which has plenty of bike stands.

17. Clissold House, a grand 19th-century home in Clissold Park, is a lone reminder of Stoke Newington's rural past. A café (open 9 am–5 pm winter, 9 am–7 pm summer) serves tea and cakes.

18. Retracing your steps to the bridge leading up to the house, cross it and ride straight across the park to Mountgrove Road where there is a curious vintage bike shop, **Sargent & Co**.

19. Entering Arsenal football club territory on Gillespie Road you pass the old **Highbury Stadium** on the left, and then the new **Emirates Stadium** as you look to the right on Highbury Hill.

20. Turning right at the monument to Queen Victoria, you enter **Highbury Fields** and have

Above: *Clissold House, a 19th-century reminder of Stoke Newington's rural past.*

a last chance for an outdoor café stop along Church Path on the left, before returning to Highbury & Islington station.

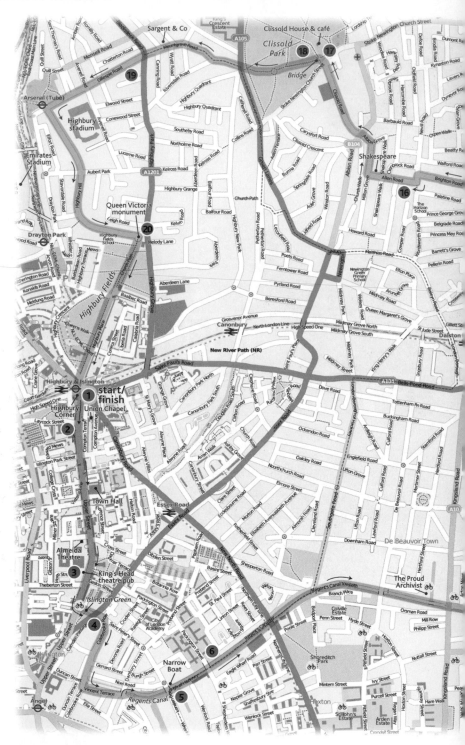

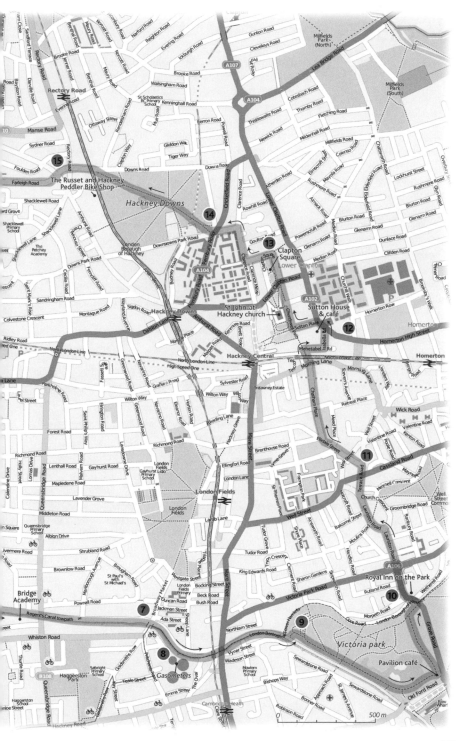

Limehouse Cut

The Limehouse area is named after the lime kilns that dominated this part of London in the 15th century. Later, in the Victorian era, Limehouse Dock was so busy you could walk across what is now the marina by hopping from boat to boat. Many of the area's residents were sailors; there was also a large Chinese population working in the docks. Today Limehouse Basin, where the ride starts and finishes, is full of expensive yachts and equally valuable flats. The relaxed ride is traffic-free and fairly short but it can be linked with other rides in this book: at Limehouse Basin you can join the Thames Path and near Victoria Park you can follow Regent's Canal (page 182) or the Lee Valley (page 60). For a full day's ride, you can link tag this ride onto the Royal Docks and Greenway ride page 70). Sections of the canals can be desolate during weekdays so take care – avoid cycling late in the day, or else ride in company. The ride is suitable for most bikes but it includes a stepped ramp which has to be walked.

1. Limehouse station is conveniently located 100 metres (110 yd) from the start of the ride. As you exit, go underneath the bridge arch within the station and turn left, away from the **Railway Tavern**, as soon as you get outside. You have to walk down the one-way street (Ratcliffe Lane) to Branch Road, which you cross to enter **Limehouse Marina** directly opposite.

2. Turn right (away from the metal bridge) and follow the path around the marina, which leads to a footbridge across the mouth of the canal and, beyond it, a rotating road bridge along Narrow St. Just to the right of the rotating bridge is **The Narrow**, a Gordon Ramsay bar/restaurant that has fine riverside views and railings to chain your bike.

3. Turn left after crossing the foot bridge and follow the marina on the other side of the canal until you see the sign, next to a small park, for **Limehouse Cut**, the oldest canal in Britain (1766). Stay on the right (east) side of the canal and go beneath the Commercial Road bridge.

4. The canal runs straight as a die until you reach the award-winning floating towpath under the A12. Arriving at **Bow Lock** you have to walk up a white bridge (the stone ridges were there to help horses) with views of **Canary Wharf** and nearby gasometers.

5. Soon after Bow Lock you see **Three Mills**, believed to be the largest tidal mill still in existence. Built in 1776, it was used for flour milling and for distilling. You can visit the **Miller's House** on Sundays (11–4 pm) and there is also a

LOCAL INFO

Start point: Limehouse station
Length: 13 km (8 m) including Victoria Park
Time: 1.5 hours
Type of ride: Easy. Traffic-free along towpaths

Sights and places to visit
- Limehouse Marina
- Three Mills, Three Mill Lane E3 3DU. Tel 020 8980 4626
- Olympic Park Vista, Greenway
- Victoria Park
- Ragged School Museum 46–50 Copperfield Road E3 4RR. Tel 020 8980 6405

Eating and drinking
- The Narrow, 44 Narrow St E14 8DP. Tel 020 7592 7950
- Miller's House café, see Three Mills, above.
- Royal Inn on the Park, 111 Lauriston Road E9 7HJ. Tel 020 8985 3321
- Pavilion café, Crown Gate West, Victoria Park, 111 Lauriston Road, E9 7JH. Tel 020 8985 3321
- Palm Tree, Haverfield Road E3 5BH. Tel 020 8980 2918

Rail stations: Limehouse, Hackney Wick, Cambridge Heath
Underground stations: Bromley by Bow, Limehouse DLR (cycle carriage off-peak)

café (open Sundays May – Oct. 11 am–4 pm).

There are bike stands by the canal. Behind the mills is **Three Mills Studios** where the TV series *London's Burning* was made. Leaving the mills, cross the bridge opposite and go back onto the canal (to the right), heading north.

6. You cross underneath the Bow Flyover on another award-winning suspended pedestrian and cycling bridge (LCC lobbied for its installation) which spares you even looking at the heavy motor traffic above.

7. As you come to two huge sewer pipes (Northern Outfall Sewer, 1863) above the canal it's worth leaving the canal (path on the right) to see the **Olympic Stadium** from the Greenway (connection to the QE Olympic Park ride page 64)

8. Returning to the canal you arrive at **Old Ford Locks**. Staying on the east side of the canal you

Above: *Three Mills, one of the largest tidal mills still in existence.*

come to a bridge. Take the path up onto the bridge and cross over to the other side, then double back on yourself past very colourful graffiti to the Hertford Union Canal. Alternatively, you can go straight on under the bridge to follow the River Lee northwards (see the Lee Valley ride, page 60).

9. After another graffiti wall exit the canal in **Victoria Park** through Lockhouse Gate at the canal-keeper's cottage via a narrow path, just beyond the cottage, that doubles back to the pedestrian bridge. If Victoria Park is closed (after dark), you can stay on the canal path until you reach a bridge/canal junction where, taking the left arm of the canal, you join the

Above: *Boys riding across the suspended bridge underneath Bow Flyover.*
Left: *A very tall Victorian brick sewer-vent chimney towers over the cycle path along the canal by Mile End Park.*

southbound Regent's Canal and follow the Limehouse Basin signs.

10. Riding along tree-lined avenues anticlockwise around Victoria Park (which is only open during daylight hours), you will see dozens of runners and cyclists. The Park was the first public open space in London laid out by Sir James Pennethorne in 1845. It was used in the film *Pride* to represent Hyde Park.

11. Just as you pass through a gate by the road that splits the park you'll see, to the right, the

Royal Inn on the Park, a favourite with Tower Hamlets Wheelers – leave your bikes in the garden if you are stopping.

12. Continuing around the park you come to the lake, fountain and pleasant **Pavilion café** (with bike stands). On an island in the centre of the lake is **Pennethorne's Pagoda**, rebuilt just before London's 2012 Olympic Games and reached by a bridge not built in 1845 but reconstructed from his drawings

13. Opposite the lake, 50 metres (55 yd) before the café, is an entrance to the canal. Turn left on the canal itself and ride up the bridge ramp, then down again to head south along Regent's Canal, following the signs for Limehouse Basin (don't make the mistake of turning left along the Hertford canal).

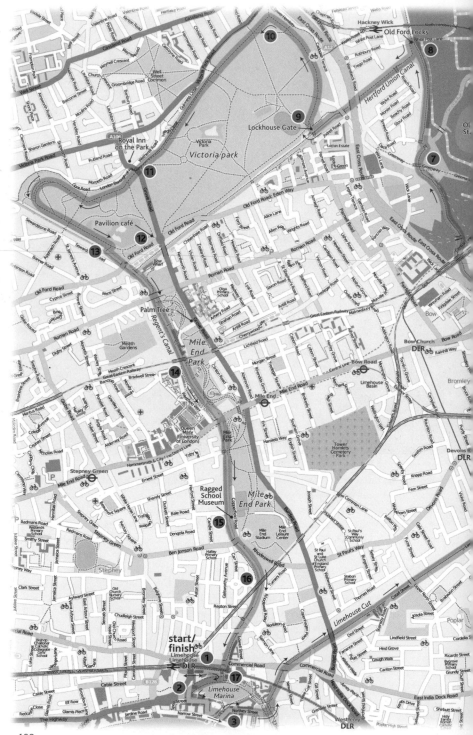

14. The canal runs alongside **Mile End Park**, which has an ecology park. Nearby is the pleasant **Palm Tree pub**, and good views of the Canary Wharf towers.

15. After several locks you arrive at the **Ragged School Museum** (open Wed, Thu 10 am–5 pm and on the 1st Sun of the month 2–5 pm, free), which has a reconstructed Victorian classroom as well as a café, bike stands and, directly opposite, a fish sculpture made out of cans.

16. Stay on the canal, passing the curious brick sewer-vent chimney, until you cross under Commercial Road, which brings you back into Limehouse Marina.

17. Cross over the metal footbridge to the right and follow the side of the marina towards the road – Branch St takes you back to where you started at Limehouse station.

Below: *A leafy ride along Regent's Canal, where there are a number of permanently moored residential canal boats.*

London Landmarks I

London grew up around the Thames, spreading westwards from the old city centre near the Tower of London to Westminster and beyond. The street plan in the old City of London remains medieval despite the Great Fire of 1666 and the bombs that damaged the area in World War II. By combining some minor streets and taking advantage of the river, this ride shows off works by some of London's great modern architects (James Stirling, Norman Foster and Richard Rogers) along with iconic buildings of the medieval, Baroque and Victorian periods. The riverside walkway has sections where cycling is permitted and sections where it isn't (these are subject to change), including the section from London Bridge to Tower Bridge. If you prefer to ride all the way there is an alternative and faster road route parallel to the Thames (see *Local Cycling Guide* 7).

1. Starting at **Charing Cross station**, cross the road and walk down Adelaide Street and then turn right into Chandos Place.

2. A left at Bedford Street and right into King St brings you to **Covent Garden**, London's oldest square, originally designed by Inigo Jones in 1631 along with the perfectly proportioned church of **St Paul's**. In the church portico, street performers show off their skills throughout the day. Walking through the old flower market immortalized in George Bernard Shaw's *Pygmalion* you reach Bow St (bike stands are near the magistrates' court on the left) where you turn right. The **London**

Below: Tower Bridge – a Victorian technical marvel.

Transport Museum, which includes bicycles as well as double-decker buses, is on the right as you leave the piazza (open Mon–Thu, Sat, Sun 10 am–6 pm, Fri 11 am–6 pm, entrance fee).

3. As you come to the Strand you'll probably congregate with other cyclists waiting to cross over **Waterloo Bridge**.

4. Beware of fast traffic on the bridge – it's worth walking across to enjoy the spectacular views of the **City of London** and **St Paul's Cathedral**. To the west you can see the **Houses of Parliament** and London's iconic **Big Ben**.

5. Just as the bridge comes to an end, and before the busy roundabout, turn off very sharp left down the cycle path. Go across the road towards the riverside where you can have a bite or drink at the

National Film Theatre underneath the bridge arch (bike stands nearby). Cyclists gather here on the last Friday of each month for the regular Critical Mass ride around town.

6. Going east by the river takes you past Blackfriars Bridge to the **Tate Modern** gallery, one of Britain's most popular tourist attractions. There are plenty of bike stands and the café on level 3 has the perfect view of St Paul's.

7. After passing the **Globe Theatre** (a replica of Shakespeare's theatre) there's the popular 18th-century **Anchor pub** (bike stands around the corner). Along cobbled Clink St you'll see the remains of the old Archbishop's palace and, via a walking section, a replica of Sir Francis Drake's *Golden Hind*. To ride, follow the signs for NCN4 along Whitehall Walk.

8. Walking or riding you come to the Gothic **Southwark Cathedral**. It was once a priory and became a cathedral in 1905.

9. Passing under London Bridge you have a choice of walking along the riverfront (turn left down a passageway adjoining the west side of the Deco-style **St Olaf House**) and enjoying fine views of Tower Bridge, or riding along Tooley St, which is often congested, so take care.

10. City Hall (by Norman Foster) is open to the public on weekdays (Mon–Thu 8.30 am–6 pm, Fri 8.30 am–5.30 pm, free) and you can see every London house on a giant map of the city at basement level. There are bike stands behind the building and a pleasant outdoor café next door.

11. If walking on the riverfront take Weavers Lane, behind City Hall, down to Tooley Street, then turn onto **Tower Bridge** and cross with care. Keep left after the bridge. You can admire the medieval Tower of London or visit if time permits (bike stands near the visitor shop). The royal chapel of **St Peter** there is one of London's earliest churches.

12. Follow the road around the Tower, through the lights; to the left you can see **The Shard** (of light) currently London's tallest building, and as the Tower precinct ends, just after the green spired church, fork right into Great Tower Street where cycling westwards is permitted. After passing **St Margaret Pattens Church**, take care turning third right into Philpott Lane.

LOCAL INFO

Local Cycle Guide: 1
Start point: Charing Cross station
Length: 12 km (7½ m)
Time: 1.5 hours
Type of ride: Easy but with several busy streets (especially on weekdays). All surfaces are hard, either road or proper cycle path, and so suitable for most types of bike.

Sights and places to visit
- Tower of London, Tower Hill EC3N 4AB. Tel 0870 756 6060
- Tate Modern, Bankside SE1 9TG. Tel 020 7887 8888
- Guildhall, Gresham Street EC2V 7HH. Tel 020 7606 3030
- St Paul's Cathedral, Chapter House EC4M 8AD. Tel 020 7236 4128
- Inner Temple, EC4Y 7HL. Tel 020 77978250
- London Transport Museum, Covent Garden Piazza, WC2E 7BB. Tel 020 7379 6344

Eating and drinking
- Food for Thought, 31 Neal St WC2H 9PR. Tel 020 7836 0239
- National Film Theatre, South Bank Centre, Belvedere Rd, SE1 8XT. Tel 020 7928 3535
- Espresso bar, Level 4, Tate Modern, see above
- The Anchor, 34 Park St SE1 9EF. Tel 020 7407 1577
- Parkside kiosk, Potters Fields Park Tooley St, SE1 2RL. Tel 020 7407 9751
- Seven Stars, 53 Carey St WC2A 7JB. Tel 020 7242 8521

Rail stations: Charing Cross, Waterloo, London Bridge, City Thameslink
Underground stations: Charing Cross, Waterloo, London Bridge, St Paul's, Tower Hill, Bank, Covent Garden

13. On your right you pass the **Walkie Talkie** building (to see the spectacular views from the top book on-line, for free, at *https://skygardentickets. com/skygardenpublic_ui/events/*) and then, just off to the left, during weekdays **Leadenhall Market** is packed with hungry executives. The **Paul patisserie** serves nice croissants and the **Lamb Tavern** is a favourite watering hole.

14. Carry on up Lime St, past Sir Richard Rogers'

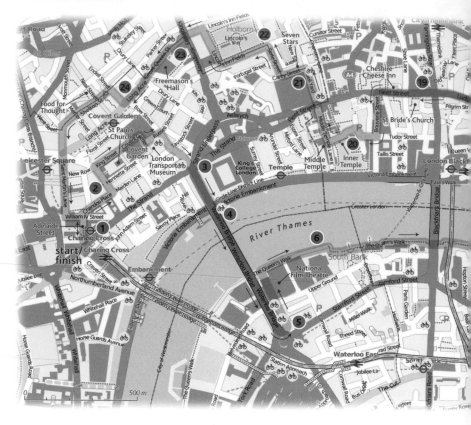

Lloyds of London; all services such as lifts, WCs and ventilator shafts are on the outside to create more space inside. Opposite you will see the **Gherkin**, named after its shape and colour. Turn left into Cornhill, passing in front of the **Cheesegrater**.

15. The junction outside the **Bank of England** is very busy. You may wish to walk across and admire the venerable Bank, the columned **Mansion House**, **Royal Exchange** and its new neighbour **No. 1 Poultry**, designed by Sir James Stirling.

16. A right fork into Poultry and then a right turn at the lights into King Street takes you to the medieval **Guildhall**, which is the seat of the City of London administration (bike stands outside).

17. Return to the road and turn right (West) into Gresham Street then take the fourth left into Foster Lane to cross over Cheapside into New Change.

18. Cycle clockwise around **St Paul's Cathedral**, taking care at the right turn. Wren's Baroque masterpiece (open Mon–Sat, 8.30 am–4 pm, entrance fee) has a superb view from the top.

19. Continuing west past St Paul's you cross Farringdon St and pass **St Bride's Church**, another Wren work. Its spire is believed to have inspired the multi-tiered wedding cake. Almost opposite is the **Cheshire Cheese Inn**, on Fleet St, frequented by Charles Dickens.

20. After the hustle of Fleet St, turn left into Bouverie St and right into Tudor St to reach the **Inner Temple Inns of Court**, which are an oasis of calm. Wander around (you can have a bite at the **Pegasus** during the week) and head west to Middle Temple Lane where you turn right (north) and emerge via a gate (use latch at weekends) into Fleet St. Crossing the road, walk across a short stretch of pavement to Bell Yard.

21. Turning left, the **Seven Stars pub** on Carey St is popular with LCC members. Just after the Pub, turn right into Serle Street and then left into Lincoln Inn Fields.

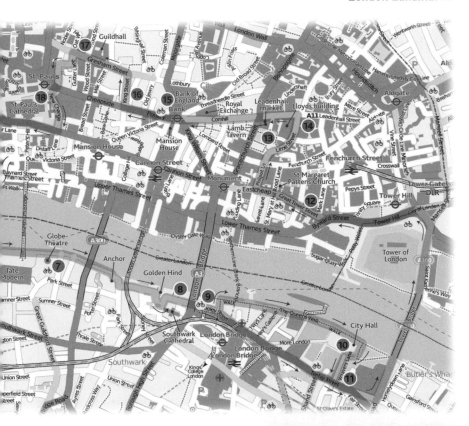

22. Lincoln's Inn, one of the four Inns of Court, dates back to the 16th century. It's open Mon–Fri to the public. Architect **Sir John Soane** built and lived at no. 13 (now a museum, open Tues–Sat 10 am–5 pm, free admission). Pass a fine Palladian house by Inigo Jones (nos. 59–60) as you round the square and exit left at its North (furthest) corner into Remnant Street.

23. Going straight across Kingsway into Great Queen St, where you can visit the **Freemasons' Hall** and see the Masonic shop across the road.

24. Cross Drury Lane, a right turn into Endell Street and left into Shelton Street takes you past trendy Neal St where **Food for Thought** (on the left) serves excellent takeaway veggie food. Left into St Martin's Lane and left again at its end into William IV Street brings you back to Adelaide Road and Charing Cross station.

Right: *Covent Garden, where bicycle taxis and tourists abound.*

London Landmarks II

This classic tour shows how wonderful it can be to visit historic London on a bicycle: see dozens of the capital's great sights in an afternoon while avoiding most of the traffic that congests the central streets. Buckingham Palace, Westminster Abbey and the Royal Hospital in Chelsea are all on the route, along with St James's Palace and the Serpentine in Hyde Park. Westminster Cyclists consider the section of route through Hyde Park to be one of the capital's most attractive cycle rides. For security reasons the police do not permit cycle parking in the streets around Whitehall and Parliament – bikes attached to railings are removed. You will find the nearest bike stands in Great Smith St and others just west of the National Gallery in Cockspur Street.

1. Start outside the entrance to the Gothic **Westminster Abbey**, where coronations and state funerals take place. The Abbey's construction was started in 1245 by King Henry III in Gothic style – it has numerous later additions. Cross the road at the traffic signal into Storey's Gate, and then take care at the junction with Great George St, where you turn left and immediately right.

2. Riding down Horse Guards Road, where the annual **Trooping the Colour** military display takes place, you pass the backs of both the **Foreign Office** and **Downing St** and you can visit the **Cabinet War Rooms** (nearest bike stands near Inn the Park). On the right is **Horse Guards Parade**, where the Queen's Life Guard is changed daily at 11 am (Mon–Sat). The gate in the centre leads through to Whitehall. Passing through the gate you can see the façade of the **Banqueting House**, by Inigo Jones, which was planned as the centrepiece of a larger palace. Returning to Horse Guards Road, on the other side of the road is **St James's Park** (WCs) and the pleasant **Inn on the Park café** (cycle parking nearby).

3. At the junction with The Mall, cross right over the carriageway and use the segregated track to the left that leads past the Tudor **St James's Palace**, up to **Buckingham Palace**, designed by Regency architect John Nash but somewhat spoiled by a later front extension. Changing of the Guard takes place here at 11.30 am on days listed at www.changing-the-guard.com. You can visit Buck House, as locals call it, in August and September and the adjoining **Queen's Gallery** throughout the year (bike stands in Buckingham Gate). The cycle track takes you to the right behind Canada Gate along the side of Green Park, following the route of the Cycle Superhighway.

4. At Hyde Park Corner, there is a special crossing for cyclists that takes you under **Wellington Arch** (which you can visit) and over to Hyde Park itself.

5. Inside the park turn right and left to follow the road north of the **Serpentine**, which can be

Left: *The London Eye towers over Horse Guards Parade, where changing of the guard takes place every day but Sunday.*

LOCAL INFO

Local Cycle Guide: 7
Start point: Westminster Abbey
Length: 12 km (7½ m)
Time: 2 hours
Type of ride: Easy. Mostly quiet streets and cycle paths in parks

Sights and places to visit
- Westminster Abbey, 20 Deans Yard SW1P 3PA. Tel 020 7654 4889
- Buckingham Palace, Buckingham Palace Rd, SW1A 1AA. Tel 020 7766 7300
- Wellington Arch, Grosvenor Place SW1X 7. Tel 020 7930 2726
- Natural History Museum, Cromwell Road SW7 5BD. Tel 020 7942 5000
- Chelsea Physic Garden, 66 Royal Hospital Road, SW3 4HS. Tel 020 73525646

Eating and drinking
- Inn the Park, St James's Park SW1A 2BJ. Tel 020 7451 9999
- Serpentine Bar and Kitchen, Serpentine Road, W2 2UH. Tel 020 7706 8114
- Lido café, south side of the Serpentine W2 2UH. Tel 020 7706 7098
- Anglesea Arms, 15 Selwood Terrace SW7 3QG. Tel 020 73737960
- Marquis of Granby, 41 Romney St SW1P 3RF. Tel 020 7227 0941
- Westminster Arms, 9 Storey's Gate SW1P 3AT. Tel 020 7222 8520

Rail stations: Victoria

Underground stations: Westminster, Hyde Park Corner, Knightsbridge, Sloane Square, Pimlico

spectacular at sunset. The Serpentine Kitchen and Bar are on the left (with cycle parking). A short detour just before a wooded area takes you past the old police station, now HQ for the Royal Parks. Bearing left, following the route of the Cycle Superhighway, you arrive at the Serpentine Bridge with fine views to either side. The **Lido café**, a short walk from the south side of the bridge, past the Diana, Princess of Wales, Memorial Fountain, provides an al fresco tea stop.

6. Just before the Cycle Superhighway reaches the park gate, cross over the pedestrian crossing, pass through Coalbrookdale Gate and admire the intricate craftsmanship on the **Albert Memorial**, erected by Queen Victoria in memory of her husband. Across the road you can see the **Royal Albert Hall**, where classical and pop concerts take place.

7. Exiting the park, ride down Queen's Gate (opposite) to reach the **Natural History Museum** (cycle parking outside the main entrance).

8. Riding south down Onslow Gardens you pass the Sloaney **Anglesea Arms**.

9. After crossing Fulham Road, continue along Old Church St. It's worth taking a look at **Carlyle Square** on the left.

10. On reaching the River Thames turn left and first left into **Cheyne Walk**. Nos. 38–39 were designed by C. R. Ashbee in Arts and Crafts style. Former residents of Cheyne Walk include writer George Eliot and Rolling Stone Mick Jagger.

Above: *The annual 'Tweed Run' cycle ride passes Admiralty Arch on The Mall.*

11. After joining the main road and passing through the traffic signals at the approach to the Albert Bridge, go through the cycle gap on the left into the east section of Cheyne Walk. At the end, turn half-left into Royal Hospital Road. On the right is the **Chelsea Physic Garden** (open Wed–Fri and Sun, afternoons), created to help apprentice apothecaries identify useful and medicinal plants. Its café is open April to October.

12. Continuing along Royal Hospital Road, you pass the 17th-century **Royal Hospital** built by Wren to house retired service people, known more commonly as Chelsea Pensioners. They are easy to spot, wearing their distinctive long red military overcoats and campaign medals.

13. Continue into Pimlico Road, with a Starbucks and bike stands across the road.

14. Cross Ebury Bridge with its classic view of

Battersea Power Station (architect Sir Giles Gilbert Scott). Bear left at the mini-roundabout into Warwick Way and take the second right (Alderney St). Take the fourth left (Charlwood St) and walk over the road closure.

15. The **Lillington Gardens Estate** at the junction of Vauxhall Bridge Road and Charlwood St is an admired example of high-density housing (architects Darbourne and Darke). It is worth visiting the gardens reached through passages on both sides of Charlwood St.

16. Crossing over Vauxhall Bridge Road and heading for Big Ben you circle **Vincent Square**, home to the Royal Horticultural Society at no. 80 on the far side. Turn left into Vincent St, left again into Marsham St and take care turning right into Horseferry Road.

17. Turning left after the traffic lights from Horeseferry Road into Dean Bradley St, the **Marquis of Granby** (open Mon–Fri) serves food till 9.30 pm (bike stands in Smith Square).

18. St John's Church (17th-century) in Smith Square often has classical concerts.

19. Exiting Smith Square by Lord North St, you pass elegant Georgian houses in Cowley St and, after crossing Great Peter St, **Lawrence of Arabia's** former home at no. 14 Barton St. Turn left at the end into Great College St.

20. Where the street turns left, enter the archway on the right (open daytime hours) into **Dean's Yard**, which houses Westminster School. You exit the square to arrive back in front of Westminster Abbey. The **Westminster Arms** (in Storey's Gate, opposite) is the nearest pub (bike stands in Great Smith Street).

Below: *London's biggest annual cycle ride passes Buckingham Palace.*

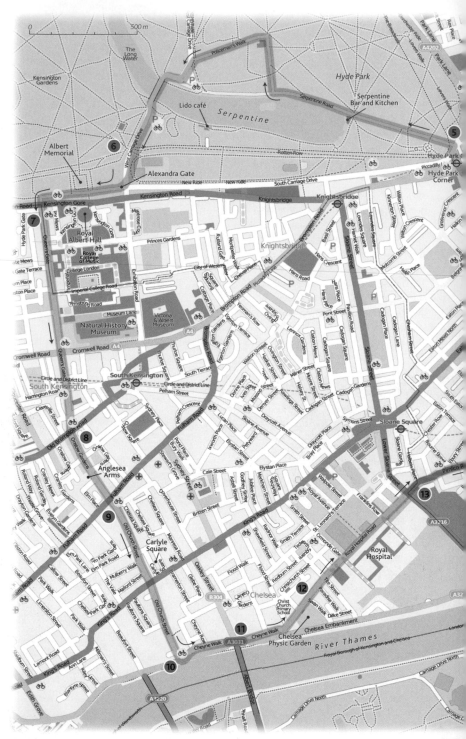

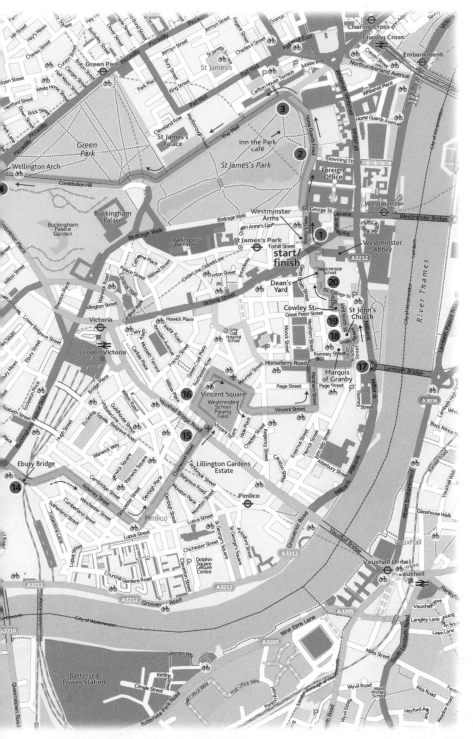

Royal Palaces and Castles: Landmarks III

This ride follows the most talked about cycle route in London. Where cyclists once had to dodge large lorries they now have their own separated space. Thanks to the work of London Cycling Campaign members and the determination of Mayor Boris Johnson, his Cycling Commissioner, and Transport for London, a former stay-away zone has become an inviting route offering some of the finest riverbank views in London.

You will see Tower Bridge, the Tower of London, the Millennium Wheel, the Houses of Parliament, Buckingham Palace and Kensington Palace. It is worth riding the two-way route in both directions to enjoy views eastwards and westwards, but you can also return along either the southern or northern routes of the Landmarks II ride (page 198) which you can join at the Tower of London (if doing this ride in the reverse direction), or at Trafalgar Square/Charing Cross by retracing your steps from Kensington Palace to Buckingham Palace and then following the segregated cycle track along The Mall to Trafalgar Square and riding or walking to Charing Cross. Cycle hire stands (see page 230) are plentiful along the route. Take care around continuing construction works which can cause diversions.

Although almost entirely segregated the route includes several junctions where you need to be watchful.

1. The route starts, appropriately, on the territory of the ancient Roman city of Londinium where London started. From **Tower Gateway station** walk over to the cycle track opposite the Tower of London and head westwards (right). A hundred yards along, next to nearby Tower Hill station, stands the largest fragment of the **Roman wall** built in AD 200 around the capital.

2. The **Tower of London** was completed in 1097 following the invasion of William the Conqueror

and was built to defend the city from attacks up the Thames. The chapel inside is one of two surviving Norman churches in London. If you want to visit the Tower there are bike stands next to the visitors' shop.

3. The route continues straightforwardly along the segregated two-way cycle track all the way to the Houses of Parliament. A short section along Castle Baynard Street veers away from the river bank and back to avoid an underpass (see step 7).

4. As you dip down along Lower Thames Street look out for a building on the river side of the road with an elegant Victorian arcade. This is the former **Billingsgate fish market** which was converted into a bank in the 1980s (and the fish trade was moved to a site near Canary Wharf).

5. A little further is **St Magnus church** one of the 51 Baroque style churches built by Sir Christopher Wren following the Great Fire in 1666. Just beyond it you pass underneath London Bridge (built 1968 – the previous one is now in Arizona crossing Lake Havasu).

6. Just past the busy junction with Queen St, which leads directly to the Guildhall (page 196), is another Wren church: **St James Garlickhythe**.

7. The cycle track diverts off Upper Thames Street to avoid the underpass by running along the quiet Castle Baynard Street (Benet Street, heading north from Castle Baynard St leads to **St Paul's Cathedral** via steps). The route returns to the segregated track just before Blackfriars Bridge and crosses the carriageway to the river side of the street.

8. You pass **Inner Temple Gardens** on your right. The location of one of London's four Inns of Court, the gardens can be entered through a gate on the right in Middle Temple Lane.

9. Just before the sleek arches of Waterloo Bridge is the neo-Classical **Somerset House**, built as government offices in the 18th and 19th centuries, it now houses the Courtauld art collection that includes several icons of Impressionism. Access is possible from Victoria Embankment.

10. Beyond Waterloo Bridge you are cycling

Left: The towers of the City of London.

LOCAL INFO

Local Cycle Guide: 1
Start point: Tower Gateway station
Length: 9 km (one way) (5.6 miles)
Time: 1 hour (one way)
Type of ride: Easy along separated track but crossing several junctions

Sights and places to visit

- Roman Wall, Tower Hill
- Tower of London, Tower Hill EC3N 4AB. Tel 0870 756 6060
- Inner Temple, EC4Y 7HL. Tel 020 7797 8250
- Somerset House, Strand, London WC2R 1LA. Tel 020 7845 4600
- Houses of Parliament, Parliament Square, W1A 1AA. Tel 020 7219 3000
- Buckingham Palace, Buckingham Palace Road, SW1A 1AA. Tel 020 7766 7303
- Serpentine Gallery, Kensington Gardens, London W2 3XA. Tel 020 7402 6075
- Kensington Palace, Kensington Gardens, London W8 4PX. Tel 0844 482 7777

Eating and drinking

- Ship and Shovell, 1-3 Craven Passage, London WC2N 5PH. Tel 020 7839 1311
- Inn the Park, St James's Park, London SW1A 2BJ. Tel 020 7451 9999
- Lido Bar and Café, Hyde Park, London W2 2UH. Tel 020 7706 7098
- Broadwalk Café, Black Lion Gate, Kensington Gardens, London W2 4RU. Tel 020 7034 0722
- Orangery, Kensington Palace, Kensington Gardens, London W8 4PX. Tel 020 3166 6000

Rail stations: Tower Gateway (DLR), Cannon St, Blackfriars, Charing Cross, Victoria

Underground stations: Tower Hill, Monument, Canon St, Blackfriars, Temple, Charing Cross, Hyde Park Corner, High St. Kensington

---

along what was riverbed in the 18th century before the Thames channel was narrowed, creating the park on the right. For a locally favoured refreshment stop you can try the relaxed **Ship and Shovell** in Craven Passage, just off Craven Street behind Hungerford rail and pedestrian bridge.

11. Across the river is the **South Bank** complex of concert halls, theatres and galleries built in the 50s(to celebrate the 1951 Festival of Britain), 60s and 70s (Sir Dennis Lasdun's Brutalist **National Theatre**). A little further on the south bank is the **London Eye** or Millennium Wheel, Europe's largest (135m) Ferris wheel.

12. Ahead you have a great view of **Big Ben**, the clock tower of the largely neo-Gothic **Houses of Parliament (Westminster Hall** is 14th century Gothic) built 1835-60 by Sir Charles Barry and Augustus Pugin. Visiting is permitted (free tickets for debates; fee for tours) but there is usually a long queue (cycles left in Parliament Square will be removed but there are bike stands on the right just before you reach Big Ben).

13. At Big Ben the cycle track turns right past the Italianate **Foreign Office** and **Home Office** to reach St James's Park. The **Inn the Park café** was built of larch wood by Hopkins Architects. If not stopping, follow the track to **Buckingham Palace** (open to visitors in August and

Above: *The defensive walls of the capital's iconic castle – the Tower of London.*

September; changing of the guard, days listed at *changingoftheguard.com*, at 11.30) whose more attractive front façade and forecourt, designed by Regency architect John Nash, has been hidden by the familiar, though dull, front extension by Edward Blore.

14. At Buckingham Palace you are guided by the track towards busy Hyde Park Corner which you cross beneath the **Wellington Arch** and enter Hyde Park (open 5 am – midnight).

15. Depart from the cycle superhighway, which continues along South Carriage Drive, and join one of London's most attractive cycle paths (on the other side of the zebra crossing), which runs next to the **Serpentine Lake**.

16. On the right you pass the **Lido Café** where you can stop off for a tea or coffee by the waterside and then see the **Princess Diana Memorial Fountain**.

17. Crossing over into Kensington Gardens (open 6 am – dusk) you pass the **Serpentine Gallery** (free entry Tues – Sun, 10 am – 6 pm). Nearby is the **Serpentine Sackler Gallery** which houses a restaurant, **The Magazine**, under a wave-like pavilion by architect Zaha Hadid. Elements of its origin as a gunpowder store are visible inside.

18. The final stop is **Kensington Palace**, by Sir Christopher Wren, once the home of Princess Diana. There is a choice of eating places with up-market **Orangery** (attributed to Nicholas Hawksmoor) behind the Palace and the **Broadwalk Café**, a little to the north of it.

Above: *Riding the 'East-West cycle superhighway' by London's memorable Big Ben clock tower.*
Left: *The London Eye built to celebrate the Millennium.*

Fashionable Quarters: Notting Hill and Chelsea

In the 1960s and 70s, King's Road in Chelsea and Portobello Road in Notting Hill were the places to be seen. The Rolling Stones sang about the 'Chelsea Drugstore' and the Clash strummed guitars in Notting Hill. Today, both areas are highly gentrified with elegant streets and well-manicured gardens, and the movie *Notting Hill* was shot in and around the area. This ride incorporates most of the parks in this part of London. You can choose a shorter version of the ride by trimming off the northern part.

1. Starting at the charming **Marylebone station** with its flower stall and coffee shops, head north, following the bike route signs for St John's Wood to cross Lisson Grove by the justly famous **Sea Shell fish and chip shop** (now with an adjoining restaurant) at no. 49.

2. Go straight across Lisson Grove and head down Shroton St to the left of the Sea Shell. Make a right and then a left into Ashmill St,

and then left and right into Penfold St. Another left and right brings you quickly to St John's Wood, a clearly affluent part of town with smart Victorian terraces. Take care turning right into St John's Wood Road and then turn first left

Below: *Elegant shops in the heart of fashionable Notting Hill, made famous by the movie of the same name.*

to enjoy the greenery and Victorian homes of Hamilton Terrace.

3. Turn left at the church into Abercorn Place, and go across busy Maida Vale into Elgin Avenue where there's **Elgin Café** near Maida Vale station. Bike route signs for Notting Hill take you over the busy Harrow Road (A404) and the Grand Union Canal (which leads to Camden). From the canal bridge you can see **Trellick Tower**, the much-loved and hated creation of Erno Goldfinger.

4. Turning right into Westbourne Park Road brings you into the heart of **Notting Hill**. You'll find bike stands at the north end of **Portobello Road's market**, which is most crowded on Saturday and Sunday mornings. Coffee shops abound and there is also the **Castle pub**. Next to Starbucks at no. 280, is the once-blue now black door featured in the movie *Notting Hill*.

5. After Portobello Road you cross Ladbroke Grove, which is the centre of the annual **Notting Hill Carnival** that takes place on the August Bank Holiday weekend. Turn left at the T-junction with Clarendon Road.

6. About 400 metres (440 yd) down Clarendon Road, turn right. The pleasant **Julie's restaurant and bar** are on the opposite side of the road. Then, turn left into Portland Road.

7. Cross the road and walk along busy Holland Park Avenue until you see the narrow shared-use path, on the right, leading uphill. This takes you past the elegant **Holland Park**. There is a nice café in Holland Park, but there is no cycling allowed.

8. Following the side-street route to Cromwell Road (note the pretty pastel-coloured houses in Blithfield St) you can stop off at the **Devonshire Arms** before negotiating Cromwell Road on foot – turn left and immediate right.

9. Continue straight on past Courtfield Gardens, then turn right at the square with grand houses in the 'Pont Street Dutch' style and into Bramham Gardens. Then follow a clever bike route (bike signs on the road) leading straight into **Brompton Cemetery** (take care crossing Old Brompton Road).

10. The cemetery, consecrated in 1840, opens from 8 am till dusk and includes an unusual octagonal chapel.

LOCAL INFO

Local Cycle Guide: 7
Start point: Marylebone station
Length: 17 km (10½ m)
Time: 2 hours
Type of ride: Easy, mostly quiet streets. Some busy roads that can be walked

Sights and places to visit
- Portobello Road market
- Brompton Cemetery
- Victoria and Albert Museum, Cromwell Road, South Kensington SW7 2RL. Tel 020 7942 2000
- Natural History Museum, Cromwell Road SW7 5BD. Tel 020 7942 5000
- Science Museum, Exhibition Road SW7 2DD. Tel 0870 870 4868
- Serpentine Gallery, Kensington Gardens W2 3XA. Tel 020 7402 6075
- Hyde Park

Eating and drinking
- Sea Shell, 49–51 Lisson Grove NW1 6UH. Tel 020 7224 9000
- The Castle, 225 Portobello Road W11 1LU. Tel 020 7221 7103
- Devonshire Arms, 37 Marloes Road W8 6LA. Tel 020 7937 0710
- Julie's Restaurant & Bar, 135 Portland Road, W11 4LW. Tel 020 7229 8331
- Daquise, 20 Thurloe St SW7 2LT. Tel 020 7589 6117
- Ognisko, 55 Prince's Gate SW7 2PN. Tel 020 7589 4635

Rail stations: Marylebone, Paddington, West Brompton

Underground stations: South Kensington, Marylebone, Maida Vale, Westbourne Park, Earl's Court

11. Turn right then left to cross Fulham Road into Hortensia Road. You pass a Queen Anne-style school building, now the called the **Carlisle Building**.

12. Turn left into the busy King's Road, where pop stars and models promenaded in the 1960s. You turn off it just before the trendy **World's End gastro pub** into Langton Street and turn right immediately.

(to page 216)

A (from page 214)
(to page 215) ↑B

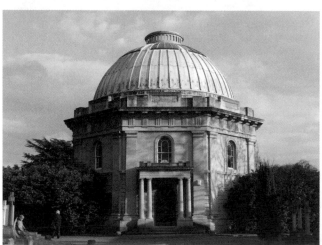

Left: *The Octagonal Chapel along the route through Brompton Cemetery.*

13. Walk through Lamont Road passage to return to the King's Road, where you will find bike stands and opportunities to eat and drink at the **Bluebird 'gastro style' steakhouse and bar** or the local Starbucks.

14. Turn left into the Vale and right into Mallord Street. Writer A. A. Milne, creator of *Winnie the Pooh*, lived at no. 17.

15. Turning left into Old Church St, at no. 64 you can admire the sadly much-altered, early Modern building by Russian-born architects Lubetkin and Chermayev.

16. Turn right into South Parade and left into Dovehouse St. Then take care crossing Old Brompton Road and follow the route to South Kensington past the neo-Gothic **St Paul's church** in Onslow Square.

17. Negotiating South Kensington to Exhibition Road (on foot can be convenient) you can stop off at London's first Polish restaurant, **Daquise**, at 20 Thurloe St – it serves excellent potato pancakes and borscht. There are bike stands near the station or by the **Victoria and Albert Museum** (the V&A).

18. The V&A, built by a number of architects in different styles in the late 19th and early 20th centuries, has a nice café and ever-changing exhibitions on the decorative arts spanning many centuries and many cultures (free, except for special exhibitions).

19. Opposite the V&A are the **Natural History Museum** (bike stands outside, free admission, except for special exhibitions) and the **Science Museum** (free, except for special exhibitions).

20. Continue straight up Exhibition Road. For a step into Poland's political past, drop in at **Ognisko** (no. 55), where World War II generals would choose vodkas.

21. The new **Imperial College building** is by Sir Norman Foster, architect of the Gherkin.

22. Enter Hyde Park and follow the bike route on the pavement northwards. You can take a dip in the **Serpentine** (temperature permitting) and have tea in the café next to it. Nearby is the **Serpentine Gallery**.

23. Continue clockwise around the park. Works on Crossrail may cause diversions as you turn left out of the park by the cycle crossing at

Above: *Intricate Victorian craftsmanship on the Albert Memorial built in honour of the much-loved and mourned consort of Queen Victoria. The Albert Hall, across the street, was also erected in his memory.*

Albion Gate.

24. A right and a half-left at the junction take you to Bryanston Square, where you turn left and head north.

25. When you reach the church in Wyndham Place you have a choice of walking across the pavement next to it or following the road clockwise around it, and then heading northwards back to Marylebone station.

Arts and Crafts and Palaces: Kensington and Chelsea

London's answer to the Gaudi buildings in Barcelona and the Art Nouveau buildings of Brussels is the architecture of the less well-known, but equally fascinating, Arts and Crafts movement. Arts and Crafts preceded Art Nouveau in the late 19th century and was based on the writings of English philosopher John Ruskin. The style stepped away from the classical architecture of the 18th century, allowing form to follow function, and architects such as Norman Shaw and Charles Voysey designed asymmetrical buildings drawing on the Tudor and Queen Anne periods. This ride takes you past some of the best examples of Britain's Arts and Crafts architecture. You will also see original Baroque and medieval designs at Kensington and Fulham palaces, which are both open to visitors.

1. Sloane Square, where the ride starts, used to be the centre point of debutante London. It's within walking distance of the elegant shops on Sloane Street and the restaurants and bars of Chelsea. Walk across to Sloane St and admire the Arts and Crafts church of **Holy Trinity** by J. D. Sedding. The interior is effectively a gallery of Arts and Crafts work (the stained glass is by Edward Burne-Jones).

2. Turning left into Cadogan Gate and right at the far side of Cadogan Square, nos. 60, 62, 68 and 70 are buildings (1887) in the Arts and Crafts 'Pont Street Dutch' style by architect Norman Shaw.

3. At the north end of Cadogan Square, turn right into Pont Street, left into Hans Place and left into Hans Road, walking up the one-way section behind the Edwardian glamour of Harrods department store. At nos. 14 and 16 are two Arts and Crafts works (1891) by **Charles Voysey**. Every detail is hand-crafted including the floral design on the door and the sculpture inside the porch. A Voysey rival, Arthur Mackmurdo, designed no. 12 after Voysey had an argument with the client.

4. Turn left at Brompton Road and cross the road on foot at the first crossing. Turn the corner into Montpelier Street, turn left into Montpelier Place and left into Montpelier Walk before walking 20 metres (25 yd) along Rutland St and going up three steps through a 'hole in the wall' on the right. Emerging from the hole, turn left along Rutland Mews East and right

LOCAL INFO

Local Cycle Guide: 2
Start point: Sloane Square station
Length: 18 km (11 m)
Time: 3 hours
Type of ride: Easy. Mostly quiet streets, some one-ways that have to be walked

Sights and places to visit
- Arts and Crafts houses and churches
- Albert Memorial
- Serpentine Gallery, Kensington Gardens W2 3XA. Tel 020 7402 6075
- Kensington Palace W8 4PX. Tel 0870 751 5170
- Fulham Palace, Bishop's Avenue SW6 6EA. Tel 020 7736 8140

Eating and drinking
- Palace Café, Kensington Palace, W8 4PX. Tel 020 3166 6112
- Builders Arms, 1 Kensington Court Place W8 5BJ. Tel 020 7937 6213
- C'est Ici, 47 Palliser Road W14 9EB. Tel 020 7381 4837
- Fulham Palace café, see Fulham Palace, above
- The Sands End, 135–137 Stephendale Road, SW6 2PR. Tel 020 7731 7823

Rail/Overground stations: West Brompton, Imperial Wharf

Underground stations: Sloane Square, High Street Kensington, Earl's Court, Barons Court, Putney Bridge

into **Ennismore Gardens**.

5. The **Russian Orthodox Church**, on the right, has Art and Crafts wall decoration by Heywood Sumner.

6. Across from Ennismore Gardens you enter **Hyde Park** via a gate. Turn left and pass through another gate (6 am–dusk) to see the **Albert Memorial**, by Sir George Gilbert Scott, a tribute to Queen Victoria's husband and a magnificent exhibition of Arts and Crafts skills. On

Above: A rare building by Arts and Crafts pioneer and Charles Vorsey rival, Arthur Mackmurdo.

the other side of Kensington Gore, just before the **Albert Hall**, are two early works by Norman Shaw: the **Royal Geographical Society** building (1873) and **Albert Mansions** (1879).

7. Returning to the park gate, turn left and re-enter the park at the next gate on the left.

Follow the cycle path past the Serpentine Gallery (bike stands outside, free entrance 10 am–6 pm daily) through **Kensington Gardens** as far as the palace, designed by Sir Christopher Wren in classical style (open daily 10 am–6 pm summer, 10 am–5 pm winter; entrance fee). There is a café at the palace and cycle parking at the NE corner of the Sunken Garden (both to the right).

8. Ride past the south (left) side of the palace and leave the park. Go straight ahead through a barrier and turn left at the end of the road. At no. 1 **Palace Green** (by Kensington High St) is a rare London work by Arts and Crafts pioneer Philip Webb.

9. Cross Kensington High St on foot and walk down the passage opposite to **Kensington Court**. On reaching the road, turn left and first right (still called **Kensington Court**). The road takes you past the popular **Builders' Arms**.

10. A short walk through a passage at the end of **Stanford St** takes you to Cornwall Gardens where you turn right into the mews through an arch, to emerge in **Lexham Gardens** via another short passage on the right. Turn right through

Above: *Kensington Palace, designed by Sir Christopher Wren, was once the home of Diana, Princess of Wales.*

Lexham Gardens and left into Marloes Road.

11. Turn left at the busy **Cromwell Road** and immediately right into Knaresborough Place — or cross on foot. Then follow a signposted cycle route with several contraflow sections through Courtfield Gardens and Laverton Place, turning right through Bramham Gardens, Earl's Court Square and Kempsford Gardens to Old Brompton Road, opposite the entrance to Brompton Cemetery.

12. Take care turning right and, going straight ahead through the double roundabout at North End Road, look out for the signed cycle route directing you right into **Mulgrave Road**. At the end, turn left into Bramber Road, which bends right to become Normand Road. At the end of this street, turn right and left into Vereker Road. Turn left at the end into Barons Court Road and fork left, following the one-way street, Barton Road, at the end of which, turn right into Palliser Road.

13. Just as you reach Barons Court station there is the welcoming café **C'est Ici**, which has bike stands outside. Turn left before the station and left again into St Dunstan's Road

14. As **St Dunstan's Road** curves right note no. 17, which is an early work by Charles Voysey featuring his trademark roughcast concrete exterior that was much copied. Check out the porch supports, which show Voysey's own profile (horizontally).

15. Cross Fulham Palace Road into Winslow Road and turn left into Manbre Road, which becomes Rannoch Road after a road closure. Continue to the end and then turn right and left through another closure into Woodlawn Road. Take the second right (Queensmill Road), which bends left to become Stevenage Road. Eventually you come to **Bishop's Park** (7.30 am–dusk), which you enter just past the Fulham football stadium. The cycle path through the park runs past the medieval **Fulham Palace** (open Mon, Tue, Sat, Sun afternoons, free), which has a nice café in the grounds (bike stands at the entrance).

16. Opposite **All Saints Church**, at the park exit, cross on foot into the riverside section of the park and go through the tunnel under Putney Bridge and another under the rail bridge in Ranelagh Road. The marked bike route takes you past **Hurlingham Park**, a famous polo venue.

17. In Stephendale Road the **Sands End pub** (opposite Byam St) has bike stands.

18. The **National Cycle Route** (NCN4) is marked clearly until you arrive at the new developments in Chelsea Harbour. Cross under the rail bridge at Imperial Wharf station (which appears to be no-entry but is not) and turn right at the power station.

19. As you reach the busy **Cheyne Walk** you can cycle on the shared-use pavement. Just past Battersea Bridge and a church on the left, cross over into the crescent (still Cheyne Walk). At nos. 38 and 39 are the meticulously finished houses by Arts and Crafts philosopher C. R. Ashbee.

20. You can then walk up the one-way Cheyne Row and **Glebe Place** (or cycle in a loop via Oakley Road) to see some of the Arts and Crafts

houses and artists' studios (architect C. R. Mac-intosh lived at no. 48; 35 is by Philip Webb).

21. Turn right into the **King's Road** then left after 50 metres (55 yd) into Dovehouse St. Turn right into Britten Street, cross Sydney Street, turn left into Astell Street and right into Cale Street.

22. It's worth a short detour via Elystan St to see the entertaining **Michelin Building** (F. Epinasse 1905), with its white tiles and tyre decoration. Take care down Sloane Avenue. Otherwise take the left fork into Whiteheads Grove, which becomes Cadogan Street. Turn right at the mini roundabout into Cadogan Gardens, which leads back to Sloane Square. **The Studio House** at no. 25 Cadogan Gardens by Arthur Mackmurdo (1893), is the final Arts and Crafts (though turning classical) masterpiece of the route.

Below: The interior of Holy Trinity Church by Sloane Square, is a gallery to Arts and Crafts accomplishments.

Cycling Parks for Children

Parks are an ideal location for teaching children how to cycle and, at a later stage, how to cycle confidently and safely. Children under ten are allowed to cycle in most parks but not all parks allow adults to accompany children on bikes. That said, there are more than a hundred parks in London where adult cycling is permitted – the easiest way of checking your local park regulations is to look on the relevant *Local Cycling Guide* (see page 234 for information) where most of the accessible park routes are marked in green. Note that not all routes where cycling is permitted are marked, and you may wish to check with the relevant council. Below are some larger inner London parks where cycling is permitted, and note that Richmond Park, Bushy Park and the Lee Valley are all suitable for cycling with children and are covered as separate rides in this book.

BATTERSEA PARK SW11
6.30 am–10.30 pm
Battersea Park has a full complement of facilities including cycle hire at weekends and a children's zoo (entrance fee). The café is large and located by an artificial lake. Adults are allowed to ride on the road around the park on which there is no motor traffic aside from park vehicles. The park is totally flat and one side of it fronts onto the Thames. The Wandsworth Cyclists group frequently organizes events in

the park during Bike Week in June (see page 110 for more details about the park).

Café: La Gondola al Parco Tel 020 7978 1655
Cycle Hire: London Recumbents, located near the children's zoo
Tel 020 7228 6843
Rail station: Battersea Park station,
2 min walk
Car parking: On Carriage Drive – 4 locations

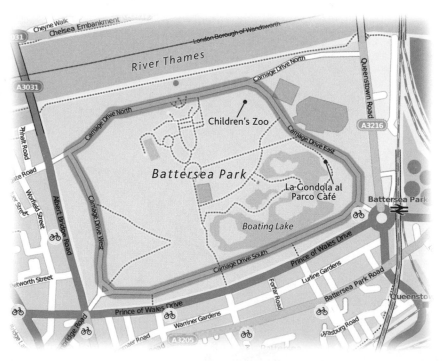

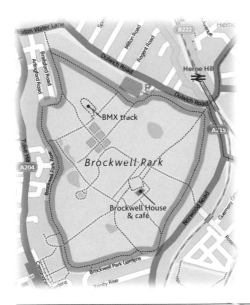

BROCKWELL PARK SE24

7.30 am–dusk

Brockwell Park has a hill but otherwise is ideal for cycling with children – the paths are wide, there are small lakes and plenty of swings. The café in Brockwell House is open daily; WCs next door. The small paved area near the house is sometimes used for cycle training. (See page 105 for more details of the park.)

Café: Brockwell Park café
SE 24, Tel 020 8671 5217
Rail station: Herne Hill,
2 min walk
Car parking: By the Lido in Dulwich Road

BURGESS PARK SE5

Open 24 hours; café 9 am – 5 pm weekdays; 10 am – 5 pm weekends

Burgess Park, which includes part of the former Surrey Canal, is fairly small but centrally located and has a popular BMX track. You can cycle from one end of the park to the other on a wide path without any motor traffic (a tunnel goes under Wells Way). There are tennis courts at the Addington Square end and the changing rooms next to them have a WC. You can ride off-road from the park to Peckham Rye along Surrey Canal (see Lambeth and Dulwich Parks ride, page 104).

Café: Park Life Café, Burgess Park, 3 Chumleigh St, SE5 0RJ, Tel 020 7252 6556
Rail station: Elephant and Castle, 25 min walk.
Car parking: Chumleigh Gardens

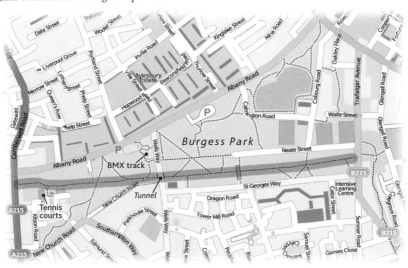

DULWICH PARK SE21

8 am–dusk

Dulwich park has everything a cycling family might need:
a pleasant café and bicycle hire; London Recumbents offers
a range of hire bikes including recumbent and side-by-side
bikes. There is a lake and a flower garden.

Café: Pavilion café, Tel 020 8299 1383
Cycle Hire: London Recumbents, Tel 020 8299 6636
Rail station: West Dulwich, 10 min walk
Car parking: Old College Gate, College Road

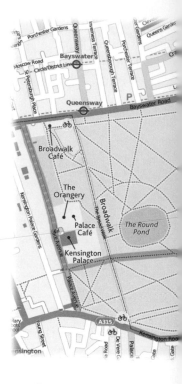

FINSBURY PARK N4

6.30 am–dusk

The road around this park has no traffic
and the recently refurbished café, next to a
boating lake, is very pleasant (with WCs). You
can also follow, from the park, the entirely
off-road Parkland Walk route from the bridge
next to the Tennis Courts (see the North London Heights ride, page 172). This is on rough
ground and not suitable for small children,
but older children on BMX-type bikes will
enjoy it – it is uphill. On some weekends you
can hire all-ability bikes at the tarmac-covered
area opposite the café.

Café: Finsbury Park café, Tel 020 8880 2681
Pedal Power: Cycling club for adults and
children with learning disabilities. Meets
fortnightly at the park. Contact Jo Roach
Tel 020 8809 7718, info@pedalpowercc.org
Rail station: Finsbury Park,
2 min walk
Car parking: Street parking only

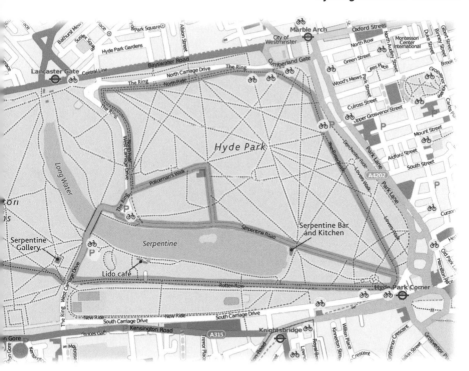

HYDE PARK W2

5 am–midnight

Young children are allowed to cycle anywhere in the park but adult cycling is restricted to the marked paths and roads. These are very attractive, especially those by the Serpentine lake and are a must for any cyclist in London. The section of the route around the park on the north side, along the Ring, is on road and is unsuitable for young children but they can use the parallel walking path. Otherwise, the routes are all traffic-free.

There are two very pleasant cafés by the Serpentine, both of which have WCs outside. The popular cycle paths parallel to Park Lane and along the south side of the Serpentine can get busy with cyclists and joggers during rush hour.

Cafés: Lido (south side) Tel 020 7706 7098;
Serpentine Bar and Kitchen (east side of Serpentine) Tel 020 7706 8114
Rail station: Paddington, 15 min walk
Car parking: West Carriage Drive
KENSINGTON GARDENS SW7
6 am–dusk

Kensington Gardens is adjacent to Hyde Park so you may want to combine these two parks into one ride. Cycling by adults is permitted on the Broadwalk and along a path from the Serpentine Gallery to Kensington Palace. The ride alongside the lake is perfect for pictures. The Palace Café and the Orangery restaurant behind Kensington Palace are pricey but pleasant.

Cafés: Broadwalk café, Tel 020 7034 0722;
The Orangery, Tel 020 3166 6113;
Palace Café, (no phone listed)
Rail station: Paddington, 15 min walk
Car parking: West Carriage Drive, Kensington Palace Gardens

PARLIAMENT HILL FIELDS NW5

Accessible from Hampstead Heath

24 hours

While this route is short it is ideal for children, with nearby swings and a convenient café. There are WCs across from the café at the east end of the path. To reach the path from Hampstead

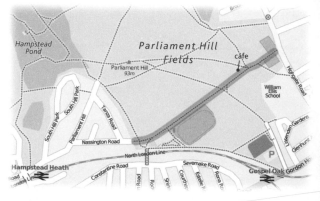

Ponds you can ride along the Hampstead Cycleway up to Parliament Hill – you then have to walk up and down hill to reach the cycle path.

Café: Parliament Hill Café, east end of path by Highgate Road, Tel 020 7485 6606

Rail station: Hampstead Heath, 15 min walk.

Car parking: East Heath Road

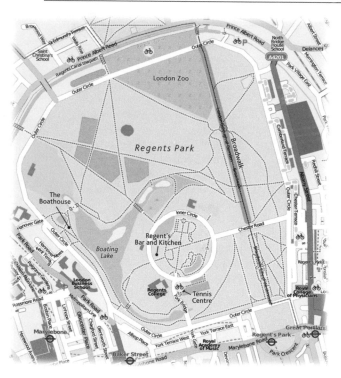

REGENT'S PARK NW1

5 am–dusk

At present, cycling by adults is only permitted along the Broad Walk. The attraction of this very wide path is that it offers lovely views of the Nash terraces and leads to the zoo. Slightly older children may be able to ride down Chester Road and Inner Circle to the pleasant Garden café in Queen Mary's Gardens. The café hidden in the tennis centre at the south end of the park is less crowded.

Cafés: Regent's Bar and Kitchen Tel 0207 935 5729; **The Boathouse** Tel 020 7724 4069; **Tennis Centre** Tel 0207 486 4216

Rail station: Euston, 20 min walk

Underground: Regent's Park, Bakerloo Line

Car parking: Outer Circle of the park

VICTORIA PARK E9

6 am–dusk

Vicky Park, as everyone calls it, is a favourite with cyclists who use the circular road within it for exercise. The park is divided by a road with traffic but you can cross it on foot. The area near the lake is particularly attractive for children. There are two play areas: one for smaller children on the west side just above the Pavilion café and the other for older children just above the Park café at The Hub. Next to the café is a skate park.

Cafés: Pavilion café. Tel 020 8980 0030; **Park café**, The Hub Building, Victoria Park East, E9. Tel 0758 288 1095
Cycle hire: Bikeworks All Ability Cycling Club on Saturdays, Tel 0208 980 7998
Rail stations: Cambridge Heath, 10 min walk; Hackney Wick, 10–15 min walk
Car parking: Street only

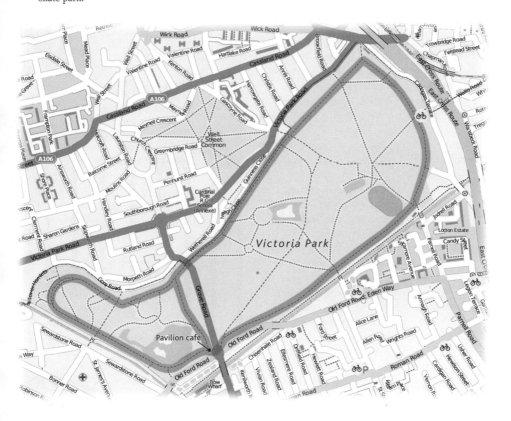

SANTANDER CYCLES

London's self-service, bike-sharing scheme for short journeys

Launched in 2010, Santander Cycles is the second-largest bike-sharing scheme in Europe and is rapidly becoming a popular way to travel to work, pop to the shops at the weekend or simply see the sights of London. Whether you're an old hand or new to two wheels it is easy to hire a bike, ride it where you like and return it to any docking station. There are over 11,000 bikes at more than 750 docking stations. Stations are located every 300–500 metres from one another from Shepherds' Bush in the west to Stratford in the east and from Camden Town down to Wandsworth Town.

A number of the rides in this book are in the hire zone, notably the London Landmarks rides and the QE Olympic Park ride. A break during your journey can allow you to drop a bike off at a docking station and later pick up another one to continue your trip and take advantage of the much lower cost of separate short journeys.

Santander Cycles, popularly known as Boris bikes (after the former Mayor of London, Boris Johnson), have front and rear brakes and reflectors. Lights come on when you start pedalling and stay on for two minutes when you stop. The bicycles also have three gears, a basket with an elastic cord, adjustable saddle, mud guards/fenders and a chain protector. Each cycle is numbered for identification and monitoring. One disadvantage of the hire bikes is that, because they are designed to be durable, they are relatively heavy and not well suited to hills (but there are virtually no hills in the hire zone). Their advantage is that they are maintained regularly and are relatively comfortable on flat roads. Locks are not provided with the bicycles because TfL anticipates that both tourists and commuters will be docking their bicycles securely at

Right: *Santander cycles are great for tourists and locals alike.*

the end of each journey in one of the many docking points.

How to hire a bike

You don't have to be a member to use the scheme; simply go to any docking station with your bank card and touch the screen to get started. Select 'Hire a cycle' and follow the on-screen instructions to get a printed release code that you then type into the docking point's keypad to release your chosen bike. You can hire up to four bikes at the same time (although you will need separate release codes for each bike).

For even quicker hire, the Santander Cycles app allows you to send bike release codes straight to your smartphone. Simply download the app and register for pay as you pedal or yearly membership. Use the app to 'hire now' from a nearby docking station and get your release code. It also has a map showing the status of nearby docking stations and sends handy notifications at the end of each journey.

If you are a regular user you can register online and request a membership key. Visit *tfl.gov.uk/santandercycles* for more information on membership.

You can hire a bike for as little as £2 a day and this includes as many 30-minute journeys as you like for free. So if you dock your bike every half an hour and wait five minutes between rides, you can travel all day and only pay £2. If any journey is longer than 30 minutes, it costs £2 for each extra 30 minutes or less.

For longer periods and all-day use you are better off hiring a bike from one of the commercial bicycle rental companies listed in the next section.

When you return a bike remember to push it firmly into the docking point and wait for a green light to appear. This means you have successfully docked your bike. If you don't get the green light TfL may continue to charge you for your journey. If you are having any problems call the Santander Cycles Contact Centre on 0343 222 6666 (charges may apply) and they will help.

You must be 18 to hire a bike and 14 to ride one, however, if you are planning a family bike ride you may be able to bring the children's bikes to your start point by rail or underground (see Transporting Your Bike, page 26).

Tips

1. Each bike release code is valid for 10 minutes and can only be used at the docking station you chose to hire from.
2. To release the bikes it is often easier to lift the saddle as you pull the bike.
3. The bikes have lights that come on automatically when you start pedalling.
4. If you don't get a green light when you dock a bike, call the Contact Centre on 0343 222 6666 (charges may apply) straight away and they will help.
5. Yearly membership is £90 and includes all 30-minute journeys for 12 months.
6. Parks are great places to give cycling a go but be sure to stick to the designated cycle paths or you may be fined.
7. Santander offers news and competitions—@SantanderCycles.
8. It has become a convention to mark a faulty bike by reversing the saddle when docking. This alerts the maintenance staff and stops others from using it.

For more information regarding Santander Cycles visit *tfl.gov.uk/santandercycles*.

Right: *This map shows the extent of the scheme throughout the capital. There are some 700 docking stations throughout the city, so that you will never be far from a hire bike.*

Santander Cycles scheme overview

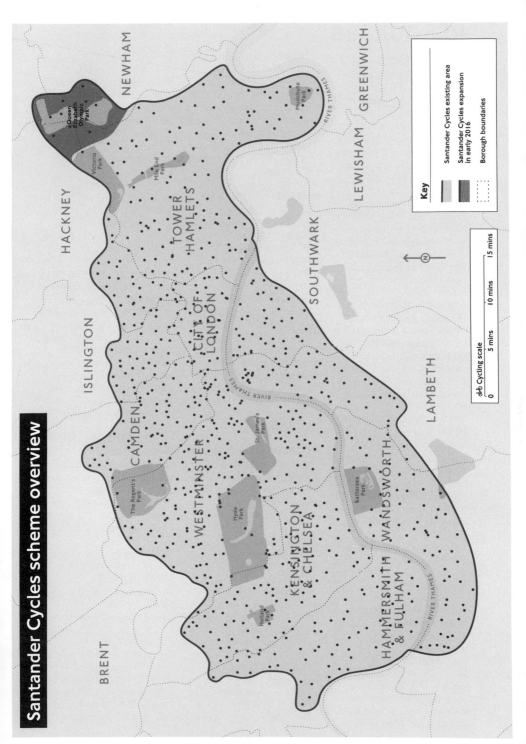

Key

Santander Cycles existing area

Santander Cycles expansion in early 2016

Borough boundaries

Cycling scale

0   5 mins   10 mins   15 mins

N

NEWHAM

GREENWICH

LEWISHAM

HACKNEY

Queen Elizabeth Olympic Park

Victoria Park

Mudchute Park

Mile End Park

TOWER HAMLETS

SOUTHWARK

ISLINGTON

CITY OF LONDON

RIVER THAMES

RIVER THAMES

CAMDEN

WESTMINSTER

St James's Park

LAMBETH

The Regent's Park

Hyde Park

KENSINGTON & CHELSEA

Battersea Park

WANDSWORTH

Holland Park

HAMMERSMITH & FULHAM

RIVER THAMES

BRENT

RESOURCES

Key Contacts

LONDON CYCLING CAMPAIGN (LCC)

*2 Newhams Row, SE1 3UZ,
Tel 020 7234 9310
www.lcc.org.uk*
This is the major cycling organization in London, with more than 12,000 members, and it campaigns to make London a world-class cycling city. Membership benefits include London's best cycling magazine, access to free legal advice, third-party insurance, and free social rides and events. The LCC website has a regularly updated rides and events page as well detailed advice on all aspects of cycling, from theft prevention to campaigning for local improvements. You can download a free all-ability cycling booklet. LCC runs community and social projects and also offers consultancy services. Membership costs £40 waged, £19 unwaged.

LOCAL CYCLING GROUPS IN LONDON

There are welcoming local branches of LCC in each London borough, and most groups have their own websites with details of rides and events. All groups and websites can be found on LCC website (see box opposite).

TRANSPORT FOR LONDON

Distributor of the *Local Cycling Guides* (14 free maps) and funding provider for cycle infrastructure facilities across London. Order new guides at *www.tfl.gov.uk/cycleguides* or call 0343 222 1234.

BIKEWORKS

138-140 Cambridge Heath Road, E1 5QJ, Tel 020 8980 7998, www.bikeworks.org.uk.
Runs community cycling programmes including employ-

ability for disadvantaged groups, all-ability cycling, bicycle ReUse and recycling, and school cycle training. Also offers repair services, sale of new and refurbished bikes and cycle maintenance courses. **Community Centre in Tower Hamlets** offering cycle training and cycle hire.

BRITISH CYCLING

Stuart Street, Manchester M11 4DQ, Tel 0161 274 2000; info@britishcycling.org.uk, www. britishcycling.org.uk
Information and advice about sports cycling.

COMPANION CYCLING

Companion Cycling, c/o 9 Harvey Drive, Hampton Middlesex TW12 2FB Tel 07961 344545 (voicemail) info@companioncycling.co.uk www.companioncycling.org.uk
Charity that enables people with special needs to cycle on specially adapted cycles in Bushy Park, SW London.

CYCLINGINSTRUCTOR.COM

One-on-one and group cycle training. *74 Munster Rd, London SW6 4EP, Tel 0845 652 0421; www.cyclinginstructor.com, info@cyclinginstructor.com*

CYCLE TRAINING UK

Arch 16 Almond Road, Bermondsey, London, SE16 3LR, Tel 020 7231 6005, info@cycletraining.co.uk www.cycletraining.co.uk.
Provider of one-on-one and group cycle training and official trainer of cycle instructors.

CYCLING FOR ALL

Twice-weekly cycle sessions at Croydon Sports Arena run by Wheels for Wellbeing (see below). *www.cyclingforall.org*

CYCLING UK

National organization for cyclists. Campaigns for improvements, provides info and advice to members.
Parklands, Railton Road Guildford, Surrey GU2 9JX, Tel 01483 238 337, cycling@ctc.org.uk, www.ctc.org.uk

HANDCYCLING ASSOCIATION UK

www.handcyclinguk.org.uk
Promotes recreational and competitive handcycling.

LONDON RECUMBENTS

Hire and sale of recumbent and special needs cycles.
Dulwich Park Centre, Ranger's Yard, Dulwich Park, London SE21 7BQ, Tel 0208 299 6636 Battersea Park Centre, North Carriage Drive, nearest entrance Chelsea Bridge, London SW11 4NJ, Tel 0207 498 6543, info@ londonrecumbents.com, www.londonrecumbents.co.uk

LONDON SCHOOL OF CYCLING

One-on-one and group training, and basic maintenance training. *Tel 0208 801 8628, Patrick@londonschoolofcycling .co.uk, www.londonschoolofcycling.co.uk*

MERTON SPORTS AND SOCIAL CLUB, TANDEM SECTION

Roy Benjamin, Tel 020 8540 3959 webmaster@mssc.org.uk www.mssc.org.uk/tandems.html

PEDAL POWER

Cycling club for adults and children with learning disabilities. Meets fortnightly at Finsbury Park. *Contact Jo Roach on 020 8809 7718, info@pedalpowercc .org, www.pedalpowercc.org*

SUSTRANS
National cycle network and details of traffic-free routes, including safe routes to school. *70 Cowcross Street, London, EC1M 6EJ, Tel 020 7017 2350, info@sustrans.org.uk, london@sustrans.org.uk*

TANDEM CLUB
Club with more than 6,000 members across the UK. Significant number of disabled members. *www.tandem-club.org.uk, Tel 01522 695781 Disability Liaison Officer, disabilities@tandem-club.org.uk*

URBAN CYCLE PARKING
www.urbancycleparking.org.uk Website providing information about cycle parking locations and enabling users to suggest locations for additional parking stands.

WEBSITES: BIKE ROUTES
www.cyclestreets.net opencyclemap.org www.bikely.com www.camdencyclists.org.uk www.lcc.org.uk – route planner on homepage.

WHEELS FOR WELLBEING
Charity that supports disabled cycling in London. *Lambeth Accord, 336 Brixton Road, London SW9 7AA, Tel 020 7346 8482 info@wheelsforwellbeing.org.uk www.wheelsforwellbeing.org.uk*

WHIZZ-KIDZ
Provides funding for tricycles (as well as wheelchairs and walking frames) for disabled children. *4th Floor, Portland House, Bressenden Place, London, SW1E 5BH Tel 020 7233 6600, info@whizz-kidz.org.uk www.whizz-kidz.org.uk*

LOCAL BOROUGH CYCLING GROUPS IN LONDON

Barking and Dagenham STIBASA
www.stibasa.org.uk

Barnet Cyclists
www.barnetlcc.jalbum.net

Bexley Cyclists
www.ramblingrides.wordpress.com

Brent Cyclists
www.brentcyclists.org.uk

Bromley Cyclists
www.bromleycyclists.org

Camden Cycling Campaign
www.camdencyclists.org.uk

City Cyclists
www.citycyclists.org.uk

Croydon LCC
www.croydoncyclists.org.uk

Ealing Cycling Campaign
www.ealingcycling.org.uk

Enfield Cyclists
www.enfieldcc.co.uk

Greenwich Cyclists
www.greenwichcyclists.org.uk

Hackney Cyclists
www.hackney-cyclists.org.uk

Hammersmith and Fulham Cyclists
www.hfcyclists.org.uk

Haringey Cyclists
www.haringeycyclists.org

Harrow Cyclists
www.harrowcyclists.org.uk

Havering LCC
www.haveringcyclists.org

Hillingdon Cyclists
www.lcc.org.uk/boroughs/hillingdon

Hounslow LCC
www.lcc.org.uk/boroughs/hounslow

Islington Cyclists Action Group
www.icag.org.uk

Kensington and Chelsea Cyclists
www.lcc.org.uk/boroughs/kensington-and-chelsea

Kingston Cycling Campaign
www.lcc.org.uk/boroughs/kingston-upon-thames

Lambeth Cyclists
www.lambethcyclists.org.uk

Lewisham Cyclists
www.lewishamcyclists.co.uk

Merton Cycling Campaign
www.mertoncycling.org.uk

Newham Cycling Campaign
www.newhamcyclists.org.uk

Redbridge LCC
www.lcc.org.uk/boroughs/redbridge

Richmond LCC
www.richmondlcc.co.uk

Southwark Cyclists
www.southwarkcyclists.org.uk

Sutton Cyclism
www.lcc.org.uk/boroughs/Sutton

Tower Hamlets Wheelers
www.towerhamletswheelers.org.uk

Waltham Forest Cycling Campaign
www.lcc.org.uk/boroughs/waltham-forest

Wandsworth Cycling Campaign
www.wandsworthcyclists.org.uk

Westminster Cycling Campaign
www.westminstercyclists.org.uk

Major London Cycle Shops

50Cycles Electric Bikes London, 345 Upper Richmond Road West, SW14 8QN. Tel 0333 900 5050, www.50cycles.com

A Fudge & Sons, 176 Chiswick High Rd, W4 1PR. Tel 0208 994 1485

A&S Cycles, 1 Chatsworth Road, Lower Clapton, E5 0LH. Tel 020 8985 0042, www.aandscycles.com

About the Bike, 124B Dalston Lane, E8 1NG. Tel 020 7254 2513, www.aboutthebike.co.uk

Action Bikes, 437 Upper Richmond Road, East Sheen, SW14 7PJ. Tel 020 8876 5566, www.actionbikes.co.uk

Action Bikes, Dacre House, 19 Dacre Street, Victoria, SW1H 0DJ. Tel 020 7799 2233, www.actionbikes.co.uk

Action Bikes, 54-56 Whitton High Street, Whitton, TW2 7LT. Tel 020 8894 0174, www.actionbikes.co.uk

Action Bikes, 23-26 Embankment Place, WC2N 6NN. Tel 020 7930 2525, www.actionbikes.co.uk

Armourtex Cycles, 14-16 Rowe Lane, Urswick Road, E9 6EL. Tel 020 8986 2028, www.armourtexcycles.co.uk

Balfe's Bikes, 388 Kennington Road, SE11 4LD. Tel 020 7820 0028, www.balfesbikes.co.uk

Balfe's Bikes, 36 East Dulwich Road, SE22 9AX. Tel 0207 732 4170, www.balfesbikes.co.uk

Balfe's Bikes, 87 Streatham Hill, SE22 9AX. Tel 0208 671 1984, www.balfesbikes.co.uk

Barclays for Bikes, 515 Kingsland Road, E8 4AR. Tel 020 7241 3131

Better Health Bikes, 13 Stean Street, Haggerston, E8 4ED. Tel 020 7254 9103, www.betterhealthbikes.org.uk

Bicycle Repair Shop, 17 The Vale, W3 7SH. Tel 0208 749 7344, www.bicyclerepairstation.com

Bicycle Repair Station, 2a Goldsmith Road, W3 6PX. Tel 0203 556 5384, www.bicyclerepairstation.com

Bicycle Workshop, 27 All Saints Road, W11 1HE. Tel 0207 229 4850, www.bicycleworkshop.co.uk

Bike and Run, 134 High Road, N2 9ED. Tel 020 8883 5945, www.bikeandrun.co.uk

Bike House, 10 Fortess Road, NW5 2ES. Tel 020 7267 7399, www.bikehouse-london.com

Bike Mech, Castle Climbing Centre, Green Lanes, N4 2HA. Tel 07762 270616, www.bikemech.co.uk

Bike Plus, 429 Brighton Road, South Croydon, CR2 6EU. Tel 020 8763 1988, www.bikeplus.co.uk

Bike Shack, 26 Ruckholt Road, Leyton, E10 6RF. Tel 0845 8062373, www.cycleshoplondon.com

Bikefix, 48 Lambs Conduit Street, WC1N 3LJ. Tel 020 7405 1218, www.bikefix.co.uk

Bikes and Bits, 66 Mortlake High St, SW14 8HR, Tel 0208 878 6695

Bikes R Us Mobile repair, Mobile repair service North London area. Tel 020 8882 8288

Bikewise, 61 Swakeleys Road, Uxbridge, UB10 8DQ. Tel 01895 675376, www.bikewisegb.com

Bikeworks, 138-140 Cambridge Heath Road, E1 5QJ. Tel 020 8980 7998, www.bikeworks.org.uk

Blue Door Cycles, 5 and 7 Central Hill, SE19 1BG. Tel 020 8670 9767, www.bluedoorbicycles.com

Bon Velo, 27 Half Moon Lane, Herne Hill, SE24 9JU. Tel 020 7733 9453, www.bonvelo.co.uk

Brick Lane Bikes, 118 Bethnal Green Road, E2 6DG. Tel 020 7033 9053, www.bricklanebikes.co.uk

Bright Cycles, 57 Approach Road, Raynes Park, SW20 8BA. Tel 020 8542 4076, www.brightcycles.co.uk

Bright Cycles, 137 Kingston Road, New Malden, KT3 3NX. Tel 020 8949 4632, www.brightcycles.co.uk

Brixton Cycles, 296-298 Brixton Road, SW9 6AG. Tel 020 7733 6055, www.brixtoncycles.co.uk

Broadway Bikes, 250 West Hendon Broadway, NW9 6BG. Tel 020 8931 3925, www.broadwaybikes.co.uk

Bromley Bike Co., 27 Widmore Road, Bromley, BR1 1RW 020. Tel 8460 4852, www.bromleybike.com

Brompton Junction, 76 Long Acre, WC2E 9JS. Tel 020 7836 5700, www.bromptonjunction.com/London

Burts Cycles, 77-79 High Street, Hampton Hill, Middlesex, TW12 1NH. Tel 020 8979 2124, www.burtscycles.co.uk

Camden Cycles, 251 Eversholt Street, NW1 1BA. Tel 020 7388 7899, www.camdencycles.co.uk

Chelsea Bikes, 427 Kings Road, SW10 0LR. Tel 020 7376 3700, www.chelseabikes.co.uk

Cloud 9 Cycles, 38 Store Street, WC1E 7DB. Tel 020 3205 0190, www.cloud9cycles.com

Compton Cycles, 23-25 Catford Hill, SE6 4NU. Tel 020 8690 0141, www.comptoncycles.co.uk

Condor Cycles, 51 Grays Inn Road, WC1X 8PP. Tel 020 7269 6820, www.condorcycles.com

Corridori, 203 Fir Tree Road, Epsom, KT17 3LB. Tel 01737 373227, www.corridori.co.uk

Crazy Horse Bike Workshop, 275 Balham High Road, SW17 7BD. Tel 020 8767 5614, www.crazyhorsebikeworkshop.co.uk

Cycle Junxion, 84C Lillie Rd, SW6 1TL. Tel 020 3475 7778, www.cyclejunxion.co.uk

Cycle King, 26-40 Brighton Road, South Croydon, CR2 6AA. Tel 020 8649 9002, www.cycleking.co.uk

Cycle King, 451-455 Rayners Lane, Pinner, HA5 4ET. Tel 020 8868 6262, www.cycleking.co.uk

Cycle King, 173 Hillside, NW10 8LL. Tel 020 8965 5544, www.cycleking.co.uk

Cycle King, 1088-1090 High Road, Chadwell Heath, RM6 4AB. Tel 020 8597 6834, www.cycleking.co.uk

Cycle PS, 41 Camberwell Church Street, SE5 8TR. Tel 020 3719 5736, www.cycle-ps.co.uk

Cycle PS, 179 Battersea High Street, SW11 3JS. Tel 0207 738 9991, www.cycle-ps.co.uk

Cycle Store, Shepherds Bush Green, 101 Uxbridge Road, W12 8NL. Tel 0208 743 5265, www.cyclestorew12.com

Cyclecare Kensington, 54 Earl's Court Road, W8 6EJ. Tel 020 7460 0495, www.cyclecarekensington.co.uk

Cycledelik, Unit 30, 63 Jeddo Road, W12 9EE. Tel 3331230500, www.cycledelik.com

CycleLab, 18a Pitfield Street, N1 6EY, Tel 020 3222 0016. www.cyclelab.co.uk

Cyclelife, 8 Bittacey Hill, NW7 1LB. Tel 020 8346 5784, www.cyclelife.com

CyclesUK, 135 Creek Road, SE8 3BU. Tel 0208 692 3148, www.cyclesuk.com

CycleSurgery, Lee Valley Velo Park, Abercrombie Road, Queen Elizabeth Olympic Park, Stratford, E20 3AB. Tel 020 8001 0000, www.cyclesurgery.com

CycleSurgery, Unit 4, 230-250 Purley Way, Croydon, CR0 4XG. Tel 020 8253 0180, www.cyclesurgery.com

CycleSurgery, 12-13 Bishops Square, E1 6EG. Tel 020 7392 8920, www.cyclesurgery.com

CycleSurgery, Brody House, Strype Street, E1 7LQ. Tel 020 7375 3088, www.cyclesurgery.com

CycleSurgery, 72 Chiswell Street, EC1Y 4AB. Tel 020 7562 8500, www.cyclesurgery.com

CycleSurgery, 72 Upper Thames Street, EC4R 3TA. Tel 020 7246 6880, www.cyclesurgery.com

CycleSurgery, 200 Pentonville Road, N1 9EN. Tel 020 7713 1312, www.cyclesurgery.com

CycleSurgery, 70 Holloway Road, N7 8JG. Tel 020 7697 2848, www.cyclesurgery.com

CycleSurgery, 44 Chalk Farm Road, NW1 8AJ. Tel 020 7485 1000, www.cyclesurgery.com

CycleSurgery, 275 West End Lane, NW6 1QS. Tel 020 7431 4300, www.cyclesurgery.com

CycleSurgery, 63-65 Garratt Lane, Wandsworth, SW18 4GR. Tel 020 8877 4990, www.cyclesurgery.com

CycleSurgery, 26 Palace Street, SW1E 5JD. Tel 020 7630 4959, www.cyclesurgery.com

CycleSurgery, 658 - 662 Fulham Road, SW6 5RX. Tel 0207 371 0730, www.cyclesurgery.com

CycleSurgery, 30 West 12 Shopping Centre, Shepherds Bush Green, W12 8PP. Tel 020 8749 5700, ww.cyclesurgery.com

CycleSurgery, 42-48 Great Portland Street, W1W 7LZ. Tel 020 7436 9727, www.cyclesurgery.com

CycleSurgery, 186 Kensington High Street, W8 7RG. Tel 020 7368 5188, www.cyclesurgery.com

CycleSurgery, 3 Procter Street, WC1V 6DW. Tel 020 7269 7070, www.cyclesurgery.com

CycleSurgery, Brettenham House, Lancaster Place, WC2E 7EN. Tel 020 7836 9883, www.cyclesurgery.com

CycleSurgery - Specialized Concept Store, 11 Mercer Street, WC2H 9QJ. Tel 020 7438 9450, www.cyclesurgery.com

Cycleworx, 79 Replingham Rd, Southfields, SW18 5LU. Tel 020 8616 4049, www.cycleworx.co.uk

Cyclopolis, 54 Balham High Road, SW12 9AQ. Tel 020 8673 7153, www.cyclopolis.co.uk

Daycocks, 143 Stoke Newington Road, Stoke Newigton, N16 8BP. Tel 020 7254 3380

Day's Cycles, 213 Dawes Rd, SW6 7QZ. Tel 0207 385 3870

Decathlon, Southside Shopping, Center Wandsworth, SW18 4TF. Tel 0208 870 5135, www.decathlon.co.uk

East Central Cycles, 18 Exmouth Market, EC1R 4QE. Tel 020 7837 0651, www.eastcentralcycles.co.uk

Edwardes, 221-225 Camberwell Road, SE5 0HG. Tel 020 7703 3676, www.edwardescycles.com

Elswood Cycleworks, 98 Lower Richmond Road, SW15 1LN. Tel 020 8789 9837, www.elswoodcycleworks.com

Evans Cycles, 1 Market Street, E1 6AA. Tel 020 7426 0391, www.evanscycles.com

Evans Cycles, 30 South Colonade, Canary Wharf, E14 5EZ. Tel 0870 1644037, www.evanscycles.com

Evans Cycles, 5 Cullum Street, EC3 7JJ. Tel 020 7283 6750, www.evanscycles.com

Evans Cycles, 1 Farringdon Street, EC4M 7LD. Tel 020 7248 2349, www.evanscycles.com

Evans Cycles, 48 Richmond Road, Kingston, KT2 5EE. Tel 020 8549 2559, www.evanscycles.com

Evans Cycles, 4-6 Pancras Road, N1C 4BJ. Tel 020 3040 2010, www.evanscycles.com

Evans Cycles, 31-35 Crouch End Hill, N8 8DH. Tel 020 8341 1306, www.evanscycles.com

Evans Cycles, 86 Chalk Farm Road, NW1 8AR. Tel 020 7229 3253, www.evanscycles.com

Evans Cycles, 240 Watford Way, NW4 4UB. Tel 020 8732 8609, www.evanscycles.com

Evans Cycles, 6 Tooley Street, SE1 2SY. Tel 020 7403 4610, www.evanscycles.com

Evans Cycles, 77-81 The Cut, SE1 8LL. Tel 020 7928 4785, www.evanscycles.com

Evans Cycles, 111-115 Waterloo Road, SE1 8UL. Tel 020 7928 2208, www.evanscycles.com

Evans Cycles, 43A East Dulwich Road, SE22 9AN. Tel 020 3040 4830, www.evanscycles.com

Evans Cycles, 167-173 Wandsworth High Street, Wandsworth, SW18 4LB. Tel 020 8877 1878, www.evanscycles.com

Evans Cycles, 6-12 Gladstone Road, Wimbledon, SW19 1QT. Tel 020 8417 0604, www.evanscycles.com

Evans Cycles, 320 Vauxhall Bridge Road, SW1V 1AA. Tel 020 7976 6298, www.evanscycles.com

Evans Cycles, 65-79 Clapham High Street, Clapham, SW4 7TG. Tel 020 7720 4139, www.evanscycles.com

Evans Cycles, 13-15 Jerdan Place, SW6 1BE. Tel 020 7384 5550, www.evanscycles.com

Evans Cycles, 113-114 High Street, TW8 8AT, www.evanscycles.com

Evans Cycles, 51-52 Rathbone Place, W1T 1JP. Tel 020 7580 4107, www.evanscycles.com

Evans Cycles, 62 Mortimer Street, W1W 7RR. Tel 020 7637 1940, www.evanscycles.com

Evans Cycles, 106 Westbourne Grove, W2 5RU. Tel 020 7229 3253, www.evanscycles.com

Evans Cycles, 548-550 Chiswick High Road, W4 5RG. Tel 0870 060 5489, www.evanscycles.com

Evans Cycles, 178 High Holborn,WC1V 7AA. Tel 020 7836 5585, www.evanscycles.com

Everyone Bikes, 176 Northcote Road, SW11 6RE. Tel 020 7924 5636, www.everyonebikes.co.uk

Finches, 25-29 Perry Vale, SE23 2NE. Tel 020 8699 6768, www.finches-ski.com

Finsbury Cycles Ltd, 185 Seven Sisters Road, N4 3NS. Tel 020 7263 0007, www.finsburycycles.moonfruit.com

Fitzrovia Bicycles, 136 -138 New Cavendish Street, W1W 6YD. Tel 020 7631 5060, www.fitzroviabicycles.com

Flagbikes, 324 Battersea Park Road, SW11 3BX. Tel 020 7738 9469, www. flagbikes.com

Fudges Cycle Store , 564-566 Harrow Road, W9 3QH. Tel 020 8969 5991, www.fudgescyclestore.com

Get A Grip Bicycle Workshop, 19 Lavender Hill, Clapham, SW11 5QW. Tel 020 722 34 888, www.getagripbicyclework shop.co.uk

Giant Camden, 75-77 Kentish Town Road, NW1 8NY. Tel 020 7485 4488, www.giant-camden.co.uk

Giant Store, 200 Aldersgate Street, EC1A 4HD. http://www.giant-stpauls.co.uk

Global Esprit, 525 Garratt Lane, SW18 4SR. Tel 020 7870 2227, www.globalesprit-sw18.co.uk

Halfords, 166-168 Stoke Newington High Street, N16 7JL. Tel 020 7923 8820, www.halfords.com

Halford's Cycle Republic, 286 Euston Road, NW1 3DP. Tel 0207 388 3323, www.halfords.com/

Halford's Cycle Republic, 26-30 Kings Street, TW1 3SN. Tel 0208 891 9130, www.halfords.com

Halford's Cycle Republic, 43 Margaret Street, W1W 8SB. Tel 0207 323 1563, www.halfords.com

Halfpipe, 40 Golborne Rd, W10 5PR. Tel 020 8969 2999, www.halfpipelondon.com

Heales Cycles, 477 Hale End Road, E4 9PT. Tel 020 8527 1592, www.healescycles.co.uk

Herne Hill Bicycles, 83 Norwood Road, SE24 9AA. Tel 020 8671 6900, www.hhbikes.co.uk

Holdsworth, 132 Lower Richmond Road, SW15 1LN. Tel 2087881060

Holloway Cycles, 290 Holloway Road, N7 6NJ. Tel 020 7700 6611/22

Hub Velo, 217 Lower Clapton Road, E5 8EG. Tel 020 3490 2110, www.hub-velo.co.uk

Jazz Cycles, 50 Mill Lane, NW6 1NJ. Tel 020 7998 8969, www.facebook.com/jazzcycles

Justebikes, 318 Portobello Road, W10 5RU. Tel 0208 960 9848, www.justebikes.co.uk

Kinoko, Unit 122, Conlan Street, W10 5AP. Tel 0207 243 6088, www.kinokostore.com

Le Beau Velo, Basement East, 36-42 New Inn Yard, EC2A 3EY. Tel 020 3239 2311, www.lebeauvelo.co.uk

Lock 7, 5 Broadway Marrket Mews, E8 4TS. www.lock-7.com

London Bicycle Workshop, 97-99 Clerkenwell Road, EC1R 5BX. Tel 020 7998 8738,www .londonbicycleworkshop.com

London Bike Kitchen, 28 Whitmore Road, N1 5QA. Tel 020 8127 3808, www.lbk.org.uk

London Fields Cycles, 281 Mare Street, E8 1PJ. Tel 020 8525 0077, www.londonfieldscycles.co.uk

London Green Cycles, Chester Court, Albany Street, NW1 4BU. Tel 020 7935 6934, www.londongreencycles.co.uk

London Joggers, 21-25 Goldhawk Road , W12 8QQ. Tel 0208 749 1032, www.londonbikesuk.com

London Recumbents, Rangers Yard, Dulwich Park, College Row, SE21 7BQ. Tel 020 8299 6636, www .londonrecumbents.co.uk

London Recumbents, Battersea Park, Carriage Drive North, SW11 4NJ. Tel 020 7228 6843, www.londonrecumbents.com

Look Mum No Hands!, 49 Old Street, EC1V 9HX. Tel 020 7253 1025, www.lookmumnohands.com

Love Bikes, 137 Church Walk, N16 8QW. Tel 07841 421905, www.lovebikes.com

Luciano Cycles, 97-99 Battersea Rise, Clapham Junction, SW11 1HW. Tel 0207 228 4279, www.lucianocycles.co.uk

Lunar Cycles, 66 Wilkin Street Mews, NW5 3NN. Tel 0207 482 1515, www.lunarcycles.co.uk

Mamachari, 18 Ashwin Street, E8 3DL.Tel 020 7254 0080, www.mamachari.co.uk

Mamachari Walthamstow, 163 Forest Rd, E17 6HE. Tel 020 8531 2585, www.mamachari.co.uk

Micycle East, 58 Southgate Road, N1 3JF. Tel 020 7249 1212, www.micycle.org.uk

Micycle N1, 47 Barnsbury Street, N1 1TP. Tel 020 7684 0671, www.micycle.org.uk

Micycle N4, 8 Ferme Park Road, N4 4ED. Tel 020 8347 9180, www.micycle.org.uk

Moores Cycles, 61 London Road, Twickenham, TW1 3SZ. Tel 020 8744 0175, www.moorescycles.co.uk

Moores Cycles, 214 Kingston Road, Teddington, TW11 9JF. Tel 020 8977 2925, www.moorescycles.co.uk

Moores Cycles, 3-5 St Johns Road, TW7 6NA. Tel 020 8560 7131, www.moorescycles.co.uk

Moose Cycles, 48 High Street, Colliers Wood, SW19 2BY. Tel 0208 544 9166, www.moosecycles.com

Mosquito Bikes, 123 Essex Road, N1 2SN. Tel 020 7226 8765, www.mosquito-bikes.co.uk

On Your Bike, The Vaults, Montague Close, SE1 9DA. Tel 020 7378 6669, www.onyourbike.com

Paul's Custom Cycles, 121 Bellenden Road, SE15 4QY. Tel 020 7732 3300, www.paulscustomcycles.co.uk

Pearson Cycle Specialists, 126 High Street, Sutton, SM1 1LU. Tel 020 8642 2095, www.pearsoncycles.co.uk

Pearson Performance, 232 Upper Richmond Road West, SW14 8AG. Tel 020 8642 2095, www.pearsoncycles.co.uk

Pedal-It, 288-290 Lee High Road, SE13 5 PJ. Tel 020 8852 6680, www.pedal-it.co.uk

Perlie Rides, 137 Well Street, E9 7LJ.Tel 020 8525 5694, www.perlierides.com

Phoenix Cycles, 59a Battersea Bridge Road, SW11 3AU. Tel 020 7738 2766, www.phoenix-cycles.co.uk

Pretorius Bikes, Arch 441/442, 2 Drysdale Street, N1 6NA. Tel 020 3538 3882, www.pretoriusbikes.com

Psubliminal, 17 Balham High Road, Balham, SW12 9AJ. Tel 0208 772 0707, www.psubliminal.co.uk

Push Cycles, 35c Newington Green, N16 9PR. Tel 020 7249 1351, www.pushcycles.com

Putney Cycles, 208 Upper Richmond Road, Putney, SW15 6TD. Tel 020 8785 1086, www.putneycycles.com

ReCycling , 110 Elephant Road, SE17 1LB. Tel 020 7703 7001, www.re-cycling.co.uk

Robinsons Cycles, 172 Jamaica Road, SE16 4RT. Tel 020 7237 4679

S&S Cycles, 29 Chapel Market, N1 9EN. Tel 020 7278 1631, www .mountainbikelondon.co.uk

SBC Cycles, 41 Cropley Street, East London, Greater London N1 7HT. Tel 020 7253 0339

SE20 Cycles, 78 High Street, Penge, SE20 7HB. Tel 07711015102, www.se20cycles.com

Shorter Rochford, 65-67 Woodhouse Road, Sidcup, N12 9ET. Tel 020 8445 9182, www.shorter-rochford.co.uk

Sidcup Cycle Centre, 142-146 Station Road, DA15 7AB. Tel 020 8300 8113, www.sidcupcycles.co.uk

Skinny Eric's Cycleworks, 16 Felstead Street, E9 5LT. Tel 020 3417 0252, www.skinnyerics.co.uk

Smith Brothers, 14a Church Road, Wimbledon, SW19 5DL. Tel 020 8946 2270

South Bank Cycles, 194 Wandsworth Road, SW8 2JU. Tel 020 7622 3069, www.southbankcycles.com

Sparks, 5 Bank Buildings, High Street, Middlesex, NW10 4LT. Tel 020 8838 5858, www.sparksbicycles.co.uk

Specialized Concept Store, 47-49 High Street, Ruislip, Surrey, HA4 7BD. Tel 01895 623333, www.specializedconceptstore .co.uk/ruislip-store#contact

Specialized Concept Store, 36-40 Richmond Road, Kingston upon Thames, KT2 5EE. Tel 020 8549 5888, www.specializedconceptstore .co.uk/kingston-store#contact

Squeaky Chains CIC, 33 Rushworth Street, SE1 0RB. Tel 0207 9027974, www.squeakychains.com

Stratton Cycles, 101 East Hill, Wandsworth, SW18 2QB. Tel 020 8874 1381, www.strattoncycles.com

The Bicycle Man Ltd, 61-67 Old Street, Ground Floor West, EC1V 9HW. Tel 020 7253 7322, www.thebicycleman.co.uk

The Cycle Store, 201 Woodhouse Road, N12 9AY. Tel 020 8368 3001, www.thecyclestore.co.uk

The Hackney Peddler, Hackney Downs Studios, Amhurst Terrace, E8 2BT. Tel 020 3095 9789, www.thehackneypeddler.co.uk

The London Cycle Workshop, 125 St John's Hill, SW11 1SZ. Tel 020 3441 1044, www.thelondoncycle workshop.co.uk

The London Cycle Workshop, 373 King Street, W6 9NJ. Tel 020 8834 7247, www.thelondoncycle workshop.co.uk

The Red Bike Shop, 232 St. Pauls Road, N1 2LJ. Tel 020 7226 2066, www.theredbikeshop.co.uk

There Cycling, 60 Boston Road, W7 3TR. Tel 020 8840 9228, www.there-cyclingshop.co.uk

Tokyo Bike, 87-89 Tabernacle Street, EC2A 4BA. Tel 020 7251 6842, www.tokyobike.co.uk

Top Riders, 12 Savoy Parade, EN1 1RT. Tel 020 8363 8618, www.topriderscycles.co.uk

Two Wheels Good, 165 Stoke Newington Church Street, N16 0UL. Tel 020 7249 2200, www.twowheelsgood.co.uk

Vaidas Bicycles, 74 Honor Oak Park, SE23 1DY. Tel 020 3417 0436, www.vaidasbicycles.com

Velorution, 75-77 Great Portland Street, W1W 7LR. Tel 207 148 5572, www.velorution.com

Velorution at Selfridges, Lower Ground Floor, 400 Oxford Street, W1W 1AS. Tel 020 7318 3774, www.velorution.com

Volt BMX, 2 Cazenove Road, N16 6BD. Tel 020 7275 8660, www.voltbmx.com

Wilsons, 32 Peckham High Street, SE15 5DP. Tel 020 7639 1338, www.wilsonscycles.com

Woolsey of Acton, 281 Acton Lane, W4 5DH. Tel 020 8994 6893, www.woolseyofacton.co.uk

Commercial Cycle Hire

More than a million Londoners have their own bikes, but if you aren't one of them you can always hire one. The London Cycle Hire scheme set up by the Mayor and Transport for London (TfL) enables Londoners and visitors to the city to use reliable bicycles for journeys in and around central London (see page 230).

There are also a number of cycle hire companies in London which offer a wide range of ordinary and specialist bicycles. Most shops have a flexible policy on hire, with rates varying according to quality and length of hire term. Most shops offer hire of helmets, racks, panniers and other equipment.

While every effort has been made to ensure that the following information is correct, please check details with the shop before you hire. It's best to pre-book.

Action Bikes
19 Dacre Street, SW1H 0DJ
Tel 020 7799 2233
(also at Embankment, Wimbledon and Staines)
info@actionbikes.co.uk,
www.actionbikes.co.uk
Bikes: One model – the Brompton L6 folder. Includes lock, lights, helmet and rain cover. Prices: £15 a day, £30 per weekend and £50 a week; folding, hybrid or road bikes at £35 per day, £100 per week

Brompton Dock
www.bromptonbikehire.com
Enquiries: bdsupport@ bromptonbikehire.co.uk
Tel 0208 232 3931

Good value Brompton folder hire from several rail stations including: Croydon, Ealing Broadway, Peckham Rye, Turnham Green, Walthamstow Central. Price: £5 per day plus £1 annual membership

Go Pedal!
Bikes delivered to and collected from most areas of London
Tel 07850 796 320
info@gopedal.co.uk,
www.gopedal.co.uk
Bikes: 3-speed, fat-tyre city cruisers
Prices: see website; around £40 a day, including delivery/ collection, helmet, lock

London Bicycle Tour Company
1a Gabriels Wharf, 56 Upper Ground, SE1 9PP
Tel 020 7928 6838
www.londonbicycle.com
mail@londonbicycle.com
Bikes: Hybrids, mountain bikes and traditional-style. Tandems also available
Prices: From £3.50 per hour, £20 per day, £50 per week

London Recumbents
Battersea Park, Carriage Drive North, SW11 4NJ
Tel 020 7228 6843
Dulwich Park, College Rd, SE21 7BQ
Tel 020 8299 6636
www.londonrecumbents.co.uk
Bikes: Specialize in special needs and recumbent bikes
Prices: £8 (regular cycles, kids' banana bikes) to £20 per hour (side-by-side and recumbents)

On Your Bike
The Vaults, Montague Cl, London SE1 9DA (below the south end of London Bridge)
Tel 020 7378 6669
hire@onyourbike.net
www.onyourbike.net
Bikes: Comfort-style hybrids
Prices: Hybrid £18 per day, £49 per week

Richmond Station
Richmond Station Cycle Centre, Richmond Station, Kew Road, Richmond, Surrey TW9 2NA
Tel 020 8332 0123
www.richmondcyclecentre .co.uk
Price: £21 per day; £16 per half day

Smith Brothers
14 Church Road, Wimbledon, SW19 5DL
Tel 020 8946 2270
Bikes: Hybrids
Prices: £15 for 1 day, £30 for 3 days, £60 a week

INDEX

About the Author

A Londoner who has enjoyed cycling in the capital since childhood, Tom Bogdanowicz is a journalist, photographer and cycling advocate. He leads guided rides for the London Cycling Campaign (LCC) and its local groups, is a regular contributor to the *London Cyclist* magazine and writes articles on cycling, travel and architecture for newspapers and magazines. He is co-author of the *Off-road Bicycle Book*, author of *Fred, the Magic Bicycle*, and appears on radio and TV as a cycling expert. In addition to working for LCC he has also been part of the team at Cycling UK, the national cyclists' organization, and covered cycling issues for US broadcasters CNN and ABC.

About the London Cycling Campaign

The London Cycling Campaign (LCC) is the capital's leading cycling organization with a network of local groups and an extensive programme of guided rides and social events. Its aim is to make London a world-class cycling city. LCC developed the very popular series of London cycle maps now published by Transport for London.

Dedicated to Adam, Andrej, Ania, Dušan, Milan and Rachel with thanks for their support and patience.

ACKNOWLEDGEMENTS
A big thank-you to the LCC members and staff who made this book possible.

This book could not have been published without the help of dozens of LCC members who devised the rides and often lobbied hard to make sections of routes accessible to cyclists. The prolific Colin Wing designed rides in central, west and south London. Alan Ball was my riverside guide, Anthony Austin showed the way in Greenwich, Jonathan Rowland and Paul Luton found hidden gems in Richmond, and David Lomas and Ealing Cyclists produced perfection in Ealing. Frances Renton revealed the parks of Bexley, and Phil Loy and Alastair Hanton were the experts in southeast London. Gill James, Rob Lister and Caroline Fenton covered northeast London, Jeremy Parker and the Barnet crowd accompanied me in Barnet, and Jean Dollimore and Stefano Casalotti advised on routes in Camden. Bernard Macdonnell masterminded the 2012 ride, Barry Mason inspired many rides and ride leaders, Susie Morrow and Mike Grahn took care of Wandsworth and the Wandle, and Rob James and Roger Mace provided ideas in Kingston. Rachel Bower, Oliver Schick and Colin Wing did some superb editing. David Dansky of Cycle Training UK advised on the cycling technique section. Che Sutherland, Rosie Downes and others put together the LCC booklets that served as a blueprint for the text sections of the book. Koy Thomson, Simon Brammer, Charlie Lloyd, Ian Callaghan, Andy Cawdell and the LCC board supported the project from the start. Ashok Sinha helped LCC secure infrastructure improvements that are visible in the third edition and Katrin Wedenpohl contributed to the research. For the third edition, thanks are owed too to the many route riders who helped check and update all the routes: Paul Luton, Rob Lister, Caroline Fenton, Roger Mace, Rob James, Colin Wing, Jeremy Parker, Phil Loy, and David Giddings. LCC's whole team has always been ready to help when needed and provided cover during my leave of absence.

TfL's cycling team helped with maps and advice, and London's dedicated cycling officers, as well as others at the Royal Parks, GLA and British Waterways Authority, worked to make many of the routes cycle-friendly. Sustrans's work has developed rides along many London greenways including those along the rivers Wandle, Ravensbourne, Thames and Lee. Many contributors to the book are CTC (now Cycling UK) as well as LCC members and that national organization works hard to improve conditions for cycling in the UK.

Many thanks are due to the team at the publisher, Guy Hobbs, Rosemary Wilkinson, Ross Hilton, Ian Wood, Marilyn Inglis and Phil Kay, who identified a great idea and worked hard to make it a reality. Also thanks to designer Lucy Parissi and illustrator and cartographer Steve Dew. Family and friends provided support during the writing process and Sylvia Mejri, Carole Welch, Alun Jones and Rebecca Mitchell deserve special thanks for their invaluable help, advice and comments. Finally, many thanks to Colleen Dorsey, editor of this updated edition, Alan Giagnocavo, the publisher of IMM Lifestyle Books and David Fisk, designer.

Co-authors
Colin Wing co-authored the Enfield Gentry ride and provided significant input on others, Phil Loy co-authored the Waterlink Way ride, Paul Luton wrote the Crane River ride assisted by Jonathan Rowland.

Photo credits
Many thanks to the LCC members, friends and strangers who appear in the photos.
All photographs in the book were taken by the author Tom Bogdanowicz except **page 27**: © Alamy Picture library; **pages 230–231**: © Transport for London

Map credits
Transport for London: maps on pages 28 and 233.
All other maps by Steve Dew or David Fisk (pages 68–69, 76–79, 208–211) using base maps by OpenStreetMap, © OpenStreetMap and contributors and IMM Lifestyle Books.
Licensed under CC-BY-SA.